The Slave Trade, Abolition and the Long History of International Criminal Law

Modern international criminal law typically traces its origins to the twentieth-century Nuremberg and Tokyo trials, excluding the slave trade and abolition. Yet, as this book shows, the slave trade and abolition resound in international criminal law in multiple ways. Its central focus lies in a close examination of the often-controversial litigation, in the first part of the nineteenth century, arising from British efforts to capture slave ships, much of it before Mixed Commissions. With archival-based research into this litigation, it explores the legal construction of so-called 'recaptives' (slaves found on board captured slave ships). The book argues that, notwithstanding its promise of freedom, the law actually constructed recaptives restrictively. In particular, it focused on questions of intervention rather than recaptives' rights. At the same time it shows how a critical reading of the archive reveals that recaptives contributed to litigation in important, but hitherto largely unrecognized, ways. The book is, however, not simply a contribution to the history of international law. Efforts to deliver justice through international criminal law continue to face considerable challenges and raise testing questions about the construction – and alternative construction – of victims.

By inscribing the recaptive in international criminal legal history, the book offers an original contribution to these contentious issues and a reflection on critical international criminal legal history writing and its accompanying methodological and political choices.

Dr Emily Haslam is a Senior Lecturer in International Law at Kent Law School. Her research interests lie in the field of international criminal law, international legal history and civil society. She has extensive experience teaching international law, international criminal law and transnational criminal law.

The Slave Trade, Abolition and the Long History of International Criminal Law

The Recaptive and the Victim

Emily Haslam

Routledge
Taylor & Francis Group
LONDON AND NEW YORK

First published 2020
by Routledge
2 Park Square, Milton Park, Abingdon, Oxon OX14 4RN

and by Routledge
52 Vanderbilt Avenue, New York, NY 10017

Routledge is an imprint of the Taylor & Francis Group, an informa business

First issued in paperback 2021

British Library Cataloguing-in-Publication Data
A catalogue record for this book is available from the British Library

Library of Congress Cataloging-in-Publication Data
A catalog record for this book has been requested

ISBN: 978-1-138-34889-9 (hbk)
ISBN: 978-1-03-208874-7 (pbk)
ISBN: 978-0-429-43648-2 (ebk)

Typeset in Galliard
by Apex CoVantage, LLC

Contents

Acknowledgements

In completing this book, I am hugely indebted to colleagues and friends who have generously supported and encouraged me over the many years it has taken me to complete it. Donatella Alessandrini, Kate Bedford, Davina Cooper, Marie Dembour, Maria Drakopoulou, Rod Edmunds, Luis Eslava, Emily Grabham, Nick Grief, Didi Herman, Suhraiya Jivraj, Sara Kendall, Ed Kirton-Darling, Rose Parfitt, Nick Piška, the late Bryan Scattergood, Sally Sheldon, Charlotte Skeet, Sophie Vigneron, Dermot Walsh and Toni Williams readily read drafts and discussed ideas with me. Their comments, insights and encouragement have been invaluable. In completing this project, I have also benefited from discussions with many people. I would like to express my sincere thanks to Jose Bellido, Robert Burrell, Eleanor Curran, Chris Morrison, the late Bruce Mouser, Christine Schwöbel-Patel, Marike Sherwood, Thomas Skouteris and Immi Tallgren. I am extremely grateful to the anonymous reviewers for their time and insights which have helped me to strengthen the book significantly. Needless to say, all errors are my own. I would also like to thank the Society of Legal Scholars for an award from the Research Activities Fund and the University of Kent for a Faculty Small Grant which enabled me to conduct much of the archival work that underpins this project. The book has also benefited from the collegiate and inspiring environment at Kent Law School. My thanks also go to Yvonne Rigby, who provided invaluable research assistance, and Marie Selwood for her excellent editorial assistance. I would also like to thank the staff at Routledge, particularly Katherine Carpenter, Alison Kirk and Emily Summers. Finally, I would like to thank my parents, John and Muriel Haslam, for nurturing a love of knowledge and Terry Gibson for his immense support, encouragement and patience.

Parts of this book draw on some previously published work. Aspects of my discussion of Mixed Commissions, in particular my account of the *Sinceridade, Activo, Perpetuo Defensor* and *Maria da Gloria* cases in parts of Chapters 4 and 5 draw on material and ideas previously published in Haslam, (2016) 'International Criminal Law and Legal Memories of Abolition: Intervention, Mixed Commission Courts and "Emancipation"', *Journal of the History of International Law* 18: 420–447. I explored some preliminary ideas about the slave trade, silences, international criminal legal history and victims in the context of criminal prosecutions for slave trading in Haslam, 'Silences in international criminal legal histories and the construction of the victim subject of international criminal law: The nineteenth-century slave trading trial of Joseph Peters' in C. Schwöbel (ed.), *Critical Approaches to International Criminal Law: An Introduction*, London: Routledge. Some of the claims made about international criminal legal history writing draw on some of the methodological arguments which are developed further and for a different purpose in Haslam, (2019) 'Writing More Inclusive Histories of International Criminal Law: Lessons From the Transatlantic Slave Trade' in I. Tallgren and T. Skouteris (eds), *The New Histories of International Criminal Law: Retrials*, Oxford: Oxford University Press.

1 Rethinking international criminal legal history

Introduction

The British ship, the *Snake*, captured the slave ship, the *Maria da Gloria*, not far from Rio de Janeiro in November 1833.[1] On board were over 400 slaves, or recaptives, as they were also known (that is slaves found on board slave ships captured – in this case – by the British Navy) (HM Commissioners to Palmerston 31 March 1834; Haslam 2016: 439–440). At least half of this wretched human cargo was young children (Bethell 1970: 135). The British captors brought the *Maria da Gloria* and the recaptives before a British- Brazilian Mixed Commission which had been established at Rio de Janeiro. This Commission decided that it had no jurisdiction over the *Maria da Gloria* because it considered the ship to be Portuguese (HM Commissioners to Palmerston 31 March 1834: 33). Therefore, the British captors sailed the *Maria da Gloria* and the recaptives across the Atlantic to Sierra Leone, the site of a British-Portuguese Mixed Commission. They reached Sierra Leone 46 days later (Burroughs 2010: 110). The British-Portuguese Mixed Commission at Sierra Leone ordered the *Maria da Gloria* to be returned to the master of the *Maria da Gloria*. Portugal had only agreed to the capture and detention of slave ships north of the Equator, but as the *Snake* had captured the *Maria da Gloria* south of the Equator, the seizure and detention of the *Maria da Gloria* was unlawful. The Commission, therefore – albeit very unwillingly – ordered the recaptives to be returned with the ship. On 9 April 1834, 240 slaves crossed the Atlantic for the third time on board the *Maria da Gloria*. Over 100 of the slaves originally trafficked had died. Sixty-four of the sickest slaves remained in Sierra Leone. British Commissioners hoped that this case would form the basis of representations on the part of the British government to Portugal to abolish the slave trade completely and to further empower the Royal Navy (HM Commissioners to Palmerston 9 April 1834: 45–46).

The case of the *Maria da Gloria* was unusual.[2] Recaptives found on board the *Maria da Gloria* were subject to orders of in-person restoration and exceptionally sailed across the Atlantic three times. At the same time, the case typifies how recaptives' paths to emancipation depended upon the legality of intervention and not upon the condition of slavery *per se* or the possession on the part of recaptives of rights to freedom (Haslam 2016). To that extent they were constructed as objects of intervention. Slaves on ships captured by the Navy become recaptives. But the transition to recaptivity did not necessarily represent an assertion of their humanity, nor guarantee their liberation.

The aim of this book is to inscribe the figure of the recaptive into international criminal legal histories. This is controversial because the slave trade was not an international crime during this period of abolition. Moreover, the origins of modern international criminal law are typically considered to be found in the legal principles established by the Nuremberg and Tokyo Tribunals (Haslam 2016: 422). In 2001, the UN World Conference Against Racism acknowledged in the non-binding Durban Declaration that 'slavery and the slave trade are a crime against humanity and *should* always have been so' (Durban Declaration 2001, emphasis added).[3] Yet the Preamble to the Rome Statute, which came into force a year later, notes that: '*during this century* millions of children, women and men have been victims of unimaginable atrocities that deeply shock the conscience of humanity' (Rome Statute 1998 emphasis added). The silence in the Rome Statute about the history of the transatlantic slave trade and slavery and its victims is emblematic of the synonymy of international criminal law with the twentieth century in the dominant international legal mindset. This book takes a different approach by emphasising the importance of writing the slave trade, slavery and abolition into international criminal legal histories. Many commentators consider slavery and slave trading to be international and transnational crimes today.[4] Understanding the history of abolition can, therefore, shed vital light on the development of contemporary approaches to modern slavery and human trafficking. However, the aim of this book is less to contribute to histories of modern slavery and human trafficking, about which there is already an extensive literature,[5] than to emphasise the importance of including the slave trade and abolition – and more specifically here the recaptive – in international criminal legal histories more generally. First this is a matter of justice: although the time for doing 'justice' to recaptives is long past, victims of the slave trade should be remembered in international criminal legal histories.[6] Second, analyses of the legal construction of recaptives can contribute to contemporary debates about the construction and representation of victims in international criminal law.

From a doctrinal perspective, however, these aims are controversial because, as mentioned previously, the slave trade was not a crime under the law of nations during this period. By inscribing the recaptive into international criminal legal history, this book consequently offers a reflection on the construction of history in the discipline of international criminal law and on the construction of the discipline of international criminal law through its official as well as other histories. Thus, the book is concerned with the role that histories – both those that are told and those that remain untold – play in the construction of the discipline and the power relations that underpin those histories. It rests on the assumption that the writing of history – and international criminal legal histories are no exception – involves a series of choices that are contingent and ultimately political. These choices reflect a particular set of current preoccupations and give rise to some important silences. It is therefore necessary to identify silences in the dominant historical narratives and the archives on which they rely. The preoccupation of this book is with the construction and representation of victims. Although not limited to international criminal law, concerns about the representation of victims are particularly live in this field because a central part of international criminal law's claims to legitimacy has come to rest upon its claim to do justice for victims (Sagan 2010:12–13; Kendall and Nouwen 2014: 239–241). Despite this, the ability of international criminal justice to satisfy victims' demands in practice has proved challenging (Clarke 2015: 292; Fletcher 2015: 303; Schwöbel-Patel 2016: 252). Recent years have, therefore, seen a growing body of critical scholarship on the construction of victims in international criminal law (Kendall and Nouwen 2014; Fletcher 2015; Schwöbel-Patel 2016). This important work has tended to draw inspiration from theoretical, critical and socio-legal fields. A history of the recaptive can contribute a longer-term viewpoint to this growing critique. This alternative historical starting point challenges assumptions about legal progress which can be found in much of the literature on victims in international criminal law, particularly literature which takes Nuremberg and Tokyo as its historical starting point.

A history of recaptives can challenge progress narratives in legal histories of abolition as well as in accounts of the development of victims' rights in international criminal law. That is not to say that the abolition of the slave trade did not constitute legal process, but that abolition was a partial and incomplete project which gave rise to injustices of its own.[7] Central to the compromises in the legal construction of recaptives was that international abolition law found its origins in the law of prize (the law that regulated the capture of enemy property in time of war). Prize did not challenge the construction of slaves as property (Benton and Ford 2016: 122) and both it and the slave trade repression law that drew on it commodified recaptives, both directly and indirectly. Moreover, the centrality of the law of prize to abolition meant that whether recaptives were emancipated depended upon the circumstances of the capture and detention of the slave ship on which they were found rather than any recognition that recaptives possessed rights to freedom (Haslam 2016). This is evident in the case of the *Maria da Gloria* with which this book opened, a case which haunts international abolition law. Within this legal framing, it was easier for judges, when slave ships were captured unlawfully, to extend the circumstances in which intervention could take place than to directly expand the rights of recaptives as a matter of law. However, whilst slave trade repression law did little to directly recognise recaptives as rights holders or legal subjects, recaptives were not passive objects of intervention. Recaptives did seek to influence proceedings to their own ends and on occasion, as this book shows, their resistance impacted on the law.

In sum, this book explores litigation on the capture and detention of slave ships in the first part of the nineteenth century in order to interrogate the legal construction of recaptives. To do so, it takes up Stoler's challenge of reading sources both along and against the grain (Stoler 2002: 100), or in the words of Hartman writing in the context of slavery, a 'history written with and against the archive' (Hartman 2008: 12). More specifically, it relies on archival materials found at the National Records Office, Kew, in London and a range of published and unpublished cases dealing with litigation before Vice Admiralty and Mixed Commission Courts in London and Sierra Leone in the first half of the nineteenth century. Despite differences in the legal contexts, which are explored below, this book suggests that there are similarities in aspects of the legal construction of the recaptive and aspects of the representation and construction of victims today. At the least these similarities suggest causal links between the stories told – and those not told – about the past and present. More transformatively, a history of the recaptive challenges these continuities. First it inscribes recaptives' agency and resistance into international criminal legal histories. Second it provides a springboard for experimenting with alternative thinking about victims. In this book this alternative thinking, which draws in particular on the work of Guyora Binder's subversion of the gift narrative in the context of the Thirteenth Amendment to the US Constitution and Robert Meister's critique of transitional justice (Binder 1993; Meister 2012), centres around the claim that international law is indebted to recaptives. Finally, the book argues that this thinking serves as a provocation, not just to international criminal legal histories but also to contemporary thinking about victims in international criminal law.

The remainder of this chapter explores the methodological claims underpinning these arguments in more detail; that is, it argues that slavery and abolition should be included in international criminal legal histories, and it explores the political choices that lie behind this quest. To do so the chapter turns first to the preoccupation with the Nuremberg and Tokyo trials in international criminal legal histories and highlights literature that positions Mixed Commissions within a human rights law narrative. Given that the slave trade was not a crime during this period of abolition, the claim to incorporate it, and more specifically the recaptive, into international criminal legal history requires justification. The next section, therefore, considers the purposes of international criminal legal history and the meaning of international criminal law. The section outlines different approaches to international criminal law, but argues that however international criminal law is understood, the slave trade and abolition are instructive. The chapter then shifts gear and moves to consider the inscription of the figure of the recaptive into international criminal legal histories. A key argument put forward for inscribing recaptives into international criminal legal histories is that their legal treatment can place current thinking about victims within a longer-term legal history. To that end, the next section turns to outline some of the criticisms that have been levelled against the representation of victims of international crime today. The purpose of the book is not to trace a progressive or teleological legal link from international abolition law and recaptives to international criminal law and victims today. For one thing, the slave trade repression litigation examined here did not involve criminal procedures. However, the book explores the extent to which international abolition law's approach to recaptives has been transcended in contemporary thinking about victims. Inscribing the recaptive then is not just an end in itself. It also provides a source for critically thinking and rethinking about victims in international criminal law today. Much of the transformative promise of including the recaptive in international criminal legal history derives from the inscription of recaptives' agency and resistance. However, writing in recaptives' agency is neither a straightforward nor neutral exercise. The following section considers some of the political choices behind the inscription of recaptives' agency and resistance. It should be clear by now that inscribing the recaptive raises methodological dilemmas and provides a productive opportunity to think through some of the limits, possibilities and political choices inherent in critical international legal history writing. The chapter, penultimately, therefore considers some of the challenges that arise when researchers consult archival sources. It argues that a critical reading of the archive can make a distinctive contribution to international criminal legal history by opening up a series of discursive possibilities about international criminal law's past. These critical reading practices include reading along and against the grain (Stoler 2002) and interrogating silences in the archives and their effects. Finally, the chapter sets out the book's scope and terminology and outlines the remainder of the work.

International criminal legal histories

The litigation that this book explores is historically important in its own right, in international law more generally, and in human rights. This book takes another, more controversial step, seeking to inscribe the figure of the recaptive into international criminal legal history. This move is controversial because international criminal legal histories typically focus on international crimes and the enforcement of individual criminal responsibility at the international level. Therefore, they mostly trace the origins of modern international criminal law to the post-Second World War war crimes trials and, more specifically, to the Nuremberg and Tokyo Tribunals. The legacy of Nuremberg and Tokyo has not gone uncriticised and, recently, there has been some decentring of Nuremberg in international criminal legal histories.[8] However, the focus on trials dealing with the Second World War remains strong.[9] It seems that even the impressively wide-ranging Historical Origins of International Criminal Law Research Project, which aims to be the first 'comprehensive, inclusive and systematic' study of the development of international criminal law (Cohen 2014: iii), does not appear to date to have foregrounded the transatlantic slave trade.

The Nuremberg and Tokyo trials are not simply chronological starting points in international criminal legal histories.[10] Histories that position Nuremberg and Tokyo as foundational typically give rise to progressive accounts of the development of international criminal law,[11] where progress is assessed in legal-institutional terms (Haslam 2014: 180–181). What Gerry Simpson describes as the 'narrative arc from "Tokyoberg" to The Hague' (Simpson 2013: 3) lends authority to contemporary legal structures and institutional arrangements. Christine Schwöbel has suggested that the 'confidence' of international criminal lawyers derives partly from this established history (Schwöbel 2013: 174). The preoccupation with Nuremberg and Tokyo all too often can excise or relegate to the disciplinary periphery a longer history of slavery and colonialism and with that questions about racism and capitalism.[12] In contrast, inscribing slavery and abolition would centre them as a matter of course with all that that would entail (Haslam 2019: 133).[13]

In contrast to the dominant approach in international criminal legal histories, the legal scholar Jenny Martinez argues in *The Slave Trade and the Origins of International Human Rights Law* that Mixed Commission Courts were 'the first international human rights courts' (Martinez 2012: 6) with slave trade abolition 'the most successful' chapter in human rights law history (Martinez 2012: 13). She argues that international abolition contributed to the conditions of legal possibility that made Nuremberg 'jurisprudentially possible' (Martinez 2012: 138) by ensuring that human rights breaches were 'of concern to humankind generally' (Martinez 2012: 149). Martinez's claims about the significance of legal actions against the slave trade and the link between human rights and abolition have been questioned (Moyn 2014: 54–62; Alston 2013; Benton and Ford 2016: 119; Haslam 2016), but her core thesis has been accepted elsewhere (Shaikh 2012; Gross and Thomas 2017). Martinez's scholarly and animated account is an important one. However, I respectfully come to a different conclusion. Martinez recognises that slave trade repression was beset with difficulties but overall, I read her account as located within a progressive narrative frame, which can be deployed to lend further inspiration (and to some extent legitimacy) to contemporary developments.[14] My concerns lie elsewhere. At their broadest they lie in provoking debate about how international criminal legal history should account for the slave trade, the failure to criminalise it and the consequences thereof. More specifically, it is to inscribe the recaptive for his or her own sake, but also as a springboard for alternative thinking about the relationship between international criminal law and victims.

In general, whether – and more particularly how – Mixed Commissions should be written into human rights histories depends upon how human rights are perceived (Haslam 2016: 423). Historian Lauren Benton argues that abolition was linked to rights contestation largely insofar as the rights in dispute were 'the definition of property rights and legal prerogatives of slave traders and slave owners within the imperial order' (Benton 2011: 369).[15] In addition to this focus on property rights which Benton and Ford have also emphasised was detrimental to the rights of recaptives (Benton and Ford 2016: 125), as already mentioned I show how prize channelled questions about recaptives' emancipation through the prism of intervention. I recognise that Mixed Commissions emancipated tens of thousands of recaptives. However, this approach also materialised in a focus on the legality of the capture and detention of slave ships and had potentially devastating consequences for recaptives when slave ships were captured in violation of the relevant international instruments, as the *Maria da Gloria* shows.[16] From this, I also read the construction of recaptives alongside the contemporary construction of victims, thereby setting the latter within a longer legal historical context. The legal construction of recaptives (and victims) forms just one part of a broader abolition (or international criminal justice) narrative but it plays a significant role for all that.

Martinez recognises that her argument that Mixed Commissions were early human rights courts can be countered with the observation that recaptives' roles in proceedings were limited. However, she contends that this criticism does not sufficiently acknowledge the different ways in which rights are enforced on the domestic and international levels (Martinez 2012: 150). In terms of pure numbers, admittedly few recaptives participated in Mixed Commission proceedings. However, by reading against the grain, I supplement my account of recaptive–Mixed Commission relations that emphasises the silencing of recaptives with one that also suggests that recaptives played a greater role in slave trade abolition litigation than is usually acknowledged. For example, recaptives did sometimes testify and, as already mentioned, their resistance to recaptivity did on at least two occasions significantly influence legal proceedings and ensure their own freedom. Moreover, had their roles been recognised, to say nothing of slave resistance more generally, it is possible that aspects of the representation of victims in international law today might have looked different.[17]

In my view, therefore, what is at stake here is not so much whether the slave trade and abolition should be inscribed into international human rights history on the one hand, or international criminal legal history on the other. Rather the questions are to what end is it inscribed and how should its writing-in be narrated? These broad questions run through this book. Slave trade repression should be located within histories of international law more generally, and within a number of its subfields including human rights law. This book seeks to inscribe the slave trade and abolition in international criminal legal histories because the history of abolition, and more specifically for the purposes of this book the recaptive, offers insights into international criminal law, specifically ideas about subjecthood that underpins thinking (and potential thinking) about victims today. There is also strong political and normative imperative here because the legacy of the slave trade and colonialism haunts contemporary international criminal law in political, moral and material terms. From a doctrinal perspective, however, writing abolition into international criminal legal history is controversial. It requires an analysis both of the definition of international criminal law and the purpose of international criminal legal history.

Inscribing the slave trade into international criminal law

The intention of this book is to provoke debate by challenging the focus on Nuremberg and Tokyo in international criminal legal histories. This objective raises the question of how the slave trade and abolition can be included in international criminal legal history when the slave trade was not a crime under the law of nations during this period. Whether the slave trade and abolition comprise part of international criminal legal history does not just depend upon the application of the principle of non-retroactivity or customary international law, although positivist legal doctrine clearly does and should play a role here,[18] but it also turns upon the purpose of international criminal legal history on the one hand and the meaning of international criminal law on the other (Haslam 2019: 132; Haslam

2016: 422). Neither of these are absolutely and irrevocably fixed.[19] Yet, they are co-constitutive in significant respects.

The Nuremberg and Tokyo trials represent the first international criminal prosecutions of individuals for war crimes, crimes against humanity and crimes against peace, and are, therefore, often seen as the origins of modern international criminal law. The international criminal prosecution of individuals at the end of the Second World War in turn laid the foundation stones for the more concerted development of international criminal law at the end of the twentieth century.[20] The focus on Nuremberg and Tokyo in international criminal legal histories reflects a particular set of – albeit important – preoccupations: those of international prosecution, international crimes and individual criminal responsibility. However, pre–twentieth-century debates about crimes under the law of nations can also shed light on the origins and preoccupations of international criminal law, which the focus on Nuremberg and Tokyo can obscure.

During the nineteenth century, Britain failed to achieve a general recognition of the slave trade as a crime against the law of nations and was unable to secure a general agreement that the trade was piracy. However, what is excluded from definitions of international criminality can be just as significant in understanding the past doctrinal and political preoccupations of the discipline, and its current limitations and political context, as what is included (Haslam 2016: 422; Haslam 2019: 132). Moreover, in this case the scale and gravity of the slave trade renders the exclusion of the slave trade as a crime under the law of nations constitutive.

The transatlantic slave trade can be seen as the foundational crime of modernity. It was a brutal system of injustice which destroyed individuals and communities and its effects endure.[21] At least 12 million individuals were trafficked onto slave ships destined for enforced labour; 10.5 million endured the Middle Passage and arrived in the Americas (Walvin 2007: 448). Slaves, amongst other Africans, made a vital contribution to the advancement of European and American wealth, but this went hand in hand with the underdevelopment of Africa (Gutto 2013: 33), which was one of the consequences of the loss of population that resulted from the trade (Rodney 1989). The colonial conquest associated with both the slave trade and its abolition contributed to inequality in the relations between Africa and the global north. As Gutto observes, racial discrimination still persists 'in many countries where the descendants of slave traders and slave masters/mistresses dominate' (Gutto 2013: 40). International criminal law has always placed limits on the suffering it recognises,[22] even though purportedly a response to heinousness as epitomised by the claim that international crimes shock the conscience of mankind. However, to the extent that international criminal law is a response to heinousness, it seems difficult to identify a more sustained and organised international atrocity. For that reason alone, the slave trade and slave trade abolition should form a part of international criminal legal history (even if the transatlantic slave trade was not formally at the time a crime under the law of nations).[23] The failure to criminalise the transatlantic slave trade in international law and the reasons for that failure (and its ongoing effects) should take a place in international criminal legal history. Ultimately, international criminal law requires the righting of an injustice in the accounting of its history.

Moreover, even if the transatlantic slave trade was not formally a crime under the law of nations, ongoing efforts to deal with the trade's multiple legacies implicate international criminal law. In that sense the slave trade and slavery are part of international criminal law's present. Thus, the French Taubira Law recognised the French slave trade was a crime against humanity, although the French Court of Cassation subsequently considered that this law was declaratory rather than normative (Cass Crim 5 February 2013, Haslam 2019: 133). The Durban Declaration and Taubira Law are indicative of contestation, not just about the history of the slave trade but also about the scope and purpose of international criminal law itself (Haslam 2019: 132–133). They are an important part of the history and practice of international criminal law in a broad sense. The slave trade also forms part of the broader context in which debates about the relationship between the ICC and Africa take place (Haslam 2014: 182).[24] Indeed, it might be thought that proponents of a discipline often criticised for its Eurocentricity would seek to include abolition within its core narratives.

However, international crimes, international criminal prosecution and the associated and important doctrinal developments recognising the international criminal responsibility of the individual, although vitally important, need not be – in fact should not be – the sole focus of international criminal legal history. International criminal legal history is not necessarily coterminous with international criminal law in a strict sense. The act of history writing reflects current concerns. Concerns about the representation and construction of victims in international criminal law call for a longer-term view, to which this book argues a history of the recaptive can contribute. The past therefore informs the present not just through legal doctrine (was the slave trade an international crime?) but also through questions of legal subjectivity (from recaptive to victim).[25] This book shows how the slave trade exerts its presence and absence in each of these different registers, revealing vital insights about the discipline as it does so, but its main focus is on questions of legal subjectivity. Most of the book, therefore, is about the legal construction of recaptives and their roles in slave trade abolition litigation. Focusing on the construction and representation of victims suggests a broader understanding of international criminal legal history which positions contemporary international criminal law as a historically contingent approach to injustice situated within a much longer history of international institutional justice (Haslam 2016: 422). Emphasising the historically contingent nature of international criminal law in this way can also challenge the taken-for-granted assumptions that lie behind the current dominance of international criminal law as a response to injustice.[26]

Whether international criminal law is portrayed as international criminal prosecution or more broadly as a historically contingent approach to injustice, its history extends beyond the contemporary practice and definition of international criminal law in a strict sense with abolition offering rich insights into critical aspects of contemporary international criminal justice. Ultimately, this book is a provocation to orthodox histories of international criminal law and the role that these histories play in constructing ideas about international criminal law and justice today. In that sense, the slave trade and abolition form one – but not the only – possible starting point for thinking about and rethinking histories of international criminal law. To explore the particular claim put forward in this book that a history of the recaptive offers insights on the construction and representation of victims today, the next section turns to consider some of the concerns raised about the representation and construction of victims in international criminal law.

The figure of the victim in international criminal law

As previously observed, the claim to deliver justice to victims has become a central feature of contemporary international criminal law's claims to legitimacy (Sagan 2010:12–13; Kendall and Nouwen 2014: 239–241; Fletcher 2015: 302; Haslam 2014: 183; Haslam 2019: 137). Thus, the ICC's prosecutor has asserted that 'victims and the justice they deserve' are the 'sole *raison d'être* of the Court's activities' (Kendall and Nouwen 2014: 239),[27] leading Kendall and Nouwen to describe the victim as 'a new kind of sovereign' (Kendall and Nouwen 2014: 241). Scholars have shown how such claims draw on an 'imagined' (Fletcher 2015) or 'abstract' (Kendall and Nouwen 2014) victim.[28] They are also suggestive of a progress narrative (from the limited space given to victims at Nuremberg and Tokyo to the establishment of victim participation at The Hague). However, despite best intentions, in practice meeting victims' expectations of justice has proved challenging. This is partly a consequence of the important need to balance the rights of the defendant with the rights of victims, and the need for more resources. However, it can also be linked to the ways in which victims are represented, concerns which are explored in a growing body of critical scholarship (Kendall and Nouwen 2014; Fletcher 2015; Schwöbel-Patel 2016; Schwöbel-Patel 2018). This book draws on this literature, seeking to contribute to it by offering an alternative historical perspective.[29]

Critical literature has suggested that when the claim to centre victims operates as one means of legitimation for international criminal institutions, the representation and recognition of victims' agency may be limited. For one, in practice, the voices of many survivors are often absent; even victim participants rarely address the court (Kendall and Nouwen 2014: 251–252). For another, concerns have also been raised that representations of victims have drawn upon 'infantilized, feminized and racialized victim stereotypes' (Schwöbel-Patel 2018: 704) and a '*fundraising* image of victimhood' (Schwöbel-Patel 2016: 255 original emphasis). These related factors contribute to the construction of an 'ideal' victim of international criminal law as apolitical (Haslam and Edmunds 2014; Haslam 2019: 138) or defenceless and vulnerable (Schwöbel-Patel 2018: 705).[30] The concern is that international criminal legal processes therefore may not easily recognise the critical or dissenting victim (Haslam and Edmunds 2014; Kendall and Nouwen 2014: 242, 255),[31] and international criminal law's recognition of survivor agency or, what Mamdani has described elsewhere, as victims' citizenship (Mamdani 2009: 471) may be limited.[32]

The ICC's focus on situations in Africa amplifies concerns about the racialised representation of victims (Haslam 2014: 181; Schwöbel 2014: 277–278; Sagan 2010: 9; Schwöbel-Patel 2018: 710). Ann Sagan has contended that the ICC's early focus on situations in Africa is connected to a 'discursive compatibility' between depictions of African criminals and victims and 'the cosmopolitan and liberal conceptions of international criminal law' (Sagan 2010: 4).[33] For Sagan this compatibility explains the centrality of African subjects in the early years of the court's work but the result is, she argues, that the court will have to grapple with the consequences of the 'apparent compatibility between African subjects and the court's foundational narratives' (ibid. 21). The ideal victim of international criminal law is indelibly influenced by these racialised and geopolitical origins. At the same time in so far as these origins impact upon the construction of the figure of the victim more generally, the deconstruction of the ideal victim has a potential impact beyond that on African subjects.

One way to deconstruct this figure is to turn to history.[34] Slave trade repression confronted international law with multiple victims and can set the contemporary treatment of victims in international criminal law within a broader historical context. This longer-term legal institutional context includes the legally innovative bilateral Mixed Commissions on the slave trade. Mixed Commissions were not criminal (or indeed international criminal) institutions, but they do constitute part of the development of international institutional justice of which international criminal law forms a historically contingent part. They therefore form a relevant part of international criminal legal history (albeit not international criminal law) in the broader sense outlined in the previous section.

Britain and other states which permitted/had permitted the slave trade established Mixed Commissions in order to adjudicate the capture and detention of slave ships by the navies of each signatory state. Mixed Commissions had the power to confiscate slave ships and to emancipate slaves (otherwise known as condemning the ship and its cargo) or to restore them both, with compensation, to shipmasters and owners if their capture and detention was unlawful. Between 1819 and 1846, Mixed Commissions at Sierra Leone adjudicated 528 ships, condemning 499 and restoring 29 (Van Niekerk 2004b: 2000).[35] They emancipated around 65,000 recaptives (Martinez 2012: 79). The existence and operation of Mixed Commissions may have prevented many more individuals from being trafficked. However, the historical significance of Mixed Commissions for slave trade abolition is contested. For one, the question of effectiveness is not straightforward to assess.[36] For another, historians, in contrast to Martinez, have played down the effects of Mixed Commissions on abolition (Haslam 2016: 423).[37] These debates are important, but it is not necessary to resolve them for the purposes of this book because my focus is on the legal construction of the recaptive. From this perspective, the importance of Mixed Commissions lies not so much in tracing causal links between Mixed Commissions and abolition, or even Mixed

Commissions and the development of human rights and international criminal courts (Haslam 2016: 422). To the extent that this book assumes causal links, it finds them in the stories told about the discipline's past, present and future: for example, if international (criminal) legal histories had more systematically included accounts of slaves' agency and resistance, how might victims be represented in international (criminal) law today? The premise of this book then is that the stories told – and not told – about the construction of the recaptive can impact upon contemporary thinking about victims in international criminal law.

A history of the recaptive, therefore, enables us to consider the representation and construction of victims within a longer historical trajectory, particularly when international criminal law is conceived as a historically contingent response to injustice. However, the fact that Mixed Commissions were not criminal institutions may lessen their significance in international criminal legal history for some. They were, however, early international institutions which were faced with multiple victims (Haslam 2016: 423). Although this book does not, as already explained, seek to trace legal or institutional links between Mixed Commissions and international criminal institutions of the twentieth century, it is worth noting Martinez's claim that some international lawyers at least were cognisant of the Mixed Commissions when Nuremberg was being devised (Martinez 2012: 154). In any case, the representation of victims in international criminal law draws on tropes already established outside the field of international criminal law (Schwöbel-Patel 2016: 248).[38] This borrowing alone highlights the difficulty of drawing a clear line between what should and what should not be considered relevant to international criminal legal history.

However, representations of victims in international criminal law add the 'construction of a villain' (Schwöbel-Patel 2016: 256).[39] Kamari Clarke has argued that the focus on victims and perpetrators contributes to the law's focus on individual rather than structural causes of harm (Clarke 2015: 283).[40] The slave trader was not formally speaking an internationally criminal figure, although the recaptive was to some extent constructed in opposition to him. However, if the addition of a perpetrator figure focuses attention on individual rather than structural causes of harm, it is possible that the absence of a formal international criminal figure in opposition to which the recaptive was constructed could contribute to provoking greater consideration of structural causes of harm in international criminal legal history and, therefore, the present. From this perspective then the inscription of the recaptive can provoke a challenge to some of the key assumptions underpinning international criminal law. The focus of this book is on the provocation the recaptive offers to the contemporary framing of victims in criminal law. Much of this provocation centres around the inscription of recaptive agency and resistance.

Inscribing agency and resistance

Legal sources, limited though they are, point to examples of recaptives' agency in the operation of Mixed Commissions. However, international criminal legal histories rarely centre the agency of African victims (Haslam 2014: 181).[41] Historical literature more generally has acknowledged the many different roles played by slaves and former slaves in abolition, emancipation and self-emancipation from everyday struggles to uprisings (Williams 1964; Craton 1982; James 2001).[42] The Haitian Revolution, which Genovese sees as having 'propelled a revolution in black consciousness throughout the New World' (Genovese 1979: 96), stands out for the ground-breaking way it combined human rights claims with anti-racism (Wall 2012: 15).[43] International legal scholarship has, however, been slower to embrace the implications of these accounts (Haslam 2014: 183). This is in line with international law's tendency to recognise the legitimacy of particular forms of resistance only (Rajagopal 2003). The inscription of recaptives' agency and resistance in international legal histories is, therefore, well overdue. However, in general how agency should be understood, along with critiques of it, remains less well developed or theorised in international criminal law (Killean and Moffett 2017: 721). Turning to histories of slavery and abolition is particularly productive because they have given rise to rich discussions about agency (Haslam 2019: 140).

As is well recognised, identifying and representing recaptives' agency is, however, not without its problems. For example, Elizabeth Kowaleski Wallace, commenting on the creation of the transatlantic slavery gallery at the Liverpool Maritime Museum, highlights the challenges of portraying the devastating effects of the slave trade without representing slaves as 'passive, silent, and meek' (Wallace 2006: 35–36). Recaptives faced highly constrained circumstances. Recaptives were not formally parties to litigation and had very limited opportunities to use the legal system to their own ends. Killean and Moffett describe legal agency today, which they distinguish from moral and political agency 'as the power to make choices and to pursue chosen goals within legal systems' (Killean and Moffett 2017: 722). Recaptives were not legal agents in this sense. Slave trade repression treaties were extremely limited in the extent to which they recognised recaptives' subjectivity. However, recaptives did contribute to slave trade suppression litigation, and where possible they seized opportunities to influence proceedings. And on occasion, recaptives resisted. Tracing recaptives' resistance is an end in itself irrespective of the effect it had on legal development, although, as this book will argue, recaptives' resistance did contribute to the development of the law.

Aside from contributing to a more complete history then, transformative potential comes from inscribing the recaptive. Much of this promise lies in writing-in recaptives' agency and resistance because such accounts can provoke a greater recognition of survivors' agency – and its different forms – in international (criminal) law more generally. This could encourage more openness on the part of international criminal legal institutions to resistance by contemporary victims of international crime, and to alternative approaches to international criminal justice.[44] Moreover, a history of the recaptive can provide a starting point for suggesting alternative thinking about victims in international criminal law. Whilst inscribing the recaptive can contribute to challenging a racialised international legal subjectivity, writing in agency and resistance is, however, far from straightforward (Haslam 2019: 140).

Identifying recaptives' agency and resistance – and their different effects – is therefore only one stage in this corrective history. A further step is to determine the ends to which agency and resistance can and should be inscribed. Anthropologist David Scott offers profound insights on the challenges and choices that surround the inscription of narratives about agency in his pioneering analysis of C. L. R. James's *The Black Jacobins*, in which he contrasts romance and tragedy as narrative forms (Scott 2004).[45] I have argued elsewhere that this account is particularly helpful for thinking through questions about agency in international criminal law more generally (Haslam 2019: 140–141). For Scott, history writing requires an alertness to the particular 'problem-space' (Scott 2004: 97) that frames it. It is therefore an act of, and for, the present. In the case of international criminal law, as the previous section showed, the context into which narratives about the agency of recaptives are inscribed is one in which, notwithstanding the intention to turn victims – in the words of Jorda and de Hemptinne – from 'passive object' to 'potential subject matter' of international criminal proceedings through the institution of victim participation at the ICC (Jorda and de Hemptinne 2002: 1389, 1399), international law's ability to satisfy victims has been limited (Haslam 2014: 183; Haslam 2019: 141). Scott's insights provoke us to be attentive to the narrative frames and the politics underpinning them, within which recaptives' agency and resistance might be inscribed into international criminal legal histories.

Scott challenges us to think about how recaptives' agency and resistance might be written into international criminal legal histories and what these different accounts might offer us today (Haslam 2019: 140). On the one hand, inscribing recaptives' agency and resistance, and their effects on legal change, can be used to emphasise the responsiveness and inclusiveness of international law in an overall narrative of progressive (and redemptive) legal change. However, the danger of this narrative is that it can operate to legitimate the law uncritically. On the other hand, a narrative about recaptives' agency and resistance might be positioned within a more critical frame, for example by analysing the legal structures that failed to recognise recaptives' agency in the first place. More radically, a narrative might attempt to subvert those legal structures. This is the quest of the final chapter, which suggests a reframing of the relationship between recaptives and slave trade repression law. Chapter 7 then experiments with thinking about recaptives and by analogy victims as creditors. Whilst the premise of this book is that inscribing recaptives' agency and resistance offers transformative potential when agency is understood as critique, whichever approach is taken it is still necessary to consider precisely what the archive can reveal.

What one can and cannot get from the archive

This book has been inspired by approaches to international legal history writing which challenge Eurocentric narratives which have dominated the discipline. It is indebted in particular to scholars working within the Third World Approaches to

International Law school (TWAIL) in its thinking about international law's politics of knowledge production,[46] although in its chronology and use of sources it does not escape its European and specifically British framing.[47] Since its focus is on narratives about the *legal* construction of the recaptive, it draws on a range of documentary sources found in the British National Archives in Kew, London. These sources include reports of the Crown's Law Officers on the slave trade and dispatches from the Foreign and Colonial Offices. The book also draws on published and unpublished records of English Vice Admiralty and Mixed Commission Courts. Rose Parfitt has emphasised how the sources upon which traditional international legal methodology relies are inherently Eurocentric (Parfitt 2014: 299). Other sources, especially those less rooted to textual forms of remembering, would have produced other forms of knowledge, including possibly less Eurocentric kinds, although many would still have required reading against the grain.[48] However, my concern is with the legal construction of recaptives and the extent to which its influence reverberates in the legal present.

Amongst the ways in which the archive reveals its Eurocentricity is its silencing of recaptives.[49] The silencing of recaptives in litigation is reflected in the legal sources and in international (criminal) legal histories. Thus, whilst slave trade repression litigation, to say nothing of abolition more generally, generated an enormous body of documents, these records contain little about recaptives. In most slave trade abolition litigation, recaptives feature as numbers, the nameless objects of intervention, restoration, forfeiture and emancipation. Rarely does litigation (as opposed to records of Liberated Africans) record individual recaptives' names, and other details are scarcer still.[50] This silencing in the legal record contrasts with the effect that the arrival of a slave ship with recaptives on board must have had on the locations where Mixed Commissions sat. The arrival of a slave ship must have rendered recaptives, often in deplorable conditions, very present. The legal archive contains bare traces of them, unlike the wealth of material on naval officers, colonial and government officials.

Despite the silence about recaptives in the archival sources, when deployed critically, a history that draws on the authority of the written legal archive can make a distinctive contribution to international criminal legal history. This is because archives, as has been observed, have been accorded particular authority as historical sources (Mawani 2012: 349). However, such history requires approaching the archive as if it is not just a source but also a 'subject' (Stoler 2002: 93), a place not 'of knowledge retrieval but of knowledge production' (ibid: 90). As Stoler, amongst others, has made clear (ibid 93), the politics of history are inescapable from any study of the archive. This in turn requires a set of critical reading practices. These practices include reading the archive along and against the grain (Stoler 2002: 99–101; Stoler 2009: 50) and relatedly interrogating the silences in the archive and their effects.[51] These practices seek to ensure the colonial archive is read back against itself.

Reading along the archival grain, therefore, I seek to uncover the preoccupations of international abolition law in order to uncover the legal structures that conditioned recaptives' paths to emancipation or restoration. Uncovering in detail these legal structures, in this case the inherently precarious legal condition of recaptivity, can shed light on what 'rescue' by the British Royal Navy might have looked like to recaptives. Reading along the grain shows how the preoccupations of international slave trade repression law drawn from the law of prize were manifest in a legal focus on intervention and property. This focus contributed to the silencing of recaptives. It also meant that the law failed to recognise fully their humanity. Reading along the grain of the colonial legal record, therefore, contributes to accounts which render more complex (legal) humanitarian narratives about abolition, such as those which emphasise the implication of humanitarian narratives about abolition in some of the justifications for colonialism.[52]

Reading along the grain will only get us so far. It is also necessary to read against the grain and to interrogate the silences in the archive. Silences about recaptives matter not least because they contribute to the conditions of possibility in the present. Whilst this book, as I have already explained, does not seek to trace continuities in legal institutional design from Mixed Commissions to contemporary international criminal courts, it rests on the assumption that contemporary approaches to victims are influenced by silences about recaptives (amongst other victims of the slave trade) in international (criminal) legal history. To the extent to which silence contributes to contemporary thinking about victims, the book assumes causal links.

This book then rests on a critique of silences in international criminal legal histories. Silences occur in different ways and in different forms. In his seminal analysis of the role of power in the construction of history, Michel-Rolph Trouillot explains four overlapping ways in which silence comes into the 'process of historical production'. These are:

> the moment of fact creation (the making of *sources*); the moment of fact assembly (the making of *archives*); the moment of fact retrieval (the making of *narratives*); and the moment of retrospective significance (the making of *history* in the final instance).
>
> (Trouillot 2015: 26)

A historical account is for Trouillot 'a particular bundle of silences' with the consequence that challenging these different silences calls for different approaches (Trouillot 2015: 27). Trouillot emphasises the importance of making 'the silences speak for themselves'; that is to show the 'effectiveness of the original silence' (ibid: 27). Trouillot's approach to silence can provide a highly productive starting point both for thinking about how silence about slavery and abolition and recaptives affects the current constitution of international criminal law as well as for identifying ways to challenge these silences.

At the most general level, the current volume challenges international criminal law's silences about slavery and the slave trade (or the 'making of *history*' in Trouillot's words). It contests in the context of international criminal legal history what Hamilton, Harris and Reid have described as the 'taken-for-granted archive', where the archive is understood as 'the foundation of the production of knowledge in the present' (Hamilton, Harris and Reid 2002: 9). It seeks to add to the discipline's canon of 'leading' cases ('the making of *archives*' and '*narrative*' again to adopt Trouillot)[53] by contesting the mainstream criteria for identifying leading cases in international criminal legal history on the assumption that the criteria for identifying leading cases are not inevitable and can be reconsidered in the light of current concerns. Thus the cases in this book were selected not so much for their contribution to the teleological development of the law, although many of them were also important legal precedents within the Mixed Commission system. Rather, the focus was on what the cases revealed about the legal construction of recaptives, the roles recaptives played in litigation, recaptives' resistance and the preoccupations of international abolition law.

Admittedly, there are relatively few cases which evidence recaptives' resistance. However, given the preoccupations of the colonial legal archive it might be thought surprising that evidence of recaptives' agency and resistance appears at all. In any event, leading cases are by their very nature exceptional. Therefore, litigation that features even sporadic acts of resistance, especially against the logics and framework of slave trade repression law, is significant. Designating a case that features recaptives' resistance as leading does not necessarily imply a direct causal link between resistance and international legal change, although that may exist. Establishing causal links between recaptives' resistance and international legal change can acknowledge recaptives' contributions to the law. However, a relentless search for a causal connection may obscure other insights that recaptives' agency and resistance provide about the law and recaptives' engagements with it. Resistance then is also significant for its own sake.

Uncovering recaptives' agency and resistance in the case law often requires reading against the grain; that is, to read a document for meanings and standpoints its drafters would not have had (Rizzo 2017: 28). Trouillot observes that because the Haitian Revolution was 'unthinkable' for those at the time, 'the insignificance of the story is already inscribed in the sources' (Trouillot 2015: 73). Similarly, those compiling the records of slave trade repression litigation were unlikely to countenance recaptives' agency or resistance. Recognising resistance would entail accepting 'the humanity of the enslaved' (Trouillot 2015: 83) and to admit mass resistance was 'to acknowledge the possibility that something is wrong with the system' (Trouillot 2015: 84). The archival sources hide, likely for this reason, recaptives' agency and resistance in a number of ways. In some instances, they also gloss over it. For example, although scholars have analysed shipboard rebellions from other sources (Richardson 2001), slave insurrections which constitute the factual predicate of litigation but not the main legal issue are mostly barely mentioned in case reports (*The Nancy* 1810). In other cases, where recaptives' resistance was in fact relevant to legal argument, it could be more obliquely recognised, as cases examined in Chapter 5 show.[54] Thus, the Secretary of State commenting on the implications of the *Perpetuo Defensor* (Hamilton to Canning,

12 October 1826) and *Activo* (HM Commissioners to Canning, 10 June 1826) cases referred to 'unforeseen circumstances', not recaptives' resistance (Canning to HM Commissioners 30 December 1826: 7).

In its challenge to the silencing of the recaptive in international (criminal) legal history, this book offers a contribution to ongoing efforts to remember some of the victims of the slave trade. To that end it seeks to inscribe stories about recaptives, and where possible the names of individual recaptives, where they appear in the legal record, and in the form that they appear in the legal record. This project of writing the recaptive into international criminal legal history is not one which claims to recover or to give voice. As Saidiya Hartman has shown in the context of slavery (Hartman 2008: 11–12) and scholars have warned in other contexts, this is impossible (Spivak 1988; Mawani 2012: 344). The 'real' recaptive is lost forever, and to pretend otherwise would be an appropriation. This book's account of the recaptive is then in itself also full of silence. However, tracing the effects of these silences is productive. Without being able to give voice to recaptives, this book is concerned with suggesting alternative discursive possibilities about recaptives' relationships with slave trade repression law and asking what those possibilities might offer for the present. This can contribute to critical international criminal legal history by challenging assumptions about agency and by inviting reflection about continuities in the law as well as, more radically, an accounting of it. However, these analyses, drawn from reading against the grain, are possible interpretations of the past. They are not definitive claims about 'what happened'. They involve ultimately political choices, for example, about the framing of agency and resistance in the present – each with attendant risks and opportunities – as the previous section showed. These discursive possibilities can contribute to the making of alternative histories 'in the final instance', to return to Trouillot. But they too are not free from silence. However, at least these new silences – and their political consequences – can be recognised.

Scope, terminology and outline of the book

Scope

By the middle of the nineteenth century the international law on the slave trade had radically altered, with one commentator claiming that the international legal cooperation to abolish the transatlantic slave trade was one of the nineteenth century's most important international legal advances (Van Niekerk 2004a: 6). Litigation played a central role in these legal changes. This book examines litigation dealing with the British capture and detention of slave ships between 1807, when Britain abolished its trade, and the mid-1840s when the most active Mixed Commissions largely ceased to operate. Its focus is on litigation before Vice Admiralty and Mixed Commission Courts in London and Sierra Leone. Sierra Leone was the centre of the British government's attempts to abolish the slave trade. This focus on recaptivity as a matter of law and British and Mixed Commission practice represents only part of the broader recaptive experience. Historian Sharla

Fett, for example, has masterfully traced the experiences of American recaptives and their removal from America to Liberia (Fett 2017). Her important account resonates in critical ways with the treatment of recaptives before Mixed Commission Courts at Sierra Leone. Commonalities between recaptives' experiences, Fett observes, were mediated by the particularities of the law and practice of the capturing state (Fett 2017: 5).[55]

When a slave ship was captured, the captor would place a prize crew on board to sail the captured slave ship, its crew and any recaptives to the nearest Vice Admiralty Court or Mixed Commission with jurisdiction. Here the claimants (usually the master of the captured slave ship) would seek to establish title to the slave ship and its cargo and to show that there were no grounds for intervention. Vice Admiralty Courts and Mixed Commissions determined the fate of the ship, equipment and recaptives. Of all Mixed Commissions, those at Sierra Leone were the most active. Between 1819 and 1845 Mixed Commissions at Sierra Leone heard around 528 cases, whereas those at Havana and Rio de Janeiro, for example, presided over 50 and 44 cases respectively (Shaikh 2012: 48–49). Litigation on the capture and detention of slave ships was variously a tool for legal change and an object of contestation. As a historical source litigation can illustrate the impact that broader legal structures had on individuals' lives. Examining litigation therefore offers an opportunity to contribute to broader attempts to remember some of the victims of the slave trade.

However, recaptives represented only some of the individuals subjected to the horrors of the slave trade and slavery. The figure of the recaptive therefore embodies only part of a much broader history of international law's engagement with the slave trade, slavery and abolition. However, recaptives' significance justifies the attention paid to them here. First, interventions against slave ships with recaptives on board formed the legal basis and factual predicate for much of the development of early international abolition law. Second, the rescue of recaptives from the horrors of the Middle Passage has a particular symbolic significance, at least in the British public memory of abolition, which is ripe for critical interrogation. Third, positioned at the receiving end of the contradictions of international abolition law, recaptives represent a potent symbol of law's promises and limitations. While inscribing recaptives should be part of a more concerted effort to inscribe slavery and abolition into international criminal legal history, it is a particularly important starting point.

Terminology

Writing this book has involved a number of choices around terminology. This section explains these choices.

The 'recaptive' refers to slaves found on board captured slave ships and is often also used to encompass 'liberated Africans', that is post recapture (Asiegbu 1969: 23–24; Fett 2017). An element of objectification is implicit in the term, the recaptive – and therefore in the title to this book. For one thing the term recaptive is an abstraction which erases individuality.[56] For another, the term itself objectifies those recaptured. Whilst recognising these important difficulties, I continue to deploy this commonly used term. I am interested in the law's approach to those who found themselves in recaptivity. To that extent my concern is in a legal abstraction and one which continued to commodify recaptives in critical respects. I use the term recaptivity with the aim of injecting critique into the expression from a legal perspective.

My use of the term recaptive is restricted to the period between recapture and adjudication, a liminal legal state in which slaves on board ships captured by the British Navy found themselves. Fett also argues, in her rich account of American recaptives, that recaptivity was a liminal state, describing recaptivity 'as a liminal category in the border-lands between enslavement and emancipation' (Fett 2017: 186). However, her depiction of the state of recaptivity as liminal goes beyond the legal. Thus, whilst I position recaptivity as a liminal legal state between slavery and freedom or restoration, which has effects, and which all recaptives occupied albeit for varying lengths of time, Fett's focus is on a 'lived experience' (ibid: 7). American law, unlike the slave trade repression treaties entered into with Britain and explored in this book, did not provide for a change in status to liberated Africans (ibid: 24), but required recaptives to be transported outside the USA from 1819 (ibid: 17). Thus, although recaptivity avoided re-enslavement, it operated in this context 'more as a deportation order than a repatriation policy' (ibid: 29). As already mentioned, my focus on the legal – as opposed to social transitions – aims to bring the figure of the recaptive into a set of conversations about international (criminal) law's construction and representation of victims.

Notwithstanding important discussion around the term 'slave' (as opposed to 'enslaved'), I use the term 'slave' so that the two legal statuses (of slavery and recaptivity) can be distinguished. The alternative term 'enslaved' may do less to objectify individuals, but it does not enable slavery and recaptivity to be as easily distinguished because even recaptives were enslaved to the extent that formally they retained the legal status of slaves until/if they were emancipated. Judges and Mixed Commissioners also used the term 'slave'. This terminology, therefore, serves as a critical reminder that international abolition law drew on some of the same legal structures and modes of representation that supported the slave trade. Similarly, despite the fundamental illegitimacy of ownership claims, I use the term 'slave owner' or 'slave master' to describe a relationship recognised by law, including by international slave trade repression law.

As regards terminology that is more contemporary, the use of the term 'victim' is also potentially controversial. However, in the context of the ICC, the term 'victim' or 'victim participant' has a specific legal meaning, hence its deployment here. The expression 'survivor' may do more to recognise individuals' agency than the term 'victim' does. However, the term survivor may also do less to enable criticism of the structures that may have facilitated the conditions that contribute to international crime and that set the conditions of possibility for responses to it (Haslam 2019: 138). Thus, a shift in language from victim to survivor could obscure the persistence of constraints on victims' agency. It is not that the shift in language from victim to survivor cannot do vital work. However, for the particular aims of this book there may be just as much – if different – critical purchase in an attempt to redeploy the term victim, remembering of course that not all victims of international crime survive.

Other choices about terminology go beyond the focus on the human subject. This book refers to the international law of slave trade repression or the international law of slave trade abolition. Although international abolition law and international slave trade repression law are largely interchangeable, the latter is more appropriate in the context of most of the treaties this book deals with because typically they did not abolish the slave trade outright. Either shorthand is, however, to some extent, a misnomer. These developments would not have been understood at the time as a systematic body of international law dealing with slave trade repression. In their ground-breaking account of the origins of international law, Benton and Ford argue that abolition did not appeal to or result in 'clearly articulated international norms' (Benton and Ford 2016: 121), although they acknowledge the regime 'represented international legal formations' (ibid: 147). However, whilst the term 'the international law of slave trade repression/abolition' is a convenient, if arguably anachronistic shorthand, its use is justified by the inherently international nature of the subject matter, the origins of the law in the international law of prize and its development before Mixed Commissions; that is, courts based on international treaties. To some extent Mixed Commissions were less the application of prize law than a British adaptation of it. Slave trade repression was a means by which Britain exerted legal hegemony. Admittedly, the view of one state and its legal advisers could not represent a consensus amongst nations as to international law (and Mixed Commission decisions were not undisputed amongst treaty partners, as the following chapters show). At the same time, it is not unusual for the development of international law to be characterised by what Benton and Ford have described in this context as 'bald legal imperialism' (Benton and Ford 2016: 124). For all these reasons, this book uses the term international slave trade repression law.

Outline

Although the focus of this book is on litigation, the next two chapters set the inscription of the recaptive within its broader legal context by examining developments in the international law of abolition in the first part of the nineteenth century. In so doing, they offer further reflection on the construction of the discipline through its accepted and less accepted histories. Chapter 2 emphasises the legal origins of international slave trade repression law in the law of prize. In addition to some unpublished cases, the chapter draws on published cases, many of which have been discussed elsewhere (Van Alstyne 1930; Wheaton 1936: 171–177; Kern 2004; Van Niekerk 2004a). In that sense, many of these 'facts' are not new. However, the importance of (re)telling these stories lies in the inscription of these narratives into international criminal legal history, corresponding to what Trouillot might describe as 'the moment of retrospective significance' (Trouillot 2015: 26). This legal context is important because prize set the conditions for the grant or otherwise of recaptives' emancipation and in effect positioned recaptives as still commodified objects of intervention.

Chapter 3 proceeds from the assumption that conduct that is excluded from the definition of international criminality can be as significant in understanding the preoccupations of the discipline and its current limitations and political context as that which is included. Much of the debate about whether the slave trade constituted a crime centred on whether the slave trade could be considered piracy. The chapter approaches this legal question with the aim of identifying some of the power relations that underpin the construction of the discipline of international criminal law. To that end, it considers how the slave trade is accounted for through a discussion of the application of the piracy analogy. It argues that the piracy analogy operates in a contradictory way in its application to the slave trade in different registers of international criminal law. These contradictions perform a vital gatekeeping function, enabling international law to draw rhetorical benefit from the slave trade whilst relieving it of the need to account materially for it.

Together these two chapters of the book demonstrate the centrality of the law and language of the use of force in setting the conditions of possibility for international slave trade repression and early international criminal law. Chapter 3 ends by inscribing two additional forms of violence, namely: violence against recaptives by prize crews; and violent, but productive, resistance carried out by recaptives. Both these forms of violence leave international law indebted to recaptives. Both embody in graphic form two of the main ways in which recaptives appear in this book – as legal objects of intervention on the one hand and critical resisting subjects on the other. Inscribing these forms of violence, therefore, represents a critique of international slave trade repression law, albeit in different ways.

The next three chapters focus more directly on the figure of the recaptive in international slave trade repression law. The conclusions reached from this examination of the law, which takes up the challenge of reading both along and against the grain (Stoler 2002), render more complex narratives about international law and abolition that emphasise the progressive development of the law. This history of the recaptive, historically important for its own sake, also provides critical legal and historical context from which to consider contemporary thinking about victims in international criminal law in Chapter 7.

Chapter 4 shows how British Commissioners at Sierra Leone, who often sat alone, interpreted slave trade repression treaties inventively by minimising some of the fallout – at least for captors – of apparently unlawful seizures. However, although they expanded the circumstances in which captors could intervene against foreign slave ships, they were able to do less to formally expand the rights of recaptives under the treaties as a matter of law. Nevertheless, the chapter also shows that, although recaptives were not parties to the litigation, their testimony did contribute to some Mixed Commissions' decisions and, therefore, to their own emancipation. Even if they had no formal role in proceedings, there is evidence that recaptives engaged more actively in proceedings than their formal legal status would suggest.

Chapter 5 continues the examination of the state of recaptivity, a liminal and precarious legal state. Recaptivity promised recaptives emancipation but also exposed them to the latent violence of the law through the possibility of potentially devastating orders that required the return of recaptives to those claiming ownership of them. This chapter argues that when faced with slave ships captured in violation of the relevant international treaties, Mixed Commissions were able as a matter of law to do more to protect captors from claims for damages than to formally expand recaptives' opportunities for legal emancipation. Whilst in-person restoration was avoided in many cases, this was largely serendipitous. When it was not, it was disastrous. Either way, both situations demonstrate the preoccupation of the law with questions of intervention. Yet, the status of recaptivity was one in which, given the right circumstances, recaptives' resistance could make a decisive impact. This chapter emphasises two such cases, in which recaptives' resistance challenged the legal logic of slave trade repression treaties that would have returned them to their owners. However, the outcome in these cases did not prevent the appalling case of the *Maria da Gloria*. Of course, the focus on unlawfully captured ships represents only part of a bigger narrative about slave trade repression. It is however particularly revealing because it demonstrates how recaptives' legal status was determined through the prism of intervention. In that sense recaptives were constructed in effect as objects of intervention, even in those cases in which Commissioners, recaptives and colonial officials were able to avoid orders of in-person restoration.

Chapter 6 explores the legal construction of the recaptive further by focusing on the broader economies of slave trade repression. It argues that, whilst emancipation offered the promise of liberation of sorts, it did not fundamentally challenge the commodification of slaves and recaptives. Emancipation was, therefore, not simply a legal designator of freedom. It was a particular kind of freedom that had to be understood within the broader economies of abolition.

Chapters 4 to 6 offer a counter-legal history of abolition by focusing on the construction of the recaptive and the roles that recaptives played in litigation. The final chapter shifts gear by returning to the claim that the figure of the recaptive can contribute to thinking about victims in international criminal law today. This history challenges accounts of the development of the position of victims in international criminal law which are located within a progressive narrative frame, by reading the construction of the recaptive alongside the victim today. Inspired by Guyora Binder's subversion of the gift narrative in histories of the US Thirteenth Amendment (Binder 1993) and Robert Meister's critique of transitional justice (Meister 2012), the chapter experiments with positioning the recaptive – and by analogy the victim – as a figure to whom international law is indebted. The conclusion of the book returns to reflect on history writing in international criminal law.

Notes

1 The *Maria da Gloria* had no passport authorising her to slave trade and was, therefore, illegally slave trading.

2 In fact, the Advocate General advised that although the decision of the British-Portuguese Mixed Commission had been correct, the Anglo-Brazilian Mixed

Commission should have condemned the ship, which he considered to be a Brazilian enterprise. The critical issue here was nationality (discussed further in Chapter four). Instructions were later given to the British Commissary Judge at Rio to condemn similarly situated ships, instructions with which the Brazilian government initially disagreed (Bethell 1970: 139–141).

3

> We acknowledge that slavery and the slave trade, including the transatlantic slave trade, were appalling tragedies in the history of humanity not only because of their abhorrent barbarism but also in terms of their magnitude, organised nature and especially the negation of the essence of victims, and further acknowledge that slavery and the slave trade are a crime against humanity and should always have been so, especially the transatlantic slave trade and are among the major sources and manifestations of racism, racial discrimination, xenophobia and related intolerance, and that Africans and people of African descent, Asians and people of Asian descent and indigenous peoples were victims of these acts and continue to be victims of their consequences.
>
> (Article 13 Durban Declaration 2001)

4 See further, on slavery and international law, for example, Slavery Convention 1926 and Supplementary Slavery Convention 1956. It is worth nothing that Grietje Baars observes that some experts exclude the contemporary slave trade from definitions of international crimes since it is usually not committed by public actors (Baars 2014: 200).

5 See further, for example, Allain (2012) and Quirk (2012). See further UN Protocol to Prevent, Suppress and Punish Trafficking in Persons, Especially Women and Children (2000). For criticisms of the analogy between the transatlantic slave trade and contemporary trafficking and smuggling in the Mediterranean, see Martinez and Surwillo (2017). For further criticism of the '"slavery-trafficking nexus" of the new abolitionism', see Gross and Thomas (2017).

6 My approach to remembering here draws on Stacy Douglas's account of memorials and their purpose. Drawing on the work of Johannes Snyman, Douglas contrasts memorials and monuments; the former operate as 'antidotes to forgetting victims of past injustice' and the latter represent a 'decisive moment as a new beginning and embody the historical self-perception of the founders of the monument'. Significantly she argues that memorials are aimed at instilling a commitment to avoid repetition of injustice (Douglas 2011: 176–177).

7 Moreover, recognising that the abolition of the slave trade was a progressive legal development should not blind us to the persistence of slavery and slavery-like practices and the failure to resolve the question of reparations for the transatlantic slave trade.

8 See for example, the discussion of different starting points in histories of international criminal law in Simpson (2018: 13–15).

9 See, for example, Heller (2011). For an account of war crimes trials which adopts a broader historical sweep, see Heller and Simpson (2013). For discussion of abolition in international law more generally, see Allain (2007).

10 For a discussion of periodisation in international legal histories, see Diggelmann (2012). For an extensive discussion of the politics of periodisation and the politics of time, see Davis (2008). For an alternative periodisation which takes Africa as its starting point, see Gutto (2013).

11 See, further, for a critique of progress narratives in international law, Skouteris (2010) and on 'evolutionary narratives' in international law, see Johns, Joyce and Pahuja (2011: 2) and in the context of Walter Benjamin's approach to history, see Kapczynski (2005: 1082–1086).

12 For a discussion of the relationship between slavery, antislavery and capitalism, see further Sweet (2009: 27–31).

13 Baars argues that the contemporary ideology of international criminal law results in 'explanations of conflicts that exempt/exonerate the economic/capitalism' (Baars 2014: 209). Inscribing the slave trade in international criminal legal histories could contribute to challenging this ideology by inscribing questions about the relationship between capital and international crime and capital and international criminal law.

14 For example, she writes:

> Most people think of international courts as an innovation of the twentieth century, with the Nuremberg trials of the Nazi war criminals at the end of World War II being the first real effort to use international law to prosecute those accused of gross human rights abuses. But more than a century before Nuremberg, international courts in Sierra Leone, Cuba, Brazil and other places around the Atlantic heard cases related to the slave trade, the original "crime against humanity".
>
> (Martinez 2012: 6)

15 For further discussion on the relationship between historical and contemporary rights discourses, see Alston (2013: 2051–2052).

16 This argument raises more fundamentally the question whether slave trade repression should be judged by the exceptional case, such as the *Maria da Gloria,* or more typical cases at Sierra Leone, in which recaptives were emancipated, a question which depends in part upon the purpose of history, a point which is taken up in relation to the *Maria da Gloria* in Chapter 5.

17 For a similar argument in the context of the prosecution of Joseph Peters for slave trading see Haslam (2014).

18 Muhammad contests the application of the principle of non-retroactivity and the statute of limitations in the context of reparations for the transatlantic slave trade, see Muhammad (2013: 183–187). For the argument that the expression 'crimes against humanity' was used in connection with the slave trade, see Martinez (2012: 13–14); and for criticism of this argument, see Alston (2013: 2050).

19 Immi Tallgren asks, for example: 'What is international criminal law, in its histories and today? Is it rules, institutions, actors, compliance, objective, outcomes?' (Tallgren 2014: xx). For different understandings of international criminal law, see, for example, Baars (2014: 197–204).

20 On the 'institutional growth' in practice and subsequent decline of international criminal law, see Vasiliev (2015: 705); and on the 'anxiety of demise', see Mégret (2016: 199). For the argument that international criminal law is displacing rather than supplementing international human rights law and the problems with this development, see Schwöbel (2013: 171–173, 182–183).

21 See further, for example on the continuing effects, CARICOM (the Caribbean Community) Reparations Commission Press Statement of 10 December 2013. See https://caricom.org/media-center/communications/press-releases/caricom-reparations-commission-press-statement-delivered-by-professor-sir-h

22 See further, for example, on the exclusion of famine/subsistence harms from international criminal law, Marcus (2003) and Sankey (2014).

23 This is not to suggest that there is not significant critical purchase in arguing that the transatlantic slave trade should be treated as an international crime. My focus here, however, is on interrogating the legal conditions of possibility for its formal exclusion during this period of abolition and their effects.

24 The arguments for and against the claim that the ICC has focused on Africa are well rehearsed, although it should be noted that preliminary examinations are now underway in respect of a number of non-African situations. As a continent Africa has generated a significant number of ratifications to the Rome Statute. However, geopolitical realities may render some states more vulnerable to ICC

intervention than others. The political realities are exacerbated because the relationship between the United Nations Security Council and the ICC can operate to reduce significantly the possibility that situations from the Permanent Five states come before the Court because the Security Council enjoys the power to defer and refer situations to the ICC, even though its members are not all parties to the Rome Statute. Critics charge international criminal law with failing to address structural causes of crime (Clarke 2010: 627), the impact on conflict of the political and economic conduct of Western actors (Stahn 2015: 58) and the effects of colonialism on contemporary violence in Africa (Clarke 2010: 628 and Clarke and Koulen 2014: 300). See further, Okafor and Ngwaba (2015). For a regional approach, see the Malabo Protocol (African Union 2014). It is worth emphasising that African positions on the ICC are varied. See further Clarke, Knottnerus and de Volder (2017).

25 See further in the context of criminal prosecution Haslam (2014: 190).

26 For example, Mixed Commissions challenge the centrality of international *criminal* law in delivering justice. For all the criticisms of them this book outlines, they could and did make a radical change to the status of tens of thousands of victims of slavery. From this perspective, the very reason not to include Mixed Commissions in international *criminal* legal history can also be read as a reason for including them: given the importance of the claim that international criminal law delivers justice to victims.

27 Referring to the opening of investigations in Côte d'Ivoire.

28 On the 'real' and 'imagined' victim, see Fletcher (2015). On the abstract and juridified victim, see Kendall and Nouwen (2014).

29 The historical account in this book draws heavily on the courtroom treatment of recaptives. However, histories of the slave trade and slavery have other lessons too. For example, elsewhere I have argued that scholarship on the slave trade and slavery can provide important insights about agency and witnessing today, see further Haslam (2019: 137–143).

30 On the ideal victim, see Christie (1986). For the application of the ideal victim to international criminal law, see Van Wijk (2013) and Schwöbel-Patel (2018). On the Third World victim more generally, see Kapur (2002: 2).

31 Thus, referring to suggestions on the part of the ICC that non-participating victims' concerns may in some ways be represented through common legal representation, Kendall and Nouwen note that there is no 'legal avenue for resisting representation as part of an abstract collectivity', as some of the victims in one of the Kenyan cases sought to do (Kendall and Nouwen 2014: 250–251).

32 In a debate in the *International Journal of Transitional Justice*, Mahmood Mamdani drew a distinction between positing the victim as 'citizen with agency' on the one hand and 'a ward without agency' on the other. See Mamdani (2009: 471).

33 See further, on representations of Africa in international criminal proceedings, for example, Anders (2011).

34 See further (in the context of prosecution for slave trading) Haslam (2014: 181). For a discussion of literature on the slave trade and slavery which can offer a provocation from a methodological perspective to assumptions about the framing of victims today see further see Haslam (2019).

35 One hundred and fifty-five were adjudicated before the Anglo-Portuguese Mixed Commission, 241 before the British-Spanish Mixed Commission, 21 before the Anglo-Dutch Mixed Commission and 111 before the Anglo-Brazilian Mixed Commission (Van Niekerk 2004b: 200).

36 Alston notes four possible ways of assessing effectiveness. These are: numbers of emancipated slaves; numbers of those who were not enslaved because of the presence of Mixed Commissions; the experiences of liberated Africans; and the effect Mixed Commissions had on the abolition of slavery (Alston 2013: 2053–2055).

37 David Eltis observes that of the 1635 ships condemned between 1808 and 1867, only 572 were condemned by the orders of Mixed Commission Courts between 1819 and 1845 (Eltis 1987: 97). See, further, on their effect in international law, Drescher and Finkelman (2012: 904).

38 For example Makau Mutua has famously shown how the movement for human rights has been dominated by the 'savages – victims – saviors' metaphor (Mutua 2002).

39 On the co-constitutive roles of the victim, perpetrator and legal representative see Schwöbel-Patel (2018: 718).

40 Thus, Kamari Clarke argues that the addition of the perpetrator to discussions about victims results in the exclusion from international criminal law of 'larger structural forms of victimhood'. The international criminal legal victim is, consequently, 'someone who suffered physical violence against his/her individual body' (Clarke 2015: 283).

41 See further, for example, Rwandan survivor group protests against the International Criminal Tribunal for Rwanda's treatment of victims (Haslam 2014: 189). The use of the broad term 'African' in this context requires some justification. David Northrup argues that Sierra Leone was 'one of the first places in tropical Africa where people identified themselves as "Africans"' (Northrup 2006: 8).

42 Former slaves and activists, for example, Ignatius Sancho, Ottobah Cugoano and Olaudah Equiano, spoke out against slavery, as well as the condition of the poor in England. See, for example, Ramdin (1987: 9).

43 See further on resistance to, and through, law, Genovese (1975) and Vandervelde (2014). On other forms of resistance such as the 'struggle for community and family life' on the part of plantation slaves, see Glassman (1991: 278).

44 A lack of preparedness to resistance was evident in the response of the ICC to some Ugandan victims' opposition to ICC intervention. See Haslam (2014: 189). On the ICC's reaction to Ugandan civil society opposition, see Allen (2006).

45 In similar vein, writing in the context of the US Constitution, Gross observes two kinds of narratives: a 'celebratory story of people claiming the Constitution for themselves in the face of adversity, or a darker story that emphasizes the continuing violence and injustice those people met' (Gross 2008: 321).

46 See for example, Rajagopal (2003), Anghie (2005) and Gathii (2012). See further more generally on history and international law (including TWAIL): Koskenniemi (2001), Anghie (2005), Craven (2007), Lesaffer (2007) and Koskenniemi (2012). See further on international criminal legal history for example, Heller and Simpson (2013) and Tallgren (2014).

47 An alternative approach to chronology might commence with the Haitian revolution, for example. See further, for example, Wood (2010: 62).

48 See, for example, Northrup's analysis of the creation of identity amongst liberated Africans in Sierra Leone which draws on documentation from recaptives, missionaries and administrators, as well as African Americans (Northrup 2006), or Fett's rich account of American recaptivity as 'lived experience' (Fett 2017: 7). For an alternative first-hand account of capture and transportation, see, for example, Equiano (2003). For a discussion of alternative and 'nondiscursive' memory practices of the slave trade, see Shaw (2002). For an alternative approach to historical sources, such as the palaver as a collective site for reproducing historical knowledge, see Depelchin (2005): 179–180.

49 On the role of archives in the production and maintenance of colonial power, see, for example, Richards (1993), Steedman (2011: 332) and Mawani (2012: 344–345).

50 On the Registers of Liberated Africans at the Sierra Leone National Archives, and what may be read from them, see, for example, Olusoga (2016: 311) and Schwarz (2012).

51 For discussion of silence as 'a constitutive feature of discourse and practice' in the context of human rights, and the need to challenge it see Bhambra and Shilliam (2009: 3, 5–9).

52 For the argument that the 'theory of imperial trusteeship . . . found its point of departure in the 1807 [slave trade abolition] bill', see Wood (2010: 94).

53 Accounts of abolition have tended to focus on a handful of cases, notably, in the Anglo-American context, the famous *Somerset*'s case (*Somerset v Stewart* 1772) and on the role played by prominent white abolitionists, such as Granville Sharp in legal proceedings. On Sharp, see further Hoare (1820).

54 For further discussion in a different context of silences inherent in the terminology selected for use in official records, see Guberke and Hedstrom (2017: 29–30).

55 In the context of the US, recaptives were 'lawful charges of the government who were mandated for removal outside the nation' (Fett 2017: 105). See further Conrad (1973), Martinez-Fernandez (1995) and Mamigonian (2009).

56 On the victim in international criminal law as an abstraction see further Kendall and Nouwen (2014).

References

Allain, J. (2007) 'The Nineteenth Century Law of the Sea and the British Abolition of the Slave Trade', *British Yearbook of International Law* 78: 342–388.

Allain, J. (ed.) (2012) *The Legal Understanding of Slavery from the Historical to the Contemporary*, Oxford: Oxford University Press.

Allen, T. (2006) *Trial Justice: The International Criminal Court and the Lord's Resistance Army*, London and New York: Zed Books.

Alston, P. (2013) 'Does the Past Matter? On the Origins of Human Rights Law', *Harvard Law Review* 126(7): 2043–2081.

Anders, G. (2011) 'Testifying about "Uncivilized Events": Problematic Representations of Africa in the Trial against Charles Taylor', *Leiden Journal of International Law* 24(4): 937–959.

Anghie, A. (2005) *Imperialism, Sovereignty and the Making of International Law*, Cambridge: Cambridge University Press.

Asiegbu, J. U. J. (1969) *Slavery and the Politics of Liberation 1787–1861*, London: Longman.

Baars, G. (2014) 'Making ICL History: On the Need to Move beyond Pre-Fab Critiques of ICL', in C. Schwöbel (ed.), *Critical Approaches to International Criminal Law: An Introduction*, Abingdon: Routledge.

Benton, L. (2011) 'Abolition and Imperial Law, 1790–1820', *Journal of Imperial and Commonwealth History* 39(3): 355–374.

Benton, L. and Ford, L. (2016) *Rage for Order: The British Empire and the Origins of International Law 1800–1850*, Cambridge and London: Harvard University Press.

Bethell, L. (1970) *The Abolition of the Brazilian Slave Trade: Britain, Brazil and the Slave Trade Question 1807–1869*, Cambridge: Cambridge University Press.

Bhambra, G. K. and Shilliam, R. (2009) 'Introduction: "Silence" and Human Rights', in G. K. Bhambra and R. Shilliam (eds.), *Silencing Human Rights: Critical Engagements with a Contested Project*, Basingstoke, Hampshire: Palgrave Macmillan.

Binder, G. (1993) 'Did the Slaves Author the Thirteenth Amendment? An Essay in Redemptive History', *Yale Journal of Law and the Humanities* 5(2): 471–505.

Burroughs, R. (2010) 'Eyes on the Prize: Journeys in Slave Ships Taken as Prizes by the Royal Navy', *Slavery and Abolition* 31(1): 99–115.

Christie, N. (1986) 'The Ideal Victim', in E. A. Fattah (ed.), *From Crime Policy to Victim Policy*, Basingstoke: Macmillan.

Clarke, K. M. (2010) 'Rethinking Africa through Its Exclusions: The Politics of Naming Criminal Responsibility', *Anthropological Quarterly* 83(3): 625–652.

Clarke, K. M. (2015) '"We Ask for Justice, You Give Us Law": The Rule of Law, Economic Markets and the Reconfiguration of Victimhood', in C. De Vos, S. Kendall and C. Stahn (eds.), *Contested Justice: The Politics and Practice of International Criminal Court Interventions*, Cambridge: Cambridge University Press.

Clarke, K. M., Knottnerus, A. S. and de Volder, E. (eds.) (2017) *Africa and the ICC: Perceptions of Justice*, New York: Cambridge University Press.

Clarke, K. M. and Koulen, S. J. (2014) 'The Legal Politics of the Article 16 Decision: The International Criminal Court, the UN Security Council and Ontologies of a Contemporary Compromise', *African Journal of Legal Studies* 7: 297–319.

Cohen, D. (2014) 'Searching for Historical Origins of International Criminal Law', in M. Bergsmo, C. W. Ling and Y. Ping (eds.), *Historical Origins of International Criminal Law*, Volume 1, Brussels: Torkel Opshal EPublisher.

Conrad, R. (1973) 'Neither Slave Nor Free: The Emancipados of Brazil, 1818–1868', *Hispanic American Historical Review* 53(1): 50–70.

Craton, M. (1982) *Testing the Chains: Resistance to Slavery in the British West Indies*, Ithaca and London: Cornell University Press.

Craven, M. (2007) 'Introduction: International Law and Its Histories', in M. Craven, M. Fitzmaurice and M. Vogiatzi (eds.), *Time, History and International Law*, Leiden and Boston: Martinus Nijhoff.

Davis, K. (2008) *Periodization and Sovereignty: How Ideas of Feudalism and Secularization Govern the Politics of Time*, Philadelphia: University of Pennsylvania Press.

Depelchin, J. (2005) *Silences in African History: Between the Syndromes of Discovery and Abolition*, Dar Es Salaam: Mkuki Na Nyota Publishers.

Diggelmann, O. (2012) 'The Periodization of the History of International Law', in B. Fassbender and A. Peters (eds.), *The Oxford Handbook of the History of International Law*, Oxford: Oxford University Press.

Douglas, S. (2011) 'Between Constitutional Mo(nu)ments: Memorialising Past, Present and Future and the District Six Museum and Constitution Hill', *Law Critique* 22: 171–287.

Drescher, S. and Finkelman, P. (2012) 'Slavery', in B. Fassbender and A. Peters (eds.), *The Oxford Handbook of the History of International Law*, Oxford: Oxford University Press.

Eltis, D. (1987) *Economic Growth and the Ending of the Transatlantic Slave Trade*, New York: Oxford University Press.

Equiano, O. (2003) *The Interesting Narrative and Other Writings*, New York and London: Penguin.

Fett, S. M. (2017) *Recaptured Africans: Surviving Slave Ships, Detention, and Dislocation in the Final Years of the Slave Trade*, Chapel Hill: University of North Carolina Press.

Fletcher, L. (2015) 'Refracted Justice: The Imagined Victim and the International Criminal Court', in C. De Vos, S. Kendall and C. Stahn (eds.), *Contested Justice: The Politics and Practice of International Criminal Court Interventions*, Cambridge: Cambridge University Press.

Gathii, J. T. (2012) 'Africa', in B. Fassbender and A. Peters (eds.), *The Oxford Handbook of the History of International Law*, Oxford: Oxford University Press.

Genovese, E. D. (1975) *Roll, Jordan, Roll: The World the Slaves Made*, London: André Deutsch Ltd.

Genovese, E. D. (1979) *From Rebellion to Revolution: Afro-American Slave Revolts in the Making of the Modern World*, Baton Rouge and London: Louisiana State University Press.

Glassman, J. (1991) 'The Bondsman's New Clothes: The Contradictory Consciousness of Slave Resistance on the Swahili Coast', *Journal of African History* (32): 277–312.

Gross, A. (2008) 'When Is the Time of Slavery: The History of Slavery in Contemporary Legal and Political Argument', *California Law Review* 96(1): 283–321.

Gross, A. and Thomas, C. (2017) 'The New Abolitionism, International Law, and the Memory of Slavery', *Law and History Review* 35(1): 99–118.

Guberke, T. and Hedstrom, M. (2017) 'On or Off the Record? Detecting Patterns of Silence about Death in Guatemala's National Police Archive', *Archival Silence* 17(1): 27–54.

Gutto, S. (2013) 'In Search of Real Justice for Africa and Africans, and Her/Their Descendants in a World of Justice, Injustices and Impunity', *International Journal of African Renaissance Studies: Multi-, Inter- and Transdisciplinarity* 8(1): 30–45.

Hamilton, C., Harris, V. and Reid, C. (2002) 'Introduction', in C. Hamilton, V. Harris, J. Taylor, M. Pickover, G. Reid and R. Saleh (eds.), *Refiguring the Archive*, Dordrecht: Kluwer.

Hartman, S. (2008) 'Venus in Two Acts', *Small Axe*: 1–14.

Haslam, E. (2014) 'Silences in International Criminal Legal Histories and the Construction of the Victim Subject of International Criminal Law: The Nineteenth-Century Slave Trading Trial of Joseph Peters', in C. Schwöbel (ed.), *Critical Approaches to International Criminal Law: An Introduction*, London: Routledge.

Haslam, E. (2016) 'International Criminal Law and Legal Memories of Abolition: Intervention, Mixed Commission Courts and "Emancipation"', *Journal of the History of International Law* 18: 420–447.

Haslam, E. (2019) 'Writing More Inclusive Histories of International Criminal Law: Lessons from the Transatlantic Slave Trade', in I. Tallgren and T. Skouteris (eds.), *The New Histories of International Criminal Law: Retrials*, Oxford: Oxford University Press.

Haslam, E. and Edmunds, R. (2014) 'Victim Participation, Politics and the Construction of Victims at the International Criminal Court: Reflections on Proceedings in *Banda and Jerbo*', *Melbourne Journal of International Law* 14(2): 727–747.

Heller, K. J. (2011) *The Nuremberg Military Tribunals and the Origins of International Criminal Law*, Oxford: Oxford University Press.

Heller, K. J. and Simpson, G. J. (2013) *The Hidden Histories of War Crimes Trials*, Oxford: Oxford University Press.

Hoare, P. (1820) *Memoirs of Granville Sharp Esq*, London: Henry Colburn & Co.

James, C. L. R. (2001) *The Black Jacobins*, London: Penguin.

Johns, F., Joyce, R. and Pahuja, S. (2011) *Events: The Force of International Law*, Abingdon: Glasshouse.

Jorda, C. de Hemptinne, J. (2002) 'The Status and Role of the Victim', in A. Cassese, P. Gaeta and J. R. W. D. Jones (eds.), *The Rome Statute of the International Criminal Court: A Commentary*, Volume 2, Oxford: Oxford University Press.

Kapczynski, A. (2004–2005) 'Historicism, Progress, and the Redemptive Constitution', *Cardozo Law Review* 26: 1041–1117.

Kapur, R. (2002) 'The Tragedy of Victimization Rhetoric: Resurrecting the "Native" Subject in International/Post-Colonial Feminist Legal Politics', *Harvard Human Rights Journal* 15: 1–37.

Kendall, S. and Nouwen, S. (2014) 'Representational Practices at the International Criminal Court: The Gap between Juridified and Abstract Victimhood', *Law and Contemporary Problems* 76: 235–262.

Kern, H. L. (2004) 'Strategies of Legal Change: Great Britain, International Law, and the Abolition of the Transatlantic Slave Trade', *Journal of the History of International Law* 6: 233–258.

Killean, R. and Moffett, L. (2017) 'Victim Legal Representation before the ICC and ECCC', *Journal of International Criminal Justice* 15(4): 713–740.

Koskenniemi, M. (2001) *The Gentle Civilizer of Nations: The Rise and Fall of International Law 1870–1960*, Cambridge: Cambridge University Press.

Koskenniemi, M. (2012) 'A History of International Law Histories', in B. Fassbender and A. Peters (eds.), *The Oxford Handbook of the History of International Law*, Oxford: Oxford University Press.

Lesaffer, R. (2007) 'International Law and Its History: The Story of an Unrequited Love', in M. Craven, M. Fitzmaurice and M. Vogiatzi (eds.), *Time, History and International Law*, Leiden and Boston: Martinus Nijhoff.

Mamdani, M. (2009) 'Response', *International Journal of Transitional Justice* 3: 470–473.

Mamigonian, B. G. (2009) 'In the Name of Freedom: Slave Trade Abolition, the Law and the Brazilian Branch of the African Emigration Scheme (Brazil: British West Indies, 1930s-1950s)', *Slavery and Abolition* 30(1): 41–66.

Marcus, D. (2003) 'Famine Crimes in International Law', *American Journal of International Law* 97: 245–281.

Martinez, J. (2012) *The Slave Trade and the Origins of International Human Rights Law*, Oxford: Oxford University Press.

Martinez, J. and Surwillo, L. (2017) '"Like the Pirate and the Slave Trader before Him": Precedent and Analogy in Contemporary Law and Literature', *Law and History Review* 35(1): 81–98.

Martinez-Fernandez, L. (1995) 'The Havana Anglo-Spanish Mixed Commission for the Suppression of the Slave Trade and Cuba's Emancipados', *Slavery and Abolition* 16(2): 205–225.

Mawani, R. (2012) 'Law's Archive', *Annual Review of Law and Society Science* 8: 337–651.

Mégret, F. (2016) 'The Anxieties of International Criminal Justice', *Leiden Journal of International Law* 29(1): 197–221.

Meister, R. (2012) *After Evil: A Politics of Human Rights*, New York: Columbia University Press.

Moyn, S. (2014) *Human Rights and the Uses of History*, London: Verso.

Muhammad, P. (2013) 'The Trans-Atlantic Slave Trade: A Legacy Establishing a Case for International Reparations', *Columbia Journal of Race and Law* 3(2): 148–202.

Mutua, M. (2002) *Human Rights: A Political and Cultural Critique*, Philadelphia: University of Pennsylvania Press.

Northrup, D. (2006) 'Becoming African: Identity Formation among Liberated Slaves in Nineteenth-Century Sierra Leone', *Slavery and Abolition* 27(1): 1–21.

Okafor, O. and Ngwaba, U. (2015) 'The International Criminal Court as a "Transitional Justice" Mechanism in Africa: Some Critical Reflections', *International Journal of Transitional Justice* 9: 90–108.

Olusoga, D. (2016) *Black and British: A Forgotten History*, London: Macmillan.

Parfitt, R. (2014) 'The Spectre of Sources', *European Journal of International Law* 25(1): 297–306.

Quirk, J. (2012) 'Defining Slavery in All Its Forms: Historical Inquiry as Contemporary Instruction', in J. Allain (ed.), *The Legal Understanding of Slavery from the Historical to the Contemporary*, Oxford: Oxford University Press.

Rajagopal, B. (2003) *International Law from Below: Development, Social Movements and Third World Resistance*, Cambridge: Cambridge University Press.

Ramdin, R. (1987) *The Making of the Black Working Class in Britain*, Aldershot: Gower Publishing.

Richards, T. (1993) *The Imperial Archive: Knowledge and the Fantasy of Empire*, London and New York: Verso.

Richardson, D. (2001) 'Shipboard Revolts, African Authority, and the Atlantic Slave Trade', *William and Mary Quarterly* 58(1): 69–92.

Rizzo, M. (2017) 'Reading against the Grain: Finding the Voices of the Detained', *Museums and Social Issues* 12(1): 26–32.

Rodney, W. (1989) *How Europe Underdeveloped Africa*, Nairobi: East African Educational Publishers.

Sagan, A. (2010) 'African Criminals/African Victims: The Institutionalised Production of Cultural Narratives in International Criminal Law', *Millennium Journal of International Studies* 39(1): 3–21.

Sankey, D. (2014) 'Towards the Recognition of Subsistence Harms: Reassessing Current Approaches to Socio-Economic Forms of Violence in Transitional Justice', *International Journal of Transitional Justice* 8(1): 121–140.

Schwarz, S. (2012) 'Reconstructing the Life Histories of Liberated Africans: Sierra Leone in the Early Nineteenth Century', *History in Africa* 39: 175–207.

Schwöbel, C. (2013) 'The Comfort of International Criminal Law', *Law and Critique* 24(2): 169–191.

Schwöbel, C. (2014) 'The Market and Marketing Culture of International Criminal Law', in C. Schwöbel (ed.), *Critical Approaches to International Criminal Law: An Introduction*, Abingdon: Routledge.

Schwöbel-Patel, C. (2016) 'Spectacle in International Criminal Law: The Fundraising Image of Victimhood', *London Review of International Law* 4(2): 247–274.

Schwöbel-Patel, C. (2018) 'The "Ideal" Victim of International Criminal Law', *European Journal of International Law* 29(3): 703–724.

Scott, D. (2004) *Conscripts of Modernity: The Tragedy of Colonial Enlightenment*, Durham and London: Duke University Press.

Shaikh, F. (2012) 'Judicial Diplomacy', in K. Hamilton and P. Salmon (eds.), *Slavery, Diplomacy and Empire Britain and the Suppression of the Slave Trade, 1807–1975*, Eastbourne: Sussex Academic Press.

Shaw, R. (2002) *Memories of the Slave Trade: Ritual and the Historical Imagination in Sierra Leone*, Chicago and London: University of Chicago Press.

Simpson, G. J. (2013) 'History of Histories', in Kevin Jon Heller and Gerry Simpson (eds.), *The Hidden Histories of War Crimes Trials*, Oxford: Oxford University Press.

Simpson, G. J. (2018) 'The Conscience Of Civilisation, and Its Discontents', in P. Kastner (ed.), *International Criminal Law in Context*, London: Routledge.
Skouteris, T. (2010) *The Notion of Progress in International Legal Discourse*, The Hague: T.M.C. Asser Press.
Spivak, G. (1988) 'Can the Subaltern Speak?', in C. Nelson and L. Grossberg (eds.), *Marxism and the Interpretation of Culture*, Chicago: University of Chicago Press.
Stahn, C. (2015) 'Justice Civilisatrice? The ICC, Post-Colonial Theory, and Faces of "the Local"', in C. De Vos and S. Kendall (eds.), *Contested Justice: The Politics and Practice of International Criminal Court Interventions*, Cambridge: Cambridge University Press.
Steedman, C. (2011) 'After the Archive', *Comparative Critical Studies* 8: 321–340.
Stoler, A. L. (2002) 'Colonial Archives and the Arts of Governance', *Archival Science* 2 (1–2): 87–109.
Stoler, A. L. (2009) *Along the Archival Grain: Epistemic Anxieties and Colonial Common Sense*, Princeton and Oxford: Princeton University Press.
Sweet, J. W. (2009) 'The Subject of the Slave Trade: Recent Currents in the Histories of the Atlantic, Great Britain and Western Africa', *Early American Studies* 7(1): 1–45.
Tallgren, I. (2014) 'Searching for Historical Origins of International Criminal Law', in M. Bergsmo, C. W. Ling and Y. Ping (eds.), *Historical Origins of International Criminal Law*, Volume 1, Brussels: Torkel Opshal EPublisher.
Trouillot, M.-R. (2015) *Silencing the Past: Power and the Production of History*, Boston: Beacon Press.
Van Alstyne, R. W. (1930) 'The British Right of Search and the African Slave Trade', *Journal of Modern History* 2:37–47.
Vandervelde, L. (2014) *Redemption Songs: Suing for Freedom before Dred Scott*, Oxford: Oxford University Press.
Van Niekerk, J.-P. (2004a) 'British, Portuguese, and American Judge in Adderley Street: The International Legal Background to and Some Judicial Aspects of the Cape Town Mixed Commissions for the Suppression of the Transatlantic Slave Trade in the Nineteenth Century', *Comparative and International Law Journal of South Africa* 37: 1–39.
Van Niekerk, J.-P. (2004b) 'British, Portuguese, and American Judges in Adderley Street: The International Legal Background to and some Judicial Aspects of the Cape Town Mixed Commissions for the Suppression of the Transatlantic Slave Trade in the Nineteenth Century (Part 2)', *Comparative and International Law Journal of South Africa* 37: 196–225.
Van Wijk, J. (2013) 'Who is the "Little Old Lady" of International Crimes? Nils Christie's Concept of the Ideal Victim Reinterpreted', *International Review of Victimology* 19: 159–179.
Vasiliev, S. (2015) 'On Trajectories and Destinations of International Law Scholarship', *Leiden Journal of International Law* 28(4): 701–716.
Wall, I. R. (2012) *Human Rights and Constituent Power: Without Model or Warranty*, Abingdon: Routledge.
Wallace, E. K. (2006) *The British Slave Trade and Public Memory*, Chichester: Columbia University Press.
Walvin, J. (2007) 'Slave Trade', in D. Dabydeen, J. Gilmore and C. Jones (eds.), *The Oxford Companion to Black British History*, Oxford: Oxford University Press.
Wheaton, H. (1936) *Elements of International Law*, R. H. Dana (ed.), Boston: Little Brown and Oxford: Clarendon.

Williams, E. (1964) *Capitalism and Slavery*, London: Andre Deutsch Ltd.
Wood, M. (2010) *The Horrible Gift of Freedom: Atlantic Slavery and the Representation of Emancipation*, Athens, Georgia: University of Georgia Press.

International instruments

African Union, 2014 Protocol on Amendments to the Protocol on the Statute of the African Court of Justice and Human Rights.
Durban Declaration, 8 September 2001, World Conference against Racism, Racial Discrimination, Xenophobia and Related Intolerance A/Conf. 189/12.
Rome Statute on the International Criminal Court 1998, 2187 UNTS 90.
Slavery Convention 1926 60 LNTS 253.
Supplementary Convention on the Abolition of Slavery, the Slave Trade, and Institutions and Practices Similar to Slavery (Supplementary Slavery Convention 1956) 1956 266 UNTS 3.
UN Protocol to Prevent, Suppress and Punish Trafficking in Persons, Especially Women and Children UN Doc A/55/383 1 November 2000.

English cases

The Nancy (1810) 12 Eng Rep 157.
Somerset v Stewart (1772) 98 Eng Rep 499.

French case

Cass Crim, 5 February 2013, Bull Crim 2013 n 38 (case number 11–85909).

Mixed commission cases

Hamilton to Canning, 12 October 1826, in the Case of the *Perpetuo Defensor*, No. 46 with Enclosures in *Class A Correspondence with the British Commissioners at Sierra Leone, the Havannah, Rio de Janeiro, and Surinam, relating to the slave trade 1826–1827* PP 1826–27 (010) XXVI.127.
HM Commissioners to Canning, 10 June 1826, in the Case of the *Activo*, No. 42 with Enclosures in *Class A Correspondence with the British Commissioners at Sierra Leone, the Havannah, Rio de Janeiro, and Surinam, relating to the slave trade 1826–1827* PP 1826–27 (010) XXVI.127.
HM Commissioners to Palmerston, 31 March 1834, in the Case of the *Maria da Gloria*, No. 34 with Enclosures in *Class A Correspondence with the British Commissioners at Sierra Leone, the Havana, Rio de Janeiro, and Surinam, Relating to the Slave Trade 1834* PP 1835 (006) LI.1.

Documents and correspondence

Canning to HM Commissioners, 30 December 1826, The National Archives: FO 84/49, p. 7.

HM Commissioners to Palmerston 9 April 1834, No. 35 in *Class A Correspondence with the British Commissioners at Sierra Leone, the Havana, Rio de Janeiro, and Surinam, Relating to the Slave Trade 1834* PP 1835 (006) LI.1.

Internet sources

CARICOM (10 December, 2013) Reparations Commission Press Statement 10, https://caricom.org/media-center/communications/press-releases/caricom-reparations-commission-press-statement-delivered-by-professor-sir-h

2 Where it all began
Prize

Introduction

The origins of international slave trade repression law lay in the law of prize, the law that regulated the capture and detention of enemy property in war. To that extent, war was legally enabling of international abolition law. In turn, prize law had a fundamental impact on the construction of recaptives in law. This chapter sets the book's discussion of the construction of the recaptive within the context of these legal origins. In so doing, it provides an account of British efforts to mobilise against the slave trade on the international level.

To this end the chapter begins by outlining British domestic measures to prohibit the trade. It then turns to the British assault against the foreign slave trade, much of which centred, at least initially, on interventions against foreign slave ships based on the law of prize. War then legally empowered early attempts at the international suppression of the slave trade. However, prize was limited because it did not enable the seizure of foreign slave ships during peacetime. Despite this, British ships controversially and often unlawfully continued to seize foreign slave ships outside the context of war. Many of these actions were legally and diplomatically unsustainable, but Britain – not least through financial inducement – was able to persuade some major states which permitted the slave trade to come to a series of bilateral agreements that provided for the establishment of Mixed Commissions on the slave trade. The following section shows how these new institutions, which effectively replaced action against enemy slave traders with action against slave traders of treaty partners, drew upon the jurisprudence and legal structures of prize with the result that the principles drawn from war infused even peace time provisions on slave trade repression. This section focuses in particular on the London Slave Trade Commission. This particular Mixed Commission was established to compensate Portuguese owners for illegal seizures. It represents an inauspicious but telling beginning for the Mixed Commissions on the slave trade. If prize enabled slave trade repression, its legacy was, however, more problematic in respect of the construction of the recaptive in international law, to which the remainder of the book turns.

The British context

Despite its role in international abolition, Britain had been one of the major slave trading nations. British slave traders transported at least 2.6 million Africans to the Americas (Hamilton and Shaikh 2012: 2). Motivations for this turnaround are strongly disputed; since the publication of Eric Williams's *Capitalism and Slavery* (Williams 1964), the relationship between humanitarian and economic causes in particular.[1] Much is at stake in these debates. It was clear however, even to West Indian planters who had opposed the Abolition Act 1807, that British economic interests lay in international action against the slave trade (Martinez 2012: 23).

The British Parliament had passed a series of statutes aimed at ameliorating the trade from the late 1780s, notably after the infamous but ultimately inconclusive 1783 case of *Gregson v Gilbert*, otherwise known as the *Zong* (Van Niekerk 2004a: 2), in which Luke Collingwood, the master of the slave ship, allegedly ordered his crew to throw 133 sick slaves overboard (Krikler 29–31).[2] The House of Lords prevented a Bill abolishing the trade in 1792. However, by characterising the measure as a question of 'national security' and not humanity, proponents of the Foreign Slave Trade Act ensured the 1806 Act got through the House of Commons and abolitionist mobilisation and popular support ensured it passed the Lords (Martinez 2012: 22). The Act for the Abolition of the Slave Trade (Abolition Act 1807) followed. This Act prohibited British subjects and residents from participating in the transatlantic slave trade.[3] It permitted the forfeiture of their slave ships and their cargo with a £100 fine levied for each captured slave.

The Abolition Act (and the subsequent slave trade repression treaties) did not recognise any right on the part of slaves to freedom, leading Marcus Wood to describe it 'a mean-spirited and highly efficient plan for the continued exploitation of the African body' (Wood 2010: 14). The act provided that captured slaves were to be forfeited to the King 'in such Manner and Form, *as any Goods or Merchandize unlawfully imported*' albeit 'for the purpose. . . of divesting and barring all other Property' to them (s 4 Abolition Act 1807 emphasis added). Liberated slaves were to be treated like slaves taken as prize of war (s 7 Abolition Act 1807). Therefore, they were to be apprenticed for a maximum period of 14 years or enlisted *as if* they had entered the services voluntarily (s 7 Abolition Act 1807, emphasis added). Unlike those in the forces they served alongside, enlisted liberated Africans were not entitled to a pension (s 17 Abolition Act 1807). This was a limited kind of freedom. Lord Stowell recognised in the case of *The Slave Grace* that there was, 'nothing of free will. . . or free action' in compulsory apprenticeships or enlistment. Rather it was 'only a transit from one species of slavery into another' (*The Slave Grace* 1827: 182).

Subsequent legislation expanded the basic provisions of the Abolition Act. The Slave Trade Felony Act 1811 made slave trading a felony, reducing slave factors to 'pickpockets and swindlers' in the words of Thorpe CJ in the trial of Samuel Samo, the first prosecution under the Act in Sierra Leone (*The Trials of the Slave*

Traders 1813: 11). The Foreign Slave Trade Act had prohibited British investment and security in the foreign slave trade. Had it passed the Lords, a Bill in 1814 would also have made these violations a felony (HC Deb 18 April 1814; HL Deb 30 June 1814–1815). In 1824, slave trading became an act of piracy which was punishable by death (An Act for the more effectual Suppression of the African Slave Trade 1824). This was reduced in 1837 to transportation or imprisonment (An Act for abolishing the Punishment of Death 1837). In 1843, the Slave Trade Suppression Act finally confirmed that legislation prohibiting British involvement in the slave trade also applied to British subjects outside British territories (Eltis 1987: 83; Slave Trade Suppression Act 1843).

There was no shortage of legislative activity but there were, however, few prosecutions for slave trading. For example, John Bean Hannay, captain of the ship the *James* was the first convicted in England under the Slave Trade Felony Act. He was sentenced to seven years' transportation in February 1817 (*R v John Bean Hannay* 1817). In April 1812, Samuel Samo was convicted, and later pardoned, by the Sierra Leone Vice Admiralty Court (*The Trials of the Slave Traders* 1813; Haslam 2012). Carrol and Villemont were controversially brought from Mauritius to England to stand trial at the Old Bailey in January 1820 for bringing 200 slaves from Madagascar to Mauritius. The jury found them guilty after 10 minutes' deliberation and they were sentenced to 14 years' transportation (*R v Carrol and Villemont* 1820). Many of the few prosecutions that did take place seem to have been marred by concerns about legality and pardons were not uncommon (Haslam 2012; Petition of Elizabeth Bostock; Petition on behalf of the Spanish envoy).

There is considerable proof that British participation in the slave trade – to say nothing of slavery – continued after the formal abolition of the trade (Sherwood 2007). Although slavery was abolished in the West Indies in the 1830s (Slavery Abolition Act 1833), Shaw claims that up until 1929 the British permitted 'internal slavery' in the hinterland of Sierra Leone (Shaw 2002: 38). British goods also continued to fuel the slave trade. Sherwood observes that in the 1830s and 1840s around 80–90% of the goods exchanged for slaves intended for the Cuban and Brazilian trade were British made and supplied (Sherwood 2004: 55). As Lieutenant Colonel Nicolls testified in the infamous trial that led to the controversial acquittal of London merchant Pedro De Zulueta in 1843:[4] 'You cannot get slaves for money; I never saw a slave got for money: they cannot be got without British manufactured goods, supplied by British merchants' (Johnson 1844: 39).

The use of British capital and goods in the foreign slave trade, the participation of British subjects in the trade abroad and the inherently international nature of the slave trade necessitated an international response to the trade's suppression. From the outset, it was also clear that Britain was likely to be significantly economically disadvantaged if other states did not stop their nationals from slave trading (Miers 1975: 9; Haslam 2016: 425). Consequently, soon after passing the Abolition Act in 1807 the British government focused attention on the so-called foreign slave trade. However, an international response to slave trade repression required changes to international law. Although international law permitted the slave trade at the end of the eighteenth century (Martinez 2012: 17–19), by the mid-nineteenth century, international law on slave trade repression was radically altered. Slave trade suppression litigation contributed to this fundamental change.

Sierra Leone played a critical role in British efforts to effect such changes. It was the site of an often judicially interventionist Vice Admiralty Court and the most active of the Mixed Commissions on the slave trade. It was also the location of British efforts to resettle liberated Africans. In 1787, the Committee for the Relief of the Black Poor established the Province of Freedom as a settlement for former slaves from Britain and the New World. In 1791, the Sierra Leone Company took over the Province and called it Freetown. In 1792, around 1000 former slaves whom the British emancipated in return for support during the American War of Independence were settled in Sierra Leone, followed in 1800 by around 700 Jamaican maroons (Fyfe 1961: 77). The British Crown established Sierra Leone as a Crown colony in 1808 (Fyfe 1962: 97). It was to Sierra Leone that the British Navy brought captured slave ships and recaptives. During the next 60 years, 90,000 recaptives were settled in Freetown – not, it should be added, by their own choice (Schwarz 2012: 176–177). The Sierra Leone Vice Admiralty Court, or one of the Mixed Commission Courts, decided the fate and status of most of them. The exact law these courts applied – prize law, slave trade repression treaties or the Abolition Act – depended on the circumstances in which slave ships were detained and the nationality of the ship. The resulting litigation contributed to radical shifts in the status of the slave trade in international law in the first part of the nineteenth century.

War and the enabling of slave trade repression

British interventions against foreign slave ships were initially based on the law of prize. During war, belligerents could search and detain enemy ships on the high seas. Neutral ships could be visited and searched for contraband (Allain 2007: 348). Prize courts located within the seizor's jurisdiction determined whether the vessels were seized according to international law (Phillimore 1857: 393; Benton 2011: 357). During the Napoleonic Wars, British ships drew on the law of prize to seize enemy slave ships. In 1810, the test case of the *Amedie* affirmed the legality of the seizure of neutral slave ships trading with the enemy and famously shifted the burden of proof as to the legality of the trade. The Court held that the entry into force of the British prohibition had rendered the slave trade prima facie unlawful. As a result, the claimants had to demonstrate the legality of the trade because the trade could not 'abstractly speaking, be said to have a legitimate existence' (the *Amedie* 1810: 93). This decision and the case law it spawned allowed robust action against enemy slave traders and neutrals, at least where neutral states had prohibited the trade.[5]

This creative deployment of prize for abolition had uneasy origins, however. Prize had previously been used to enslave hundreds of black sailors. During much of the eighteenth century British Vice Admiralty Courts presumed that captured black mariners were slaves who could be disposed of on capture along with ships' cargoes (Foy 2010: 283). Foy describes Anglo-American prize that operated before abolition therefore as 'highly organised enterprises for the provision of coerced labour' (ibid: 380). After abolition, Britain deployed the same legal instrument to justify the search and seizure of enemy slave ships. The creative deployment of prize for abolition might be considered to transcend these dubious origins. However, prize was an inherently limited tool for abolition. As Benton and Ford have shown, it focused on the 'adjudication of property rights rather than the protection of rescued slaves' (Benton and Ford 2016: 125) and it did not challenge the construction of slaves as 'human property' (Benton and Ford 2016: 122). Moreover, this creative deployment of prize had other limits.

For one thing, the legal origins of the British assault against the foreign slave trade lay in action against British enemies.[6] Thus, the appellants in the appeal in the case of the *Gertrudis La Preciosa* claimed that they had British assurance that British allies could lawfully trade in slaves without British interference (*Gertrudis La Preciosa* 1816: 398). The case of the *Amedie*, which as previously explained confirmed the legality of the seizure of neutral slave ships, limited the usefulness for slave traders of relying on neutral flags of convenience (Van Niekerk 2004a: 10; African Institution 1811: 14). As a result, many slave traders sought to sail under the flags of Spain and Portugal, states which were British allies (Eltis 1987: 104). Although captors and courts challenged colourable (that is false) transactions,[7] it seems that by 1811 almost all of the trade sailing under the Spanish flag was in fact British or American (African Institution 1811: 31).

For another, during peace the right to visit lapsed, including the right to visit British ships colourably (that is falsely) flying the flag of another state (African Institution 1819: 6). Peace in Europe was therefore considered detrimental to international abolition (African Institution 1819: 3, 77, 79), a sentiment echoed by the respondents in the classic case of *Le Louis* (*Le Louis* 1817: 1466) which finally determined the illegality of peacetime seizures and which is explored in more detail in Chapter 3. In peacetime, intervention could only be justified against non-British slave traders if an international treaty permitted it. Until the establishment of Mixed Commissions from 1817 onwards no international treaty provided for such intervention.

Foreign Secretary George Canning ordered British ambassadors overseas to negotiate slave trade abolition treaties shortly after the Abolition Act was passed (Hamilton and Shaikh 2012: 4). However, the resulting treaties did not permit the search and detention of slave ships. For example, the 1810 Anglo-Portuguese Treaty of Amity committed Portugal to adopt 'the most efficacious means for bringing about a gradual Abolition of the Slave Trade' (Bandinel 1968: 127–128). It also prohibited Portuguese subjects from slave trading on the African coast outside Portuguese dominions and where the trade was forbidden. The treaty did not permit Portuguese ships to be detained.[8] Even so, the Vice Admiralty Court in Sierra Leone repeatedly relied on it, for example, condemning at least 24 Portuguese ships between 1810 and 1812 (Eltis 1987: 108). Spain also agreed to a treaty in 1814 to restrict the Spanish slave trade and to prohibit foreigners from participating in it, but it did not agree to British interventions against Spanish ships (Hamilton and Shaikh 2012: 7). Therefore, peacetime condemnations of Spanish ships were legally indefensible. Indeed, the partly successful appeal in the case of the *Gertrudis La Preciosa*, discussed earlier, rested on the claim that the trader had ensured that he had adhered to British-Spanish agreements (*Gertrudis La Preciosa* 1816: 399). British attempts to negotiate multilaterally a right of search also failed to bear fruit. Whilst states famously declared the slave trade 'repugnant to the principles of humanity and universal morality' at the Congress of Vienna in 1815, they recognised the need to end it only according to the 'interests, habits and even the prejudices of their subjects' (Declaration of Eight Powers 1815). Subsequent proposals for a peacetime mutual right of search were controversial. In particular, America having experienced British naval interventions and the resulting impressment of sailors into the British navy during war, feared the potential for abuse during peacetime (Martinez 2012: 46–47).

Captors, however, continued to seize slave ships and courts to condemn them. Martinez has calculated that 204 cases were tried in British Admiralty Courts between 1806 and 1817 (Martinez 2012: 26). Decisions of the Sierra Leone Vice Admiralty were controversial, seemingly all too often combining the theoretically separate grounds of prize, international treaties and the Abolition Act in broad-brush justifications.[9] This approach partly reflected the inherently international and interconnected nature of the slave trade, but it was theoretically muddled. Sir William Scott observed, in one successful appeal against condemnation, that the proceedings of the Sierra Leone Vice Admiralty were 'as mongrel a proceeding as ever presented itself to the notice of this or of any other Court' (the *Diana* 1813: 1246). By 1815 the government's legal advisor was challenging the legality of the decisions of the Sierra Leone Vice Admiralty Court (Helfman 2006: 1148–1149). Such decisions gave rise to so much diplomatic and political controversy that Britain was compelled to compensate Portugal.[10] Even so, seizures, condemnations and the controversy they generated contributed to the changing face of international abolition law. In 1815, Britain agreed to compensate Portugal for illegal detentions and condemnations and to cancel money owing on an outstanding loan, in exchange for Portugal agreeing to abolish the slave trade north of the equator, to limit its slave trade to supplying Brazil and to agree to a future treaty prohibiting the trade (Eltis 1987: 109; Hamilton and Shaikh 2012: 7). Once this had been agreed, the British government ordered the African squadron to seize Portuguese slave ships north of the equator (Eltis 1987: 109). These continued interventions, controversially affirmed by the Vice Admiralty Court in Sierra Leone, again gave rise to diplomatic concern. Decisions of the Sierra Leone Vice Admiralty Court to condemn Portuguese, Spanish and Dutch ships after 1815 were just as much lacking in authority and jurisdiction as previously, as was statutorily recognised (Appropriation of Proceeds Act 1821). As the court emphasised in the case of the *Le Louis*, what was needed was an international agreement. Agreements to establish Mixed Commissions form part of a broader network of bilateral treaties that Britain agreed with other states and African powers, with varying degrees of cooperation (Van Niekerk 2004a: 15–21).[11]

In 1817, Britain and Portugal agreed by the Additional Convention to establish British-Portuguese Mixed Commissions in Sierra Leone (1819–1844) and Rio de Janeiro (1819–1823) (Haslam 2016: 426). Britain agreed to pay Portugal £300,000 outstanding under the 1815 treaty. It also agreed to establish the London Slave Trade Commission as a means of compensating Portuguese ship and cargo owners for illegal seizures (Additional Convention (Portugal) 1817). Britain and Spain agreed to establish a British-Spanish Mixed Commission at Sierra Leone and Havana (Additional Convention (Spain) 1817). Britain agreed to compensate Spain for illegal seizures and paid a sum of £400,000, with which Spain purchased warships (Eltis 1987: 110).[12] The Additional Convention (Spain) committed Spain to abolish the Spanish slave trade north of the equator immediately and, after May 1820, to abolish it everywhere else. Other states also agreed to establish Mixed Commissions, including the Netherlands and, on its independence from Portugal, Brazil. Brazil agreed in 1826 to a treaty against the slave trade in exchange for Britain recognising its independence (Van Niekerk 2004a: 25). This treaty committed Brazil to abolish the slave trade completely from 1830 and to declare it piracy. It incorporated the Additional Convention (Portugal) which was to remain in force, barring an alternative arrangement, for 15 years after the Portuguese abolition of the slave trade (Jenner to Palmerston 28 July 1831: 330; Palmerston to HM Commissioners at Sierra Leone 16 August 1831).[13]

Separate, but similar, bilateral treaties regulated each of these Mixed Commissions (Haslam 2016: 426). Treaties provided that signatory states' navies acting under special instructions could search and detain slave ships and bring them to the nearest Mixed Commission with jurisdiction. Searching officers had to be at least of lieutenant status. Searches had to be conducted in the mildest possible way (Article 7 Portuguese Instructions 1817; Article 5 Spanish Instructions 1817). Mixed Commissions were empowered to restore slave ships and their cargoes to owners with compensation or to condemn the ship and emancipate the recaptives. Recaptives were never compensated.

Mixed Commissions did not replace the role of Vice Admiralty Courts in slave trade repression. Britain continued to resort to Vice Admiralty Courts to obtain goals that were unattainable through the Mixed Commission regime. For example, British Vice Admiralty Courts continued to hear cases that fell outside the jurisdiction of Mixed Commissions, such as cases dealing with stateless ships or ships of states not covered by a Mixed Commission agreement, such as France (Van Niekerk 2004b: 211).[14] Vice Admiralty Courts also supported the work of Mixed Commissions. For example, after the captor abandoned the prosecution of the Spanish ship the *Carolina* before the British-Spanish Mixed Commission, the *Carolina* remained in the harbour at Freetown equipped for the slave trade for so long that another officer detained it. The Sierra Leone Vice Admiralty Court then condemned it as a foreign ship, equipped for the trade in British waters (HM Commissioners to Palmerston 31 December 1839: 11). When Mixed Commissions ceased to operate, Britain also turned to Vice Admiralty Courts as it had done before the Mixed Commissions were established. On occasion, this enabled Britain to achieve goals that would have been unattainable through Mixed Commissions alone.[15]

In summary, many early British interventions against the foreign slave trade were of questionable legality, but they contributed to developments in international law and slave trade suppression. The initial actions and the Mixed Commissions to which those actions eventually gave rise found their origins in the law of prize. The deployment of prize for slave trade repression was a creative legal response developed at a time when the slave trade was widely considered lawful. However, the legal coupling of belligerency and abolition was limited and its peacetime extension was extremely controversial. The development of international abolition was, therefore, inextricably linked to the legal rights of states triggered by war. The legally enabling nature of war was recognised by the British-Spanish Mixed Commission in the case of the *Mary Anne Cassard*, captured in October 1838 with a Spanish crew but falsely flying the flag of America, a state which had not agreed to the Mixed Commission regime (HM Commissioners to Palmerston 30 November 1838). British Commissioners declared themselves incompetent to adjudicate. In a separate clarificatory report they insisted that there was no right to visit and search ships flying American flags during peacetime. Had England been at war '*with any Power*' they explained the situation would have been different because under these circumstances the *Mary Anne Cassard* could have been searched and detained, and the captor could have used his discovery that the ship was Spanish to bring it before the British-Spanish Mixed Commission which would have condemned it (ibid: 19, original emphasis). Prize determined the conditions of legal possibility according to which early international slave trade repression took place and set the tone for the subsequent development of the law. For although they were established during peacetime and had no power to draw on the rights of war, Mixed Commissions were far from a clear departure from their legal past.

Enduring prize

As discussed, from 1817, Britain developed what looked on the face of it to be a more consensual approach towards international slave trade abolition (Haslam 2016: 426). This was characterised by the recognition of mutual rights of search and the establishment of Mixed Commissions with, for example, Spain and Portugal (Additional Convention (Portugal); Additional Convention (Spain)). This more consensual version of abolition replaced enemies (and neutrals) with treaty partners. However, prize continued to exert a profound legacy.

British Commissioners at Sierra Leone borrowed from, and relied upon, arguments drawn from prize. Notwithstanding the shift to a more consensual approach, British Commissioners apparently saw no difficulty in the continued application of prize law. For example, in the *Diligente*, the British-Spanish Mixed Commission rejected claimants' arguments that it was unfair to apply the principles and decisions of wartime seizures to peacetime captures (HM Commissioners to Palmerston 20 October 1838: 17–18). The legal link between Mixed Commissions and prize is further evident in the establishment and operation of the London Slave Trade Commission. The London Slave Trade Commission, one of the first but most overlooked Mixed Commissions on the Slave Trade, exemplifies the more general focus of Mixed Commissions on questions of intervention (Haslam 2016: 429). The prioritising of questions about intervention was one of the key legal legacies of the origins of international abolition law in prize. This was an unpromising if illuminating institutional origin for subsequent Mixed Commissions on the Slave Trade.

Located at 53 Parliament Street, London, the Commission was established by the Additional Convention (Portugal), the same treaty that provided for the establishment of Mixed Commissions in Sierra Leone and elsewhere. This legacy casts a critical shadow on claims that Mixed Commissions constituted early human rights courts because the London Commission was established solely to compensate Portuguese owners for losses arising out of unlawful seizures. It had jurisdiction over seizures that took place from 1 June 1814 until the British-Portuguese Mixed Commissions were established in Sierra Leone and Rio de Janeiro. Although the jurisdiction of the London Slave Trade Commission was not limited to claims arising out of the judgments of the Vice Admiralty Court in Sierra Leone, these cases made up the greatest part of its workload and one of the Commission's first acts was to request that the court hand over all of its papers relating to seized Portuguese slave ships (Roffery to Hamilton 27 November 1819).

Not surprisingly, since they were established under the same enabling treaty, the institutional set-up of the London Slave Trade Commission was very similar to that of the Mixed Commissions that were established in Sierra Leone. The Registrar administered a uniform set of interrogatories, which were approved by the Crown's Law Officers, and Commissioners were instructed to develop additional interrogatories where necessary (Castlereagh to HM Commissioners 27 March 1819). Captors had the opportunity to justify their actions. Decisions of the Commission were final and not subject to appeal. They were taken in the first instance by one Portuguese and one British-appointed Commissary Judge. If Commissary Judges could not agree, lots were drawn for the appointment of one of two arbitrators, again appointed by Portugal and Britain. Initially, Antonio Juliao da Costa and Alexander Marsden were appointed Commissary Judges for Portugal and Britain respectively. The original appointee for the position of Portuguese Arbitrator resigned before he heard any claims so that he could be free to act as agent for claimants before the Commission. In February 1820, John Jorge was appointed in his place. Justinian Casamajor was appointed as the British arbitrator. When Casamajor died, Bartholomew Frere replaced him.[16] William Roffery, who subsequently became slave trade advisor to the Treasury, was appointed Registrar.

In principle, the mandate of the London Slave Trade Commission was to indemnify unlawful captures of slave ships which had been trading lawfully. However, in practice, compensation was paid in a number of cases in which British Commissioners had serious concerns that unlawful slave-trading voyages had taken place; where force had been used against prize crews and, at least in one case, where the captured ship had been recaptured by the master and crew (Marsden to Castlereagh 25 February 1820). For example, Marsden wrote a strongly worded protest against the decision to award the claimants damages in the *San Antonio Milagrozo* which had fallen by lot to the Portuguese arbitrator and wrote to Secretary of State Canning about his concerns. Canning, who sought legal advice, considered the decision 'strongly biased and prejudiced', but the only legal option was for the British government to raise the issue at the intergovernmental level (Marsden to Canning, with enclosures including Protest 29 March 1822: 25; Canning to Marsden 5 July 1823: 57). By 1824, the London Slave Trade Commission was wound up. It had heard nearly 30 petitions from Portuguese ship and cargo owners (Marsden 9 December 1824) and had cost Britain £225,000 (Eltis 1987: 110).

Histories of Mixed Commissions rarely detail the London Slave Trade Commission. This is regrettable. The London Slave Trade Commission shared the same foundational treaty as the Mixed Commissions established in Sierra Leone and elsewhere, although they had additional powers to emancipate recaptives. The London Slave Trade Commission was able to judge the legality of seizures and condemnations precisely because the principles on which Mixed Commissions adjudicated did not differ fundamentally from those of Vice Admiralty Courts applying prize law. Central to these principles was the question of the legality of intervention. The preoccupation of the London Slave Trade Commission with compensating Portuguese ship and cargo owners tempers the portrayal of Mixed Commissions as human rights courts in so far as human rights are identified within a legal tradition that emphasises the protection of the rights of the enslaved, rather than the property rights of slave owners.[17] It also presages the focus of Mixed Commissions in Sierra Leone on questions of intervention. Prize had an enduring influence on slave trade repression and, as subsequent chapters show, on the construction of recaptives.

Conclusion

Many of the judgments emanating from the Vice Admiralty Court in Sierra Leone (in particular) were legally problematic. However, as a tool for legal change and an object of contestation, this litigation, together with the jurisprudence of Mixed Commissions, contributed to generating significant changes in international law's approach to the slave trade in the first part of the nineteenth century. However, this creative deployment of prize came at a price. Channelling questions about the slave trade into questions about intervention had major consequences for the legal construction of the subjects of abolition. Objections to the implicit criticisms contained within this line of argument can be raised on the grounds that prize was the only tool available. More radically, it might be contended that abolition powerfully subverted prize to ensure many recaptives' liberation. However, as this book shows, the legal focus on questions of intervention could work to the detriment of recaptives to greater or lesser degrees.

This chapter's focus on the law of prize has drawn upon a broad understanding of international criminal legal history (going beyond international criminal law in a strict sense). The aim has been to examine the legal and institutional context for the construction of recaptives as the basis for subsequent discussion about contemporary approaches to victims in international criminal law. This approach then draws on the idea that the subject of history writing reflects at least in part current concerns and preoccupations. The following chapter complements this perspective on international criminal legal history by positioning international criminal law – and its history – in more orthodox terms, concerned as it is with the failure to recognise the slave trade as an international crime. Strikingly, however, in both histories, the language and law of the use of force were critical in setting the legal conditions of possibility for international slave trade repression.

Notes

1 For subsequent discussion of Williams's work, see, for example, Drescher (1977) and Davis (1999: 347–348). For a discussion of these debates and their significance, see Brown (2006: 15–16) who observes that notwithstanding criticism Williams's book 'forever stigmatized the humanitarian narrative' (ibid: 16). On the role of civil society in abolition, see Drescher (1991, 1994). Christopher Brown masterfully traces the influence on abolition of the American Revolution and the 'crisis in imperial authority' it generated, arguing that: 'Support for slavery could become an embarrassment if and when the virtue of imperial rule became a public question. At the same time, moral capital might be accrued by framing antislavery initiatives as an emblem of the national character' (Brown 2006: 27). See further on abolition and American independence Grewe (2000: 556). For further discussion on the relationship between humanitarianism and capitalism in abolition, see, for example, Haskell (1985), Ashworth (1987) and Haskell (1987).

2 Collingwood is reported to have told the crew that the ship's owners could not successfully claim insurance money in the case of a so-called 'natural death', but could if the slaves were thrown overboard for the ship's safety. Some of the slaves resisted and were shackled before being thrown into the sea. Ten jumped overboard. There were two trials: the first ordered the insurers to pay. In the second Lord Mansfield, who notoriously compared the slaves to horses, suggested otherwise. A final trial to determine the issue conclusively never took place (Fryer 1987: 127–129; Krikler 2007: 29). Granville Sharp unsuccessfully campaigned for a criminal case to be brought. See further, Walvin (2011). For a powerful argument that the *Zong* is central 'to the history of modern capital, ethics and time consciousness', see Baucom (2005: 31).

3 Subsequent acts referred to 'any persons'. This enabled the Appeal Court in *Del Campo and Martinez v Reg* to affirm the decision of the Vice Admiralty Court in Gibraltar to impose penalties under the Slave Trade Amendment and Consolidation Act 1824 on the Spanish owners of the *Cazador* because it was found in a British port equipped for the trade.

4 Pedro De Zulueta was charged under the Slave Trade Amendment and Consolidation Act 1824 with feloniously equipping, manning and navigating the ship the *Augusta* for the purposes of slave trading, sending it out for purchasing slaves and putting on the ship goods to be used in barter for slaves. Friends and London merchants who had packed the courtroom cheered and clapped on his acquittal. See further Johnson (1844) and Sherwood (2004).

5 Sir William Scott overturned the condemnation of the Swedish ship, the *Diana,* because Sweden had not prohibited the trade (the *Diana* 1813). In contrast, the captured American ship the *Anne* was condemned even though the British Abolition Act, in contrast to the US prohibition of the trade, had not yet come into force (the *Anne* 1810).

6 On the friends–foe dynamic in contemporary international criminal law, see Nouwen and Werner (2011).

7 See further the *Fortuna* 1811 (an American ship falsely flying the Portuguese flag) and the *Donna Marianna* in 1812 (a British ship with false Portuguese papers). In both cases, the condemnation of the ship and cargo was affirmed on appeal. Even though the *Fortuna* was equipped for slave trading, it had not yet taken part in it. Sir William Scott claimed as irrelevant the 'stage of the employment, whether in the inception, or the prosecution, or the consummation of it' (1242).

8 William Roffery, slave trade adviser to the Treasury, considered the central provisions of the treaty to be commercial (Roffery to HM Treasury 31 May 1826).

9 See, for example, the condemnation of the *Bon Successo* which had been seized with 251 recaptives because it violated the Treaty of Amity 1810 and because it acquired canoes from British subjects. The London Slave Trade Commission indemnified claimants (Return to the House of Commons 1824: 280–281). The court based its condemnation of the *Nostra Santada da Victoria* (reversed on appeal) on the fact that British subjects had sold 68 of the 434 recaptives on board and because the Treaty of Amity had been violated (Return to the House of Commons 1824: 280–281). The Spanish ship the *Zaragozano* was condemned in July 1810. Under the command of an American, the ship had laden provisions for the slave trade at two British ports (Vessels, Cargoes and Slaves 1808–1817: 15). In 1809, the recaptives found on board the *Penel* were condemned because they had been sold by a British man and because the ship carried more weapons than neutral ships were allowed. The rest of its cargo was restored (Vessels, Cargoes and Slaves 1808–1817: 27).

10 Amongst other concerns, claimants asserted that by the time they came to know that their ships and cargoes had been condemned at Sierra Leone, they were often out of time for an appeal (Helfman 2006: 1148).

11 See further, for example, the Treaty of Ghent 1814 in which the USA and Britain recognised the inhumanity and injustice of the slave trade and agreed to 'use their best endeavours' to abolish it (Martinez 2012: 30).

12 Between 1809 and 1819 British courts had condemned at least 43 Spanish slave ships (Eltis 1987: 109).

13 From the late 1820s Brazil contested the continued applicability of the Additional Convention (Portugal), arguing that the British-Brazilian Mixed Commission should be dissolved. As soon as it could, Brazil terminated it in March 1845. Accordingly, the Anglo-Brazilian Mixed Commission in Sierra Leone was dissolved. The Commission at Rio remained in existence for six months to resolve outstanding cases.

14 France agreed in 1831, as amended in 1833, to a geographically limited mutual right of search. Captured slave ships were to be delivered to their national state for trial. The enforcement of this agreement was controversial and France refused to renew it (Van Niekerk 2004a: 20). In 1845, a new convention replaced these previous agreements. This did not provide for a mutual right of search. Rather, France and Britain agreed to maintain roughly equal squadrons on the African coast, a significant escalation of the French West-African naval presence (Eltis 1987: 87). This treaty expired in 1855.

15 When Britain failed to agree a new treaty with Portugal which would have included an equipment clause enabling it to detain ships even where slaves were not on board, it passed the controversial Slave Trade (Portugal) Act in 1839. The so-called Palmerston's Act permitted the seizure of Portuguese and stateless slave ships, north or south of the equator, with or without slaves. Ships were brought within the jurisdiction of the High Court of Admiralty and Vice Admiralty Courts. Portugal protested but the Act induced it to agree to a new treaty in 1842. Its provisions included a mutual right of detention south of the equator, an equipment clause and the establishment of new Mixed Commissions at Cape

Town and Spanish Town (Anglo-Portuguese Treaty 1842, Van Niekerk 2004a: 29–31; Martinez 2012: 141–142). As a result, the provisions of Palmerston's Act that applied to Portuguese ships were repealed. Brazil was also unwilling to renew the slave trade repression treaty and terminated the Anglo-Brazilian Mixed Commission in 1845. Britain passed the controversial Slave Trade (Brazil) (or Lord Aberdeen's) Act in 1845. This followed the pattern of the prior Palmerston's Act. By the early 1850s the Brazilian slave trade was at an effective end. Prior to this, however, British warships had set alight and sunk Brazilian ships found equipped for the slave trade in Brazilian ports (Shaikh 2012: 54; Martinez 2012: 144). On the domestic political factors which contributed to the decision on the part of the Brazilian government to end the slave trade, see Needell (2001).

16 The death of Casamajor gave rise to a protracted procedural dispute when Da Costa insisted on the drawing of fresh lots in respect of cases which had been allocated to Casamajor (Marsden to Hamilton 23 October 1821). The legal advice that the government received was that the Additional Convention (Portugal) was aimed at giving an equal opportunity to each *national* arbitrator to participate. However, since the Regulations of the Commission provided that in case of disagreement the '*name* of one of the two Commissioners of Arbitration' was to be drawn by lots, Commissioners were directed that it would be awkward to uphold the evident spirit of the Convention in this respect without further explanation from state parties (Foreign Office to Marsden 8 March 1822: 10–11). Da Costa persisted in his opposition to the new British arbitrator assuming Casamajor's role in these cases (Da Costa to Marsden 18 April 1822; Da Costa to Marsden 20 April 1822). Eventually, Secretary of State Canning instructed Marsden to relinquish his objections to new lots in November 1822. Consequently, Jorge was appointed arbitrator in both the case of the *General Silveira* and the case of the *San Antonio Milagrozo*. The slave-trading venture in the *General Silveira* was found to be lawful and £15,270.12 compensation awarded. Even so, this was less than the sum the claimants had petitioned for, which was just over £36,000 (Marsden and Frere to Canning 28 January 1823; Marsden to Canning 17 March 1823).

17 Benton, in contrast, as already mentioned, argues that debates about rights in abolition focused on 'the definition of property rights and legal prerogatives of slave traders and slave owners within the imperial order' (Benton 2011: 369).

References

African Institution (1811) *Fifth Report of the Directors of the African Institution*, Fleet Street: Ellerton & Henderson.

African Institution (1819) *Thirteenth Report of the Directors of the African Institution*, Fleet Street: Ellerton & Henderson.

Allain, J. (2007) 'The Nineteenth Century Law of the Sea and the British Abolition of the Slave Trade', *British Yearbook of International Law* 78: 342–388.

Anonymous. *The Trials of the Slave Traders, Samuel Samo, Joseph Peters and William Tufft before the Hon Robert Thorpe, LLD with Two Letters on the Slave Trade from a Gentleman Resident at Sierra Leone to an Advocate for the Abolition in London* (1813), London: Sherwood, Neeley and Jones.

Ashworth, J. (1987) 'The Relationship between Capitalism and Humanitarianism', 92(4): 813–828.

Bandinel, J. (1968) *Some Account of the Trade in Slaves from Africa*, London: France Cass & Co Ltd.

Baucom, I. (2005) *Spectres of the Atlantic: Finance Capital, Slavery, and the Philosophy of History*, Durham: Duke University Press.

Benton, L. (2011) 'Abolition and Imperial Law 1790–1820', *Journal of Imperial and Commonwealth History* 39(3): 355–374.

Benton, L. and Ford, L. (2016) *Rage for Order: The British Empire and the Origins of International Law 1800–1850*, Cambridge and London: Harvard University Press.

Brown, C. L. (2006) *Moral Capital: Foundations of British Abolitionism*, Chapel Hill: North Carolina Press.

Davis, D. B. (1999) *The Problem of Slavery in the Age of Revolution 1770–1823*, Ithaca and London: Cornell University Press.

Drescher, S. (1977) *Econocide: British Slavery in the Era of Abolition*, Pittsburgh: University of Pittsburgh Press.

Drescher, S. (1991) 'British Way, French Way: Opinion Building and Revolution: The Second French Slave Emancipation', *American Historical Review* 96: 709–734.

Drescher, S. (1994) 'Whose Abolition? Popular Pressure and the Ending of the British Slave Trade', *Past and Present* 143: 136–166.

Eltis, D. (1987) *Economic Growth and the Ending of the Transatlantic Slave Trade*, New York and Oxford: Oxford University Press.

Foy, C. (2010) 'Eighteenth Century "Prize Negroes": From Britain to America', *Slavery and Abolition* 31(3): 379–393.

Fryer, P. (1987) *Staying Power: The History of Black People in Britain*, London and Sydney: Pluto Press.

Fyfe, C. (1961) 'Four Sierra Leone Recaptives', *Journal of African History* 2(1): 77–85.

Fyfe, C. (1962) *A History of Sierra Leone*, Oxford: Oxford University Press.

Grewe, W. (2000) *Epochs of International Law*, M. Byers (trans.), Berlin and New York: Walter de Gruyter.

Hamilton, K. and Shaikh, F. (2012) 'Introduction', in K. Hamilton and P. Salmon (eds.), *Slavery, Diplomacy and Empire: Britain and the Suppression of the Slave Trade, 1807–1975*, Eastbourne: Sussex Academic Press.

Haskell, T. (1985) 'Capitalism and the Origins of the Humanitarian Sensibility, Part 1', *American Historical Review* 90(2): 339–361.

Haskell, T. (1987) 'Convention and Hegemonic Interest in the Debate over Antislavery: A Reply to Davis and Ashworth', 92(4): 829–878.

Haslam, E. (2012) Redemption, Colonialism and International Criminal Law: The Nineteenth Century Slave Trading Trials of Samo and Peters', in D. Kirkby (ed.), *Past Law, Present Histories: From Settler Colonies to International Justice*, Canberra: Australian National University e-Press.

Haslam, E. (2016) 'International Criminal Law and Legal Memories of Abolition: Intervention, Mixed Commission Courts and "Emancipation"', *Journal of the History of International Law* 18: 420–447.

Helfman, T. (2006) 'The Court of Vice Admiralty at Sierra Leone and the Abolition of the West African Slave Trade', *Yale Law Journal* 115: 1123–1156.

Johnson, J. F. (1844) *Trial of Pedro De Zulueta, Jun, in the Central Criminal Court of the City of London, on the 27th, 28th and 30th of October, 1843, on a Charge of Slave-Trading*, London: Ward & Co and Office of the British and Foreign Anti-Slavery Society.

Krikler, J. (2007) 'The *Zong* and the Lord Chief Justice', *History Workshop Journal* 64: 29–47.

Martinez, J. (2012) *The Slave Trade and the Origins of International Human Rights Law*, Oxford: Oxford University Press.

Miers, S. (1975) *Britain and the Ending of the Slave Trade*, London: Longman.

Needell, J. (2001) 'The Abolition of the Brazilian Slave Trade in 1850: Historiography, Slave Agency and Statesmanship', *Journal of Latin American Studies* 33: 681–711.

Nouwen, S. and Werner, W. (2011) 'Doing Justice to the Political: The International Criminal Court in Uganda and Sudan', *European Journal of International Law* 21(4): 941–965.

Phillimore, R. (1857) *Commentaries upon International Law Vol III*, Philadelphia: T. & J. W. Johnson & Co.

Schwarz, S. (2012) 'Reconstructing the Life Histories of Liberated Africans: Sierra Leone in the Early Nineteenth Century', *History in Africa* 39: 175–207.

Shaikh, F. (2012) 'Judicial Diplomacy', in K. Hamilton and P. Salmon (eds.), *Slavery, Diplomacy and Empire Britain and the Suppression of the Slave Trade, 1807–1975*, Eastbourne: Sussex Academic Press.

Shaw, R. (2002) *Memories of the Slave Trade: Ritual and the Historical Imagination in Sierra Leone*, Chicago and London: University of Chicago Press.

Sherwood, M. (2004) 'Britain, the Slave Trade and Slavery, 1808–1843', *Race and Class* 46(2): 54–77.

Sherwood, M. (2007) *After Abolition: Britain and the Slave Trade since 1807*, London: I.B. Tauris & Co. Ltd.

Van Niekerk, J.-P. (2004a) 'British, Portuguese, and American Judges in Adderley Street: The International Legal Background to and Some Judicial Aspects of the Cape Town Mixed Commissions for the Suppression of the Transatlantic Slave Trade in the Nineteenth Century (Part 1)', *Comparative and International Law Journal of South Africa* 37: 1–39.

Van Niekerk, J.-P. (2004b) 'British, Portuguese, and American Judges in Adderley Street: The International Legal Background to and Some Judicial Aspects of the Cape Town Mixed Commissions for the Suppression of the Transatlantic Slave Trade in the Nineteenth Century (Part 2)', *Comparative and International Law Journal of South Africa* 37: 196–225.

Walvin, J. (2011) *The Zong: A Massacre, the Law and the End of Slavery*, New Haven and London: Yale University Press.

Williams, E. (1964) *Capitalism and Slavery*, London: Andre Deutsch Ltd.

Wood, M. (2010) *The Horrible Gift of Freedom: Atlantic Slavery and the Representation of Emancipation*, Athens: University of Georgia Press.

International instruments

Additional Convention to the Treaty of the 22 January 1815, between His Britannic Majesty and His Most Faithful Majesty, for the Purpose of Preventing Their Subjects from Engaging in Any Illicit Traffic in Slaves, 18 July 1817 (Additional Convention (Portugal)), The National Archives: FO 84/2, pp. 3–5.

Additional Convention to the Treaty Concluded at Madrid on the 5 of July 1814, between His Britannic Majesty and His Catholic Majesty, for Preventing Their Subjects from Engaging in Any Illicit Traffic in Slaves, 23 September 1817 (Additional Convention (Spain)), The National Archives: FO 84/2, pp. 11–13.

Declaration of Eight Powers 1815, 63 CTS 473 Cited in V. P. Nanda and M. C. Bassiouni, (1986) 'The Crimes of Slavery and Slave Trade', in M. C. Bassiouni (ed.), *International Criminal Law: Crimes*, New York: Transnational.

Instructions Intended for the British and Portuguese Ships of War Employed to Prevent the Illicit Traffic in Slaves (Portuguese Instructions) 1817, The National Archives: FO 84/2, pp. 6–8.
Instructions for the British and Spanish Ships of War Employed to Prevent the Illicit Traffic in Slaves (Spanish Instructions) 1817, The National Archives: FO 84/2, pp. 14–15.
Treaty between Great Britain and Portugal for the Suppression of the Traffic in Slaves 1842, (Anglo-Portuguese Treaty 1842), The National Archives: FO 93/77, 21.
Treaty of Friendship and Alliance between Great Britain and Portugal (Treaty of Amity) 1810, *British and Foreign State Papers*, 1812–1814, Volume 1: 547.

Legislation

An Act for Abolishing the Punishment of Death in Certain Cases 1837 1 Vict c 91.
An Act for the Abolition of the Slave Trade (Abolition Act 1807) 47 Geo 3 c 36.
An Act for the Abolition of Slavery Throughout British Colonies, and for Promoting the Industry of Manumitted Slaves, and for the Compensation of Persons Hitherto Entitled to the Services of Such Slaves (Slavery Abolition Act 1833) 3 & 4 Will 4 c 73 as Amended 1838 1 & 2 Vict c 19.
An Act for the Appropriation of Certain Proceeds Arising from the Capture of Vessels and Cargoes, the Property of the Subjects of the Kings of Spain, Portugal and the Netherlands, Taken and Seized in Violation of the Conventions Made with Those States, and for Granting Bounties Upon Slaves Captured in Such Vessels, and also for the Granting of Indemnity to the Captors of Certain Vessels Taken in the Prosecution of the Slave Trade (Appropriation of Proceeds Act 1821) 1 & 2 Geo 4 c 99.
An Act for the More Effectual Suppression of the African Slave Trade 1824 5 Geo 4 c 99.
An Act for the More Effectual Suppression of the Slave Trade (Slave Trade Suppression Act 1843) 6 & 7 Vict c 98.
An Act for Rendering More Effectual an Act Made in the Forty Seventh Year of His Majesty's Reign, Entitled An Act for the Abolition of the Slave Trade (Slave Trade Felony Act 1811) 51 Geo 3 c 23.
An Act to Amend an Act Intituled an Act to Carry Into Execution a Convention between His Majesty and the Emperor of Brazil, for the Regulation and final Abolition of the African Slave Trade (Slave Trade (Brazil) Act 1845) 8 & 9 Vict c 122.
An Act to Amend and Consolidate the Laws Relating to the Abolition of the Slave Trade (Slave Trade Amendment and Consolidation Act 1824) 5 Geo 4 c 113.
An Act to Prevent the Importation of Slaves by Any of HM Subjects Into Any Islands, Colonies, Plantations or Territories Belonging to Any Foreign Sovereign Power (Foreign Slave Trade Act 1806) 46 Geo 3 c 52.
Slave Trade (Portugal) Act 1839 2 & 3 Vict.

English cases

The Anne (1810) 12 Eng Rep 158.
The Amedie (1810) 12 Eng Rep 92.
Del Campo and Martinez v Reg [1837] 12 Eng Rep 907.
The Diana (1813) 165 Eng Rep 1245.

The Donna Marianna (1812) 165 Eng Rep 1244.
The Fortuna (1811) 165 Eng Rep 1240.
Gertrudis La Preciosa (1816) The National Archives: HCA 45/69, 396.
Gregson v Gilbert (1783) 99 Eng Rep 629.
Le Louis (1817) 165 Eng Rep 1464.
R v John Bean Hannay (1817) The National Archives: TS 11/947/3478.
R v Carrol and Villemont (1820) The National Archives: TS 11/761/2375.
The Slave Grace (1827) 166 Eng Rep 179.

Mixed commission cases

HM Commissioners to Palmerston, 30 November 1838 in the Case of the *Mary Anne Cassard*, No. 17 with Enclosures *Class A Correspondence with the British Commissioners at Sierra Leone, the Havana, Rio de Janeiro, and Surinam, Relating to the Slave Trade from June 30 to December 31 1839* PP 1840 (265) XLVI.9.
HM Commissioners to Palmerston in the Case of the *Diligente*, 20 October 1838, No. 10 with Enclosures *Class A (Further Series) Correspondence with the British Commissioners at Sierra Leone, the Havana, and Rio de Janeiro Relating to the Slave Trade from February 2 to May 31, 1839* PP 1839 (188), XLIX.99.

Documents and correspondence

Canning to Marsden, July 5 1823, The National Archives: FO 84/37, pp. 55–57.
Castlereagh to HM Commissioners, 27 March 1819, The National Archives: FO 84/5, pp. 5–6.
Da Costa to Marsden, 18 April 1822, The National Archives: FO 84/17, p. 46.
Da Costa to Marsden, 20 April 1822, The National Archives: FO 84/17, pp. 50–51.
Foreign Office to Marsden, 8 March 1822, The National Archives: FO 84/17, pp. 9–11.
HM Commissioners to Palmerston, 31 December 1839, No. 11 *Class A Correspondence with the British Commissioners at Sierra Leone, the Havana, Rio de Janeiro, and Surinam, Relating to the Slave Trade from May 11 to December 31 1840* PP 1841 (330) XXX.1.
Jenner to Palmerston, 28 July 1831, The National Archives: FO 83/2345, pp. 328–331.
Marsden, 9 December 1824, The National Archives: FO 84/37, pp. 170–171.
Marsden and Frere to Canning, 28 January 1823, The National Archives: FO 84/37, p. 102.
Marsden to Canning, 17 March 1823, The National Archives: FO 84/37, pp. 17–18.
Marsden to Canning, with Enclosures Including Protest, 29 March 1822, The National Archives: FO 84/37, pp. 23–24.
Marsden to Castlereagh, 25 February 1820, The National Archives: FO 84/5, pp. 100–101.
Marsden to Hamilton, 23 October 1821, The National Archives: FO 84/12, pp. 39–40.
Palmerston to HM Commissioners at Sierra Leone, 16 August 1831, The National Archives: FO 315/3, pp. 181–183.
Petition of Elizabeth Bostock on behalf of John MacQueen and Robert Bostock, The National Archives: HO 17/1/1.
Petition on behalf of the Spanish Envoy on Behalf of Francisco Marinet, The National Archives: HO 17/40/141.

Return to the House of Commons of Slaves Seized Captured and Condemned at Sierra Leone from 5 January 1814 to 21 April 1823, 1824, The National Archives: HCA 35/4, pp. 273–328.
Roffery to Hamilton, 27 November 1819, The National Archives: FO 84/5, pp. 82–83.
Roffery to HM Treasury, 31 May 1826, The National Archives: HCA 39/9, p. 40.
Vessels, Cargoes and Slaves Proceeded against in the Court of Vice Admiralty at Sierra Leone between June 1808 and March 1817, The National Archives: HCA 49/97.

Hansard

HC Deb 18 April 1814, vol 30, cols 657–658.
HL Deb 30 June 1814–1815, vol 31, cols 1062–1064.

3 The piracy analogy and the slave trade

Introduction

The transatlantic slave trade was for the most part not considered an international crime during the period of slave trade repression that this book deals with – although, as the Durban Declaration recognised, it should have been (Durban Declaration 2001) – but this does not mean that this period of slavery and abolition should be excluded from international criminal legal history.[1] Labelling an activity internationally criminal is not just a result of formal legal doctrine. It is also a historically contingent and political act. A fuller more complete history of international criminal law would, therefore, account for the exclusion of the slave trade, as modernity's foundational crime, from the category of international crimes in order to understand the discipline's past and current preoccupations, limitations and politics (Haslam 2019: 132). This chapter, therefore, returns to the discussion of the role of history in the construction of the discipline and the power relations that underpin it by reading the formal exclusion of the transatlantic slave trade from the category of crimes alongside the construction in some international legal discourse of the slave trader as archetypal international criminal.[2] It argues that this Janus-faced nature of international criminal legal discourse has operated contradictorily in different registers of international criminal law. This contradiction performs an effective gatekeeping function that enables international law to draw rhetorical benefit from the application of the piracy analogy to the slave trade, at the same time as its non-application in fact works to relieve international (criminal) law from the need to deal with the more material consequences of recognising the transatlantic slave trade as an international crime. In this way, as well as providing necessary context for the book's discussion of the legal construction of the figure of the recaptive, the chapter offers a reflection on some of the power relations underpinning the construction of international criminal law as a discipline. This and the previous chapter speak to different kinds of international criminal legal history. Strikingly, however, the law and language of the use of force played a critical role in both. Yet, accounts of the role of the use of force in abolition also reflect power relations in so far as they relegate particular forms of violence to the legal periphery. The final aim of this chapter is to inscribe them.

The chapter begins by exploring international law's failure to recognise the slave trade as an international crime. Much of the debate about whether the slave trade could be considered to be an international crime centred on the question of whether the slave trade could be equated to piracy in international law. The prevailing opinion was that it could not. Slave traders were not *hostis humani generis*. Thus, international law did not position slave traders as enemies of mankind generally, even if, as the previous chapter showed, it enabled action against enemy slave traders. Here then we see another site where the use of force – here the language of the use of force, rather than legal doctrine per se – played a role in drawing parameters to abolition. Yet, the identification of *hostis humani generis* was not just a neutral exercise. Rather, the concept can also be read as functioning to carve out the objects of rightful state violence. The next section turns to compare the exclusion of the slave trade from the category of international crimes with the representation of the slave trader as the typical international criminal. This account, together with the previous chapter, emphasises how the law and language of the use of force legally enabled abolition and set limits to it. The final section adds to accounts of the use of force in abolition by turning to violence carried out by, and against, recaptives during recaptivity.

The slave trade and piracy

International law enabled action against enemy slavers, but it did not position slave traders as enemies of mankind more generally. In practice, however, piracy and the slave trade were related. Pirates and former pirates often crewed slave ships (Van Niekerk 2004: 8), for example. If international law had recognised the slave trade as piracy, interventions on the high seas against slave ships would have been permitted during peace without the need for authorising treaties. This would have provided more effective action against slave traders, including those who were nationals of states that had not acceded to the Mixed Commission regime.

Britain failed, despite multiple attempts, to persuade other states to recognise the slave trade as piracy. States refused to declare the slave trade piracy at the Congress of Verona in 1822 (Hamilton and Shaikh 2012: 9),[3] and only five states recognised the slave trade as an act of piracy in the Treaty of London 1841 (Austria, Britain, France, Prussia and Russia), one of which (France) did not ratify it (London Treaty 1841). In 1824, Britain and America agreed to declare the slave trade piracy. However, although Britain passed national legislation to that effect, the British–US treaty was not ratified. After 1826, British bilateral slave trade repression treaties required contracting parties to recognise slave trading as piracy domestically (Benton and Ford 2016: 127). Other treaties also included provisions on piracy. However, the recognition of piracy bilaterally did not equate to an acknowledgement that the slave trade was piracy under the law of nations.

As observed in the previous chapter, the classic case of *Le Louis* finally judicially determined the illegality of peacetime seizures. This case also dealt with the question of whether slave trading could constitute piracy. Although only a snapshot of the broader debate about the slave trade and piracy, the case is interesting for what it reveals about the legal thinking around piracy at this time.

After fierce fighting the British ship, the *Queen Charlotte*, captured the French slave ship *Le Louis* in March 1816 near Cape Mesurado. Eight of the crew of the *Queen Charlotte* and three of the crew of *Le Louis* were killed (*Le Louis* 1817) and many more were wounded. The Sierra Leone Vice Admiralty Court condemned the ship, but Sir William Scott reversed this decision on appeal on the grounds that there was no proof that the prohibition of the slave trade had become French law, nor was it permitted, without an authorising treaty, to visit and search a foreign ship during peace time because the right to visit and search a foreign slave ship, as the previous chapter showed, was a belligerent right. The respondents unsuccessfully sought to argue that slave trading constituted piracy and that it was an offence against the law of nations. Scott rejected the extension of piracy to the slave trade, because even under British law, slave trading was only a transportable offence and not piracy at this time. Nor was Scott prepared to accept that, if not piracy, the slave trade was nevertheless a crime under the law of nations.

International law had been widely used to justify the slave trade. As Best J stated in *Madrazo v Willes*, a case which affirmed the right of foreigners, whose national law allowed them to trade in slaves, to recover damages in English Courts for the unlawful seizures of slave ships:

> it is impossible to say that the slave-trade is contrary to what may be called the common law of nations. It was, until lately, carried on by all the nations of Europe. A practice so sanctioned can only be rendered illegal by the consent of all the powers.
>
> (*Madrazo* v *Willes* 1820: 694)

For Best J, anti-slave trade legislation might well 'speak in just terms of indignation of the horrible traffic in human beings', but it did so 'only in the name of the British nation' (ibid: 694). International law might have enabled Britain to take action against enemy – and neutral – slavers, but it did not consider that slave traders were enemies of mankind more generally. In practice, the Sierra Leone Vice Admiralty Court's condemnations of slave ships made scant reference to the law of nations or to the law of nature. In response to the claim by the Sierra Leone Vice Admiralty Court 'that the slave trade, from motives of humanity, hath been abolished by most civilised nations, *and is not at the present time legally authorised by any*' (original emphasis), Sir William Scott observed on appeal 'the contrary' was 'notoriously the fact' (the *Diana* 1813: 1246). Such a principle was 'inconsistent with the rights of independent states, and consequently with the peace and safety of this country' (ibid: 1248).

In *Le Louis* Scott considered that piracy and slave trading were fundamentally different. Pirates, unlike slave traders, were 'the enemies of every country, and at all times; and therefore are universally subject to the extreme rights of war' (*Le Louis* 1817: 1475). Scott thought the slave trade was:

> not the act of freebooters, enemies of the human race, renouncing every country, and ravaging every country in its coasts and vessels indiscriminately, and therefore creating a universal terror and alarm; but of persons confining their transactions (reprehensible as they may be) to particular countries, without exciting the slightest apprehension in others. It is not the act of persons insulting and assaulting coasts and vessels against the will of governments and the course of their laws, but of persons resorting thither to carry on a *traffic* (as it is there most unfortunately deemed), not only recognised but invited by the institutions and administrations of those barbarous communities.
>
> (*Le Louis* 1817: 1476, original emphasis)

Scott considered that there was no right to search a slave ship during peace because there was no need for self-defence. As commentators have shown, piracy was not simply – or even – a reflection of heinous conduct (Kontorovich 2004: 186). Scott explained: 'Be the malignity of the practice what it may, it is not that of piracy, in legal consideration' (*Le Louis* 1817: 1478). All nations could seize pirates, *hostis humani generis*, because pirates engaged in universal violence. In contrast, in the case of the slave trade, as Lushington argued on behalf of the appellants, the 'acts of injustice were confined to one description of persons with whom other nations had no concern; and there was no possibility of the same acts being practised against Great Britain' (ibid: 1467).[4]

In part, the debate about slave trading and piracy was about means and ends. Scott observed that there was 'no right to prevent a suspected injustice towards another by committing an actual injustice of [one's] own' (*Le Louis* 1817: 1479).

> To press forward to a great principle by breaking through every other great principle that stands in the way of its establishment; to force the way to the liberation of Africa by trampling on the independence of other states in Europe; in short, to procure an eminent good by means that are unlawful is as little consonant to private morality as to public justice.
>
> (ibid: 1479)

The failure to extend piracy to slave trading also protected European sovereignty then.

Scholars have argued that the label *hostis humani generis* was and is a 'legal fiction' (Kontorovich 2004: 235), or a 'linguistic perversion' because it was used in a context in which it was not, strictly speaking, theoretically correct (Greene 2008: 691).[5] In that sense the concept *hostis humani generis* identified those against whom violence could be legitimately carried out. Pirates were never universal enemies, in fact (Kontorovich 2004: 235; Garrod 2014: 202), except perhaps in so far as they disturbed trade between states (Greene 2008: 701; Garrod 2014: 199).[6] Garrod explains that one state's pirates were not necessarily every states' pirates. Therefore, pirates were in fact 'the enemies of the State that labelled them as such' (Garrod 2014: 202). The label is, therefore, 'both semantically void and uniquely legally productive' (Greene 2008: 685). For Jody Greene, it operates as a means by which 'law and politics veil their relations of force, hiding the violence they sanction *against specific classes of humans* through recourse to rhetorical and fictional categories of unreal or inhuman persons', amongst whom she includes the pirate, terrorist, torturer and the slave trader (Greene 2008: 703, original emphasis).

Amongst the contestations then over the meaning of the label *hostis humani generis*, one line of scholarship has emphasised how piracy was not just – or in fact not even – about heinousness, at least in the context of the slave trade. For Kontorovich, the fact that the justification for universal jurisdiction over pirates was disconnected from the question of heinousness calls into question the use of piracy as the precedent for the development of universal jurisdiction today (Kontorovich 2004: 186). Whilst the jurisprudential basis of universal jurisdiction is important, my focus is elsewhere. It lies in unscrambling some of the power relations that contribute to the construction of international criminal law as a discipline. To this end, the next section turns to the contradictions of the piracy analogy in its application/non-application to the slave trade.

The contradictions of the piracy analogy

International law did not acknowledge slave trading to be an act of piracy during this period. Seemingly paradoxically, however, the slave trader has been taken to epitomise the international criminal in some international legal discourse, as evidenced by the well-known pronouncement in *Filartiga v Peña Irala* that: 'for purposes of civil liability, the torturer has become – like the pirate and the slave trader before him – *hostis humani generis*, an enemy of mankind' (*Filartiga v Peña Irala* 1980: 890; Haslam 2019: 133).[7] Martinez and Surwillo also describe piracy and slave trading as the 'quintessential international law violation[s] by which modern violations are judged to determine if they can proceed' (Martinez and Surwillo 2017: 88). Although *Filartiga v Peña Irala* related to civil jurisdiction, it has made a significant contribution to jurisprudence on the expansion of universal jurisdiction (Kontorovich 2004: 185; Martinez 2012: 116). The piracy analogy therefore works both in exclusionary and inclusionary ways. I argue that these inclusions and exclusions contribute to a state of affairs in which international criminal law is relieved from the material consequences of recognizing the transatlantic slave trade as an international crime.

On the one hand, the rhetorical reiteration of the pirate and the slave trader can promote a sanitised view of the role of international law in slave trade repression. Thus, it can operate less as a corrective to international law's prior support of the trade than to gloss over the failure to criminalise it. It is, in this respect, a 'false memory' (Haslam 2019: 135). On the other hand, one result of the actual failure to extend the analogy was the failure to criminalise the transatlantic slave trade. This has contributed to the widespread exclusion of the slave trade from histories of international criminal law. Excluding the slave trade from histories of international criminal law, through doctrinal – and avowedly neutral – legal reasoning, performs a vital gatekeeping function. To return to Michel-Rolph Trouillot (writing about the Haitian Revolution), this can be seen as 'archival power at its strongest, the power to define what is and what is not a serious object of research and, therefore, of mention' (Trouillot 2015: 99). Here then statements such as the Durban Declaration, which acknowledged that slavery should always have been a crime (in this case a crime against humanity), are rendered peripheral, if present at all in the history and discipline of international criminal law.

This contradiction enables international (criminal) law to reap the rhetorical benefits of the piracy analogy without implicating the more material consequences that might flow were the slave trade to have been recognised as an international crime. I argue that international law has also benefited from the abolition of the slave trade – practically and rhetorically.[8] International criminal law is no exception, with the application of the piracy analogy to the slave trader. Positioning international law also as beneficiary of abolition rather than simply agent of (progressive) legal change is a potentially powerful political move which turns progress narratives on their head. This point is developed further in Chapter 7 which experiments with framing recaptives – and by analogy – victims as creditors. To return to the argument of this chapter, the material consequences the contradiction avoids include not just reparations, but also the challenges to the configuration of international criminal law that would flow from inscribing the slave trade as an international crime and/or into international criminal legal history. Perhaps most importantly, in a context in which international criminal law typically overlooks structural violence, inscribing the slave trade has the potential to centre economic questions in international criminal law and justice. The redemptive potential of the piracy analogy might be seen therefore to lie not so much in the reiteration of its application to the slave trade, but in an acknowledgement of the failure to label the transatlantic slave trade an international crime, the reasons for that failure and its ongoing effects. In this way, the gatekeeping function of the piracy analogy can be read back on itself.

At first sight, the seizure and piracy cases that this and the previous chapter have traced speak to different kinds of international criminal legal history. These are first a longer-term account of international institutional justice. This has focused on the conditions of possibility for the legal construction of recaptives, as the basis for contributing to debates about victims in international criminal law today. The second kind of international criminal legal history has focused on international crimes in a more conventional sense. Strikingly, however, the law and language of the use of force played a critical role in setting the legal conditions of possibility for slave trade repression in both. Debates about whether the slave trade constituted piracy were essentially debates about intervention. This focus on intervention provides the link between both of these histories and points to the artificiality of drawing a bright line demarcating what falls inside and outside of international criminal legal history for all purposes. This centrality of the use of force to slave trade repression raises a series of questions about the ability of contemporary international criminal law to transcend these origins – and whether that is even desirable.[9] Although these are important questions, they are not the primary focus of this chapter, which is directed at interrogating the legal conditions of possibility for the inscription of the slave trade (and by implication the recaptive) in international criminal law. To this end, the chapter turns now to accounts about the use of force that are typically rendered peripheral in either version of international criminal legal history, an exclusion which also reflects presumptions about the legitimate use of violence.

Silenced violence

An account of the law and use of force in abolition should also include violence sometimes carried out by prize crews against recaptives, and the occasional violent resistance by recaptives to their continued detention after recapture. Typically, however, accounts of international slave trade repression law focus less on these aspects. Contesting these silences challenges the assumption that only particular forms of violence are legally productive and complicates humanitarian narratives about the use of force and the legacy of law in abolition.

On occasion, prize crews carried out disciplinary violence against recaptives (Burroughs 2010: 102). For example, in April 1830, recaptives on board the captured slave ship, the *Manzanares*, revolted in the confusion of the aftermath of the capture of the ship by the British Navy. Some of the measures taken to suppress the revolt led to serious injuries. The Mixed Commission's surgeon noted that recaptives had suffered injuries, including sabre wounds and amputations (Findlay and Smith to Aberdeen 12 May 1830: 29). When a recaptive told the British prize officer of another captured slave ship, the Portuguese *Temerario*, that recaptives were planning to mutiny, the prize master, having found knives hidden amongst the recaptives, placed many of the male leaders in irons and flogged many of them (Campbell and Lewis to Palmerston 20 March 1837: 50–51). The flogging of two of the alleged ringleaders left their backs 'excessively ulcerated and lacerated' according to the surgeon who examined the recaptives on the arrival of the *Temerario* (ibid. 50). Three recaptives, who had been restrained by ropes, suffered ulcerated wrists (ibid. 51). The prize master complained that the recaptives had been unruly and aggressive from the outset. It was also claimed that recaptives had tried to strangle each other on a number of occasions and it was suspected that two dead recaptives had been strangled (ibid.). The commander of the capturing ship, who supported the conduct of the prize officer whom he had left on board the *Temerario*, later claimed that in eight years in Africa he had not seen 'so bad a set of slaves' (ibid. 52). Initially when it adjudicated the Commission did not have access to the Commander's testimony or that of some others which supported the prize officer's conduct. Although Commissioners expressed some regret that they had not had more information before the case was adjudicated, they did not comment formally on these events because it was not necessary to do so once adjudication had taken place, although they permitted the additional information to be filed to enable the conduct of the prize officer to be put 'in a proper light' (ibid. 52).

Marcus Wood argues that violent resistance by slaves was excluded from the accounts that abolition celebrated (Wood 2010: 161), with the exception of the *Amistad* ship revolt (Wood 2010: 166). Wood's primary concern here is with visual culture, but his argument resonates more broadly. Violent resistance was only one of the ways in which slaves and recaptives resisted, but it forms an important part of the history of international (criminal) law. Moreover, violent resistance was sometimes a catalyst for legal change. The cases of the *Activo* (HM Commissioners to Canning, 10 June 1826) and *Perpetuo Defensor* (Hamilton to Canning, 12 October 1826) examined in Chapter 5 show how recaptives' sometimes reportedly violent resistance could be legally productive, even though recaptive agency was not formally legally recognised. Inscribing recaptive violence, as well as other forms of resistance, challenges the idea that recaptives were simply on the receiving end of intervention. Inscribing violence against recaptives and by recaptives contributes to broader attempts to remember the slave trade and abolition by emphasising both the suffering recaptives endured and their resistance to enslavement.

Conclusion

This and the previous chapter have set the book's discussion of the legal construction of recaptives within its legal and institutional context. Both have emphasised the centrality of the law and language of the use of force in setting the legal conditions of possibility for slave trade repression. These chapters have also sought to broaden approaches to international criminal legal history. This chapter has done so by emphasising, as Chapter 1 has done, the importance of inscribing into international criminal legal history conduct which was formally excluded from definitions of international criminality. To that end the chapter has emphasised the exclusion from the category of international crimes of the slave trade as arguably modernity's foundational crime. The chapter has also argued that the contradictions inherent in the piracy analogy's application/non-application to the slave trade bestows a rhetorical benefit on international law at the same time as it works to relieve international criminal law from the material consequences of recognizing the slave trade as an international crime and from the exclusion of the transatlantic slave trade from definitions of international criminality and international criminal legal history. The inclusion or exclusion of the slave trade from international criminal legal history is not therefore a straightforwardly legal or doctrinal issue but is also a matter of (discursive) power.

Power relations are also reflected in narratives about the use of force in abolition that omit violence against, and by, recaptives. Inscribing such narratives positions recaptives as both objects and subjects of violence. The following chapters focus more directly on the figure of the recaptive as both object and subject. They explore how, on the one hand, slave trade repression determined recaptives' status through questions about intervention and continued to commodify them to a greater or lesser extent, in effect, therefore, treating recaptives as commodified objects of intervention. On the other hand, recaptives played roles in litigation that belied this construction. The historical account that unfolds over the course of these chapters is important in its own right, but it also provides the basis for the final chapter's claim that inscribing the recaptive contributes to debates about the construction and representation of victims in international criminal law today.

Notes

1 For an exhaustive review of legal developments around the question of whether the slave trade constituted piracy and for the claim that by the mid-1840s some lawyers at least referred to the slave trade as a crime, including a crime against humanity, see Martinez 2012: 114–139.

2 In a similar vein, Martinez and Surwillo describe slave trading 'as perhaps *the* paradigmatic international human rights violation' (ibid 87).

3 At the Congress of Verona, states declared the slave trade a

> Scourge, which for too long had devastated Africa, dishonoured Europe, desecrated mankind; that they are prepared to do everything for achieving and safe-guarding the complete and definite elimination of it; that they will eagerly care for examining all serviceable measures which are compatible with the rights and interests of their subjects.
>
> (Verona Declaration 1822)

4 *Le Louis* was applied in *Buron v Denman* 1848 (discussed further in Chapter 6) and in the criminal case of *R* v *Serva* 1845, the so-called 'Spanish Pirates' case. The 'Spanish Pirates' referred to some of the Brazilian crew of two slave ships, the *Felicidade* and the *Echo*, detained by a British warship and placed on board the *Felicidade*. The Brazilian crew rose up against the British prize crew and killed them. Seven of them were found guilty in a trial in Exeter of the murder of ten English sailors and were sentenced to death. The conviction was later overturned, a controversial decision amongst the public and in Parliament. The British government then paid for the defendants to be returned to Brazil. The defendants' central argument had been that the capture of the ships had been unlawful and therefore the killing was justifiable. A number of arguments were put forward to challenge the claim that the detention of the ships was lawful, including that slave trading was neither piracy nor an offence against the Law of Nations (*R v Serva* 1845; Lloyd 1968: 85–88). See further the American case of the *Antelope* 1825.

5 At the same time the '*hostis*' was not entirely fictional in so far as it referred to an enemy, 'in the sense of a wartime foe' (Kontorovich 2004: 234), although the legal benefits of such a status were withheld from pirates (Greene 2008: 702).

6 Garrod considers that jurisdiction over pirates was based on the protective principle, enabling maritime states to protect their trade and colonial interests, see Garrod (2014: 195–196).

7 For a discussion of analogy and a provocative and insightful discussion of the turn to the slave trading analogy in the contemporary context, see Martinez and Surwillo (2017).

8 For example, subsequent international law campaigns have drawn on campaigning techniques that originated in the abolition movement (Haslam 2014: 182), although this has not been unproblematic, see for example in the context of the movement against the co-called 'white slave trade', De Vries (2005: 45). See further Doezema (2000); Doezema (2001: 23).

9 Thus, the coercive institutes of international law have continued to enable international criminal law in a number of ways; for example, the ad hoc war crimes tribunals were established by United Nations Security Council resolution and the United

Nations Security Council enjoys power to refer cases to the ICC. For further discussion of the relationship between 'international courts and national economic and military enforcement powers' see for example, Martinez (2012: 167).

References

Benton, L. and Ford, L. (2016) *Rage for Order: The British Empire and the Origins of International Law 1800–1850*, Cambridge and London: Harvard University Press.

Burroughs, R. (2010) 'Eyes on the Prize: Journeys in Slave Ships Taken as Prizes by the Royal Navy', *Slavery and Abolition* 31(1): 99–115.

De Vries, P. (2005) '"White Slaves" in a Colonial Nation: The Dutch Campaign against the Traffic in Women in the Early Twentieth Century', *Social and Legal Studies* 14(1): 39–60.

Doezema, J. (2000) 'Loose Women or Lost Women? The Re-Emergence of the Myth of White Slavery in Contemporary Discourses of Trafficking in Women', *Gender Issues* 18(1): 23–50.

Doezema, J. (2001) 'Ouch!: Western Feminists' "Wounded Attachment" to the "Third World Prostitute"', *Feminist Review* 67: 16–38.

Garrod, M. (2014) 'Piracy, the Protection of Vital State Interests and the False Foundations of Universal Jurisdiction in International Law', *Diplomacy and Statecraft* 25: 195–213.

Greene, J. (2008) 'Hostis Humani Generis', *Critical Inquiry* 34(4): 638–705.

Hamilton, K. and Shaikh, F. (2012) 'Introduction', in K. Hamilton and P. Salmon (eds.), *Slavery, Diplomacy and Empire: Britain and the Suppression of the Slave Trade, 1807–1975*, Eastbourne: Sussex Academic Press.

Haslam, E. (2014) 'Silences in International Criminal Legal Histories and the Construction of the Victim Subject of International Criminal Law: The Nineteenth-Century Slave Trading Trial of Joseph Peters', in C. Schwöbel (ed.), *Critical Approaches to International Criminal Law: An Introduction*, London: Routledge.

Haslam, E. (2019) 'Writing More Inclusive Histories of International Criminal Law: Lessons from the Transatlantic Slave Trade', in I. Tallgren and T. Skouteris (eds.), *The New Histories of International Criminal Law: Retrials*, Oxford: Oxford University Press.

Kontorovich, E. (2004) 'The Piracy Analogy: Modern Universal Jurisdiction's Hollow Foundation', *Harvard International Law Journal* 45(1): 183–237.

Lloyd, C. (1968) *The Navy and the Slave Trade: The Suppression of the African Slave Trade in the Nineteenth Century*, London: Franck Cass & Co Ltd.

Martinez, J. (2012) *The Slave Trade and the Origins of International Human Rights Law*, Oxford: Oxford University Press.

Martinez, J. and Surwillo, L. (2017) '"Like the Pirate and the Slave Trader before Him": Precedent and Analogy in Contemporary Law and Literature', *Law and History Review* 35(1): 81–98.

Trouillot, M.-R. (2015) *Silencing the Past: Power and the Production of History*, Boston: Beacon Press.

Van Niekerk, J.-P. (2004) 'British, Portuguese, and American Judge in Adderley Street: The International Legal Background to and Some Judicial Aspects of the Cape Town Mixed Commissions for the Suppression of the Transatlantic Slave Trade in the Nineteenth Century', *Comparative and International Law Journal of South Africa* 37: 1–39.

Wood, M. (2010) *The Horrible Gift of Freedom: Atlantic Slavery and the Representation of Emancipation*, Athens: University of Georgia Press.

International instruments

Durban Declaration, 8 September 2001, World Conference against Racism, Racial Discrimination, Xenophobia and Related Intolerance A/Conf. 189/12.

Treaty between Great Britain and Austria, France, Prussia and Russia for the Suppression of the African Slave Trade Signed in London 20 December 1841 (London Treaty, 1841) Hertslet, Commercial Treaties, VI, 2.

Verona Declaration on the Abolition of the Slave Trade, 28 November 1822 as Cited in W. Grewe (2000) *Epochs of International Law*, M. Byers (trans.), Berlin and New York: Walter de Gruyter.

English cases

Buron v Denman (1848) 154 Eng Rep 450.

The Diana (1813) 165 Eng Rep 1245.

Le Louis (1817) 165 Eng Rep 1464.

Madrazo v Willes (1820) 106 Eng Rep 692.

R v Serva and Nine Others, also known as the *Felicidade* (1845) 175 Eng Rep 22.

American cases

The Antelope 10 Wheat 66 1825.

Filartiga v Peña Irala 630 F2d 876 (2nd Circuit 1980).

Mixed commission cases

Campbell and Lewis to Palmerston, 20 March 1837, in the case of the *Temerario*, No. 36 with Enclosure *Class A Correspondence with the British Commissioners at Sierra Leone, the Havana, Rio de Janeiro, and Surinam, Relating to the Slave Trade* 1837 PP 1837–1838 (124) L.1.

Findlay and Smith to Aberdeen, 12 May 1830, in the case of the *Manzanares*, No. 27 with Enclosure *Class A Correspondence with the British Commissioners at Sierra Leone, the Havana, Rio de Janeiro and Surinam 1830* PP 1831 (004) XIX.321.

Hamilton to Canning, 12 October 1826, in the case of the *Perpetuo Defensor*, No. 46 with Enclosures in *Class A Correspondence with the British Commissioners at Sierra Leone, the Havannah, Rio de Janeiro, and Surinam, Relating to the Slave Trade 1826–1827* PP 1826–1827 (010) XXVI.127.

HM Commissioners to Canning, 10 June 1826, in the case of the *Activo*, Nos. 42–43 with Enclosures in *Class A Correspondence with the British Commissioners at Sierra Leone, the Havannah, Rio de Janeiro, and Surinam, Relating to the Slave Trade 1826–1827* PP 1826–1827 (010) XXVI.127.

4 Mixed commissions and the expansion of intervention

Introduction

The book now turns to focus more directly on the operation and jurisprudence of Mixed Commissions with the aim of drawing out the conditions that determined recaptives' legal lives. Its general aim is twofold: first, to identify how international slave trade repression law constructed recaptives; and, second, to identify recaptives' contributions to slave trade repression litigation. This chapter, which focuses on recaptives' testimony and the preoccupation of Mixed Commissions with intervention, also serves as an introduction to the operation of Mixed Commissions. The counter-legal history put forward here is important for its own sake, but it also provides historical context from which to consider contemporary thinking about victims in international criminal law, which is further explored in Chapter 7. The primary argument that unfolds over the course of this and the following chapter focuses on cases in which slave ships were captured in violation of the relevant slave trade repression treaties. These cases are revealing because they demonstrate the law's focus on intervention. I argue that in these cases, Mixed Commissions were more effective in expanding captors' rights to intervene, and protecting captors from damages, than in formally safeguarding the rights of recaptives as a matter of general legal principle (even though in most cases in-person restoration was fortunately avoided) (Haslam 2016). Expanding intervention and reducing damages payable for unlawful captures of unlawfully trading slave ships was intended – and may well have had – the effect of restricting the unlawful slave trade. However, it is significant that within the framework of slave trade repression law the mechanism Mixed Commissioners used in these cases did not expand directly the circumstances in which recaptives could be formally emancipated. However, despite this limited legal framing of recaptives, recaptives influenced the law in important – but largely unacknowledged – ways. This chapter emphasises the role of recaptives' testimony.

The chapter begins by briefly outlining the salient legal institutional features of Mixed Commissions, pointing to the significant advantages British Commissioners enjoyed within the system. These benefits buttressed Commissioners' ability to expand the circumstances in which slave ships could be detained. However, as the next section shows, whilst the expansion of rights to intervene would have benefited some recaptives, recaptives themselves enjoyed no procedural rights before Mixed Commissions. Despite this, recaptive evidence was called upon. Thus, whilst reading along the grain reveals the failure of slave trade repression litigation to recognise recaptives as legal subjects, reading against it suggests that recaptives' testimony played a greater role than their formal position would suggest.

The chapter turns next to the legal preoccupation of Mixed Commissions with questions of intervention. It focuses on one question that persistently faced Commissioners which was how to adjudicate apparently unlawfully captured slave ships. In these circumstances, British Commissioners, who often adjudicated without their non-British counterparts, interpreted slave trade repression treaties inventively. Their often-controversial interpretations mitigated some of the major limitations of slave trade repression treaties and minimised some of the fallout – at least for captors – of illegal seizures. However, these decisions were less successful in challenging the legal construction of recaptives and, as a result, left them in a potentially precarious legal position.

During the course of the operation of Mixed Commissions, Commissioners received advice from the government and its legal advisers, who at different moments were prepared to countenance a more or less expansive interpretation of slave trade repression treaties than the ones adopted by Mixed Commissioners in relation to specific cases.[1] The respective contributions of legal advisers and Commissioners to the development of international slave trade repression law is important for revealing a richer account of the dynamics of law development. This 'internal legal discourse' in the form of law officers' opinions was, Lauren Benton and Lisa Ford argue, more significant in determining the scope of slave trade repression than states' diplomatic communications objecting to British violations of international law (Benton and Ford 2016: 130). However, the focus of this book is not so much on the separate roles of Commissioners, the government and legal advisors in constituting slave trade repression law, although it does point to differences of opinion between them. Whoever was driving the interpretations at any one time, the legal structures generally tended towards expanding intervention and reducing compensation rather than expanding formal emancipation. Before exploring this argument further, the chapter turns to the operation of Mixed Commissions.

The operation of mixed commissions

Mixed Commissions were established to adjudicate the lawfulness of the capture of slave ships (Haslam 2016: 429). As Article 1 of the Portuguese Regulations stated, the purpose of Mixed Commissions was: 'to decide upon the legality of the detention of such Slave vessels as the cruizers of both nations shall detain', with the purpose of slave trade repression treaties being to prevent the illicit slave trade (Article 1 Additional Convention (Portugal)). Mixed Commissions were empowered to emancipate recaptives found on lawfully captured slave ships, or to return recaptives found on unlawfully captured slave ships with damages to slave owners and ships masters.

When a slave ship was captured and sailed to a Mixed Commission, just as was the case before the London Slave Trade Commission, it came before two Commissary Judges, who were appointed by each signatory state. Commissioners were expected to perform their duties 'faithfully, impartially, fairly, and without preference or favour either for Claimants or Captors, or any other persons' (Commission for a British Commissary Judge 1821: 5). If Commissioners disagreed, one of two arbitrators that each contracting state had appointed was chosen by lot. Commissioners were not necessarily lawyers. Proceedings were open and not subject to appeal (Haslam 2016: 427). Cases that went to arbitration were often decided according to the nationality of the arbitrator, leading, in the words of the Queen's Advocate, to 'very unseemly' contradictory decisions on similar facts (Dodson to Aberdeen 27 September 1843: 231). A Registrar, appointed by the government where the Mixed Commission was located, assisted the Commissioners. The Registrar asked witnesses a standard set of questions or interrogatories, which the Crown's Law Officers had approved just as they had for the London Slave Trade Commission (Castlereagh to HM Commissioners 19 February 1819: 7).

Delays in the appointment of Commissioners were a constant problem. The Sierra Leone climate was unforgiving and the operation of Mixed Commissions at Sierra Leone was marked by the absence of Commissioners and Commission staff due to sickness and deaths. When delays in the appointment of the Portuguese Commissioners hindered adjudication, it was eventually agreed by analogy with Article 14 of the Portuguese Regulations, which applied in the case of the death of one of the Commissioners, that British Commissioners could decide cases alone subject to a right of appeal to the Mixed Commission at Rio de Janeiro (Count de Palmella to Castlereagh 29 October 1819: 54–55). The right to appeal lapsed when the appointment of Commissioners was delayed by six months. This principle was applied to other Mixed Commissions, on occasion controversially. When he was appointed after a two-year delay, the Brazilian Commissary Judge Joseph de Pavia unsuccessfully challenged all of the decisions that British Commissioners had made in accordance with this practice (Shaikh 2012: 44).

When Mixed Commissions condemned a ship, the ship and its cargo were publically auctioned (Shaikh 2012: 47). Mixed Commissions had no power to exercise jurisdiction over the crews of slave ships. National courts were expected to try them (ibid: 48). The two governments of the Mixed Commission that had issued an order of condemnation shared the proceeds of sale: Britain gave its portion to captors, who also received bounties (ibid. 47). Vessels sold at public auction were frequently repurchased and used again in the slave trade. Eventually, some condemned slave ships were destroyed to avoid this (Martinez 2012: 76). Liberated Africans were given emancipation certificates and placed under the responsibility of the Liberated African Department. If a ship was not condemned, for example, because the capture was unlawful, Commissioners were not mandated to emancipate recaptives on board, even if recaptives had been the victims of illegal slave trading. This left recaptives in a precarious legal position. Where owners did not pursue claims, this was less of an issue. But even then, it was not inevitable that Mixed Commissions would decide in favour of captors. In practice, however, as Chapter 5 shows, when owners did not pursue claims it made the position of recaptives less precarious. Establishing whether the capture of a slave ship was lawful or otherwise was therefore central to the operation of Mixed Commissions. The focus on lawful intervention coupled with the tightly circumscribed circumstances within which slave trade repression treaties permitted intervention left traders plenty of opportunities to continue to trade. However, British Commissioners enjoyed a number of advantages which enabled them to mitigate some of the limitations of slave trade repression treaties.

For example, cases were frequently decided by British Commissioners alone. British judges decided 81 of the 109 cases that were adjudicated at the Sierra Leone Anglo-Brazilian Mixed Commission without their foreign counterpart due to illness or absence (Martinez 2012: 69; Alston 2013: 2047). In 1819, the Foreign Office issued a memorandum to British Commissioners detailing the recommended procedure before Mixed Commissions. In so far as possible the proceedings of Mixed Commissions conformed to that of the High Court of Admiralty (Castlereagh to HM Commissioners at Sierra Leone 20 February 1819: 25). After it became independent, Brazil objected to these Regulations for the Mixed Commissions because Portugal had not expressly adopted them. The British government's view was that the Regulations had been 'acted on and acquiesced in by the Portuguese and other Commissioners at Sierra Leone' (Aberdeen to HM Commissioners 29 June 1842: 518–519). Benton and Ford describe this as 'bald legal imperialism' (Benton and Ford 2016: 124). Moreover, the relationship between British Commissioners and the Executive was, despite instances of disagreement, largely mutually re-enforcing. Deference to the government's advice was built into Commissioners' instructions as Commissioners observed in the *Diligente* (HM Commissioners to Palmerston 20 October 1838: 23). British legal power supported and was buttressed by British naval hegemony. Although the right to detain and capture slave ships was supposed to be reciprocal, British ships captured over 95% of the vessels detained under the treaties with Portugal, Spain, the Netherlands and Brazil (Bethell 1966: 83). These advantages contributed to the conditions by which British Commissioners were able to expand the possibilities for intervention.

By expanding the situations in which interventions could be considered lawful, more recaptives could be liberated, recaptives who would otherwise have been sent across the Atlantic and forced to endure displacement, violence and forced labour. The impact of this case law may have been to prevent others from being loaded in the first place. However, the impact of Mixed Commissions on abolition is contested. Historian Samuel Moyn describes Mixed Commissions as 'a minor episode' in abolition (Moyn 2014: 55). Case law is rife with evidence that naval patrols and Mixed Commissions were limited in their ability to deter the slave trade. The master of the *Segunda Socorro* claimed that despite having made 14 slave trading journeys, he was only captured once, leading British Commissioners to describe the anti-slave trading measures as 'hopeless' (HM Commissioners to Palmerston 18 July 1833: 21). The master of the *Vibora de Cabo Verde* was detained more often. Having been brought before the British-Portuguese Mixed Commission three times, including twice in one 12-month period, he showed no intention of repudiating the trade (HM Commissioners to Palmerston 14 November 1837: 14). Commissioners Macaulay and Doherty gloomily concluded in the *Mary Anne Cassard* that efforts to abolish the trade had 'only served to increase the horrors, without at all diminishing the extent' (HM Commissioners to Palmerston 30 November 1838: 19). The question of the effectiveness of Mixed Commissions is important, but this book's primary focus is on the legal construction of the recaptive. The next section, therefore, turns to recaptives' testimony.

Recaptives and mixed commissions

Recaptives enjoyed no procedural rights before Mixed Commissions. Recaptives were not legal subjects, nor parties to litigation. For example, while the British-Portuguese Mixed Commission deliberated in the case of the *Nova Sorte*, one of the 122 recaptives on board petitioned the Commission to land him and the other recaptives. The Portuguese Commissioner was willing to grant this request – after all, the master of the *Nova Sorte* had not claimed the recaptives – but British Commissioners considered the application 'unusual' emanating as it ostensibly did from an 'illiterate' black African. Commissioners refused to grant the petition and observed that recaptives had no legal standing as third parties (Gregory to Canning 7 June 1823: 113–114). Even though the master had not claimed the recaptives, Commissioners were also alive to the possibility of an eventual order of in-person restoration, which would have been difficult to enforce if the recaptives had been landed. Recaptives had no legal standing as third parties even though the litigation concerned their future.[2] However, despite such limitations, recaptives' testimony played a significant role in some cases, and this at a time when slave testimony was generally rare in national courtrooms. At the same time, problematic language and assumptions ran through the treatment of recaptives' testimony as is evident below.

In the *Marie*, an early case before the British Dutch Mixed Commission, the Dutch Commissary Judge objected to the testimony of nine Africans (Gregory to Castlereagh 21 February 1820: 79). The British Commissary Judge thought that recaptives' evidence was not essential to the case and gave way on this point. However, within a few years, in the *Perpetuo Defensor* case, the British-Portuguese Mixed Commission was able to refer to its 'undeviating practice' of examining anyone who was likely to contribute to the establishment of the truth, including recaptives (Hamilton to Canning 12 October 1826: 66).

In the case of the *Perpetuo Defensor*, the captor sought to examine four recaptives. Claimants objected, including by arguing that slaves did not recognise a religious obligation to speak the truth and that, even with the services of an interpreter, it was impossible to ensure recaptives had understood what was asked of them. They argued that liberated Africans were insufficiently knowledgeable to translate, a contention that the Mixed Commission rejected (ibid.) As a result, four recaptives – Ogoopooloo, Adoo, Aliconday and Agarree – gave evidence. Generally, when recaptives testified they swore according to the custom of their country or upon the Holy Evangelists of Almighty God. Recaptives testified mostly by special interrogatories, which required them to respond to a set of particular questions, although they were sometimes also questioned in open court. Recaptives' testimony was, therefore, inevitably limited. Even so, its importance should not be underestimated. On occasion recaptives' testimony successfully challenged the testimony of the masters of slave ships. For example, 2 of the 336 recaptives found on the captured Portuguese ship the *San Antonio de Lisboa* gave affidavits on behalf of the captors. They described how the ship's master had placed irons around their legs and necks (Gregory and Fitzgerald to Canning 1 January 1823: 80). Their testimony contradicted the master's claims and contributed to the Commissioners' finding that the recaptives had been traded outside the geographically permitted area. As a result, the ship was condemned and 291 surviving recaptives were emancipated.

British Commissioners considered recaptives' testimony generally more trustworthy than slave traders' evidence. Writing to Lord Castlereagh regarding the case of the *St Salvador*, British Commissioners explained the 'superior credit' given to recaptives' testimony when compared to the testimony of masters, noting that 'the plain narrative of the Negro prevails by the inherent force of truth' (HM Commissioners to Castlereagh 27 June 1820: 98–99). The importance of recaptives' testimony can also be inferred from efforts on the part of slave traders to bribe recaptives. In the *St Salvador*, a Portuguese sailor repeatedly tried to bribe the recaptive, Popo, also known as Will Carr, with $100 and the promise to take him to the Gallinas if he denied that he had been enslaved. Popo's response was to ask the sailor why he had put him in irons then (Gregory to Castlereagh 27 June 1820: 91).

Mixed Commissions' openness to recaptives' testimony was noteworthy. Slaves and liberated Africans testified in criminal prosecutions for slave trading in England and Sierra Leone,[3] but in the British Caribbean, slaves were generally only permitted to give evidence either for or against slaves (Zacek 2003: 25). Drawing on Paul Finkelman's annotated bibliography of slave cases, Zacek observes that slave testimony was only used twice to convict a white person in the West Indies (Zacek 2003: 31).[4] Nonetheless, recaptives' testimony did not always work in captors' favour. For example, Gregory had been inclined to decide in favour of the condemnation of the *Nova Sorte*, but after hearing recaptives' testimony he decided that the ship and cargo should be restored to the owners, although the recaptives, whom the master did not claim, were not returned (Chapter 6) (Gregory to Canning 7 June 1823: 125).

If Mixed Commissions displayed an openness – given the context – to recaptives' testimony, opportunities to testify were limited and recaptives' testimony was 'read' through a series of problematic assumptions. Moreover, as the following chapters show, the legal framework within which recaptives testified commodified them and read their path to emancipation through the question of the legality of intervention rather than their inherent humanity. Opportunities to give evidence were limited. For example, as mentioned previously, two recaptives gave evidence in the *San Antonio de Lisboa*. The remaining 289 were effectively silenced by these proceedings. Opportunities to testify were not, and could never have been, accorded to all recaptives, given the numbers of individuals found on slave ships and the needs of Mixed Commissions. However, problematic assumptions drove the selection and interpretation of recaptives' testimony. In the case of the *Magdalena*, only the recaptive Gandé testified to the place of loading after the captor petitioned the Court that 'some of the most intelligent' recaptives be permitted to testify (the crew of the slave ship had not been sailed to Sierra Leone). In the event, the case depended almost entirely on Gande's evidence since the Registrar's view was that the others were 'not sufficiently intelligible. . . by reason of their not completely understanding the interpreter' (Gregory and Fitzgerald to Canning 31 January 1823: 86). In the case of the Brazilian ship the *Sam Joao Segunda Rosalia*, the evidence of '6 of the most intelligent Slaves', contradicted the crew as to the place of their loading and was believed (Gregory and Fitzgerald to Canning 25 March 1826: 43). Paradoxically, whilst only recaptives who were considered to be particularly intelligent were typically permitted to testify, the trustworthiness of recaptives' testimony was linked to another problematic assumption. This was that recaptives' testimony was untutored. Thus, in the *Nymfa del Mar*, Gregory considered that, even if not disinterested, a slave's evidence compared favourably to a slave trader's testimony because it was given without 'design or premeditation' (Gregory and Fitzgerald to the Marquess of Londonderry 15 September 1822: 71). This assumption that recaptives' testimony was unpremeditated is problematic. Even in these brief accounts, there is evidence that, when the opportunity presented, recaptives did not engage passively with Mixed Commissions, but seized opportunities to attempt to influence proceedings.

For one thing, recaptives may have put forward particular narratives about their enslavement in the hope of satisfying the preconditions for emancipation. Thus, faced with inconsistent and contradictory evidence from seven recaptives in the case of the *Rosalia*, Gregory acknowledged that: 'The desire of liberty, which is implanted in every human breast, may have given risen to tales which promised freedom to their fabricators' (Gregory and Fitzgerald to the Marquess of Londonderry 17 March 1822: 21). For another, recaptives may also have sought to wrest some control whilst testifying. When the claimants sought to examine Okoorie and another recaptive, Olubarloo before the British-Spanish Mixed Commission in the *Rapido* case, Okoorie declined to cooperate. He refused to be sworn and was reluctant to answer questions. However, when he was examined for the captor, Okoorie willingly engaged in the process and answered questions 'with as much intelligence as might be expected from a person of his opportunities and situation' (Findlay and Smith to Palmerston 10 November 1831:15).

The influence of recaptives and liberated Africans could be particularly pronounced when translation was needed, as claimants were all too well aware. In the case of the *Nova Sorte*, the claimants objected to the translator, Jenny Andrews. The view of the British arbitrator, Fitzgerald, was that she and other translators in this case had led the witnesses. In the same case, one of the recaptives, who could speak English, testified on his own account and interpreted for the black seaman Joachim. His translation raised concern amongst Commissioners who considered he might be biased and subsequently a new translator was used (Gregory to Canning 7 June 1823: 109, 119).

Outside the courtroom, liberated Africans were also enlisted onto Royal Naval ships and were, therefore, involved in interventions against slave ships (Lovejoy and Schwarz 2015: 22). Given this, it can be assumed that some recaptives (and perhaps many by the time they reached the Court) were informed about at least some aspects of the key legal issues, and perhaps the necessary component of 'tales which promised freedom', in the words of Gregory even if they were unaware of the finer and precise legal details. None of this is to suggest that recaptives' testimony was unreliable but that testifying recaptives may have been more aware of what was needed from them to secure their legal move from recaptive to liberated African status than Commissioners assumed. The *Activo* (HM Commissioners to Canning 10 June 1826) and *Perpetuo Defensor* (Hamilton to Canning 12 October 1826) cases explored in the next chapter, in which recaptives' resistance effectively secured their own freedom, suggests as much.

Whilst slave trade repression treaties silenced recaptives, there is enough in the legal sources to suggest that at least some recaptives engaged with Mixed Commissions more actively than the formal legal sources suggest. Moreover, in so far as recaptives' testimony played a key role in some condemnations, recaptives can also be credited with contributing to the operation and efficacy of slave trade repression litigation. An argument about the significance of recaptives to slave trade repression litigation based on a handful of cases might be seen to overstate the case. Ultimately, it is a political choice whether to emphasise a narrative of exclusion and silencing on the one hand or one of inclusion and/or agency and resistance on the other. Emphasising the importance of recaptives' involvement in Mixed Commissions acts as a counterbalance to the more general focus on captors and Commissioners in the operation of Mixed Commissions. However, the choice between inclusion/exclusion or silencing/agency is not the only one to be faced here. As the insights of David Scott considered in Chapter 1 show us (Scott 2004), the question of how recaptives' testimony is framed when it is inscribed into international legal histories is also significant. In the light of the fact that black testimony against white people was generally unusual, recaptives' testimony might be read as evidence of international law's progressive (and redemptive) potential. However, the danger of such a narrative is that it can exculpate international law – both past and present – through a narrative which emphasises a long-term commitment on the part of international law to admit the voices of African victims of crime. If Mixed Commissions were inclusive to the extent that they admitted recaptives' testimony, the terms of inclusion were limited. Recaptives' testimony reflects not so much the inclusiveness of Mixed Commissions as the way that the contributions of recaptives, their agency and resistance, operated independently from the grant of legal subjectivity. Recaptives contributed to slave trade repression despite the law's failure to recognise them as legal subjects. This is one of the vital insights to be gleaned from reading recaptives' testimony in the contemporary context. This is a context in which rhetoric about international criminal law enabling the expression of victims' agency and voice has become coupled with justifications for the international criminal legal process itself. In that sense, inscribing recaptives' testimony operates as a corrective to accounts of the past. It also works to challenge some of the claims made about agency and international criminal law in the present.

Recaptives' legal lives were conditioned not only by the absence of procedural rights but also by the emphasis international slave trade repression law put on questions of intervention. This focus presented Mixed Commissioners with particular challenges when slave ships were captured unlawfully. The final section of this chapter shifts gear to focus on the dilemmas confronting Mixed Commissions when faced with unlawfully captured ships.

The expansion of intervention

British Commissioners at Sierra Leone, frequently sitting alone, interpreted slave trade repression treaties inventively and, as a result, expanded the circumstances in which captors could intervene against slave ships under the relevant treaties. However, it was far easier within the framework of international slave trade repression law for Mixed Commissioners to expand the rights of captors in circumstances where captures breached the relevant treaties than they were able in similarly situated circumstances to expand the conditions for recaptives' formal emancipation.

The purpose of Mixed Commissions was to adjudicate the legality of detention, but slave trade repression treaties only permitted the detention of slave ships in limited circumstances. Mixed Commissions, therefore, were regularly faced with slave ships that had been detained in breach of the relevant international instruments. The adjudication of such unlawfully captured ships was significant for both captors and recaptives. For one thing, captors were liable to pay compensation for unlawful seizures, although the government underwrote claims. For another, slave trade repression treaties, strictly speaking, required that recaptives found on illegally captured ships were returned to slave owners.

Preconditions for lawful detentions were set out in the applicable slave trade repression treaties and related instructions. Slave trade repression treaties bound only those states that had signed them. The fact that a ship was unlawfully slave trading was not enough to condemn it. Nor was it sufficient that there were more slaves on board than the passport allowed (Haslam 2016: 430). Particularly noteworthy was the geographically restricted scope of the right to detain slave ships (ibid.). This limit proved critical in a series of key cases – the *Sinceridade*, the *Activo*, the *Perpetuo Defensor* and finally the *Maria da Gloria* with which this book opened.

The Additional Convention (Portugal) permitted the Portuguese slave trade in particular locations south of the equator (Article 2). Portugal only agreed to the detention of slave ships north of the Equator (Article 4 Portuguese Instructions).

It followed that a Portuguese ship that had been unlawfully slave trading north of the equator could not be detained south of it; claimants of ships detained north of the equator had to show they were trading lawfully (Castlereagh to HM Commissioners at Sierra Leone 20 February 1819: 22; Haslam 2016: 430). At the beginning, the detention of Spanish slave ships was also limited. Until the total abolition of the Spanish slave trade, the British-Spanish Mixed Commission could only condemn ships captured north of the equator (Article 2 Spanish Instructions; Haslam 2016: 430).[5] Another significant limitation to detention was that at least initially, captors were only empowered to detain a ship when it had slaves on board, a restriction which was loosened over the lives of Mixed Commissions.

Mixed Commissioners typically responded in one of three ways when ships captured in violation of the treaties came before them. Sometimes they discounted the violation as so trivial that it did not invalidate detention. On other occasions, they creatively and controversially expanded captors' rights to intervene. Finally, they ordered restoration, with a question mark over the extent of damages, but with potentially devastating consequences for recaptives. The argument that Mixed Commissioners did, and probably could do, more to expand captors' rights to intervene and to minimise captors' liabilities to pay damages than to formally expand the circumstances in which recaptives could be emancipated as a matter of law draws on these second and third responses. Admittedly the third response was unusual with orders of in-person restoration being rare. However, even those cases in which in-person restoration was avoided reveal the limitations of international abolition law. In the *Maria da Gloria* (HM Commissioners to Palmerston, 31 March 1834), where in-person restoration was not avoided, the legal resolution was disastrous.

Firstly, not all violations of slave trade repression treaties invalidated detention. For example, the Spanish slave ship the *Fabiana* was captured by a subordinate officer, although Article 5 of the Spanish Instructions required the searching officer to be at least of lieutenant status. According to the King's Advocate, Christopher Robinson: 'it was not intended that capture should be invalidated by every departure from the instructions' (King's Advocate Report on the *Fabiana* 11 May 1824: 209). Commissioners condemned the ship (HM Commissioners to Canning 9 November 1824: 36). Mixed Commissions repeatedly held that trivial violations did not invalidate a capture. Even so, the government might still be liable for damages (King's Advocate Report on the *Fabiana* 11 May 1824: 209). However, such claims could be contested. For example, the King's Advocate Jenner, advising against compensation, argued that although irregular, the capture and condemnation of the Brazilian ship the *Principe de Guine* had been just because the ship had been in 'flagrant violation' of the Additional Convention (Portugal) and had attacked the capturing ship (Jenner to Aberdeen 16 November 1830: 205–206).

Secondly, British Commissioners interpreted slave trade repression treaties to expand the circumstances in which captors could seize and detain slave ships. For example, the requirement that slavers sailed with a lawful passport enabled British Commissioners to condemn slave ships without passports in circumstances that would normally have led to a ship's restoration. Thus, when the Portuguese ship the *Despique*, which had participated in the slave trade within geographically permitted areas, was captured north of the equator, it was for the owners to demonstrate the lawfulness of the slave-trading venture. Since they did not have a royal passport authorising the *Despique* to trade in slaves, they could not do so. The *Despique* was therefore condemned and the surviving recaptives emancipated (HM Commissioners to Palmerston 5 September 1834: 57).

As already mentioned, slave trade repression treaties typically initially permitted detention only when slaves were on board. Spain agreed to an equipment clause in 1835 which allowed captors to seize ships equipped for the slave trade even if slavers had not yet loaded slaves. Brazil resisted the inclusion of such a clause. In the *Emprehendedor* in 1839, British Commissioners controversially took upon themselves the 'serious responsibility' of interpreting the 1826 Anglo-Brazilian Treaty to condemn the ship on the grounds that it was equipped for the slave trade (HM Commissioners to Palmerston 2 September 1839: 111, 112). Although the British government affirmed this decision, which formed the basis for the condemnation of about 40 Brazilian slave ships, this approach was a constant source of dispute between Brazil and Britain. As late as 1842, Queen's Advocate Dodson noted that the question whether Brazilian ships could be condemned if they had slave trading equipment on board but no slaves had been 'long since raised but never finally and satisfactorily settled' (Dodson to Aberdeen 27 September 1842: 329).

Finally, Commissioners also interpreted the question of nationality flexibly. The intricate network of bilateral treaties provided slavers significant incentives and opportunities to flag, and therefore, forum-shop. Slave ships often had numerous papers on board. Deployed strategically, enslavers could render themselves immune from the jurisdiction of a particular Mixed Commission or Mixed Commissions in general. For example, when Spain agreed to the equipment clause, many Spanish slavers took up the Portuguese flag. After the case of the *Maria da Gloria* (HM Commissioners to Palmerston, 31 March 1834),[6] the British government instructed Commissioners that the nationality of merchants was to be determined by reference to their residence and 'mercantile establishment' rather than their birthplace (Palmerston to HM Commissioners 8 October 1934: 147). Following these instructions, the British-Spanish Mixed Commission condemned a number of ostensibly Portuguese ships that were crewed by Spanish nationals and belonged to Portuguese merchants resident in Havana on the basis that they engaged in the Spanish slave trade. Commissions considered captors could choose whether to proceed on the basis of the captured ship's genuine or colourable nationality. The question of nationality was challenging when slavers flew the flag of a state that had not agreed to participate in Mixed Commissions. Spanish slavers also turned to American flags in order to avoid the force of the equipment clause.[7] Legal debates about nationality were exacerbated by ongoing political controversy between the USA and Britain about the existence of a right to visit and/or to search and seize. Not surprisingly, slave trading under the US flag increased during this period (Van Niekerk 2004: 427–429).[8]

Finally, in some circumstances Commissioners had no choice but to order restoration with potentially devastating consequences for recaptives on board. For, although Commissioners were able to alleviate some of the limits of slave trade repression treaties, there were some breaches on the part of captors they could not overlook. The case of the *Sinceridade* exemplifies this.

The British ship HMS *Bann* detained the Portuguese slave ship, the *Sinceridade* in December 1822 (Gregory and Fitzgerald to Canning 22 April 1823).[9] The slave traders had purchased 152 slaves outside the area in which the Additional Convention (Portugal) permitted Portugal to slave trade. However, the captors had detained the *Sinceridade* just south of the equator and, therefore, unlawfully. The British-Portuguese Mixed Commission, therefore, ordered the restoration of the *Sinceridade*. According to the treaty, recaptives should also have been returned. However, because so many recaptives were sick, at least half of them had been landed in Sierra Leone, making the in-person restitution of recaptives difficult. The British Arbitrator Fitzgerald, therefore, tried to persuade the parties to agree that the recaptives should not be restored in person. Once this was agreed, the question was whether compensation should be payable for the loss of the slaves. Ordering compensation could encourage the illegal slave trade but refusing it could encourage the unlawful detention of slave ships. Eventually, the parties agreed that the claimant would be compensated for the slaves if the British and Portuguese governments agreed. Commissioners therefore ordered damages in respect of the uncontentious heads of damages and reserved the issue of compensation for the loss of the slaves to the Portuguese and British governments. The British Government declared what became known as the *Sinceridade* principle:

> His Majesty's Government do not hesitate to declare their opinion, that, in point of equity, no compensation whatever can be due to traders, in case of traffick carried on under circumstances which constitute illegal trade, and doubtless on the other hand no condemnation of a vessel ought to take place, when the capture is made at a spot, not absolutely within the boundary prescribed for capture by the treaty. . . His Majesty's Government believe, that the Portuguese Government will agree with them, that such is the spirit of the treaty, particularly of the 9th article of the instructions for the Mixed Commission.
>
> (Foreign Office to King's Advocate 11 November 1826: 97)[10]

The Portuguese government neither adopted this principle nor objected to it. The British government's view was that Portugal had acquiesced in the principle that no compensation was due for incidental losses where there had been a significant breach of the Additional Convention (Portugal), even in cases in which a slave ship had been unlawfully captured south of the equator (Robinson to Canning 18 November 1826: 108). Whether this principle applied beyond Portugal depended on the views of other treaty partners. Beyond that, because the *Sinceridade* principle focused on the question of compensation, it did not protect recaptives from being restored to slave owners, absent an agreement otherwise. The resolution did more, therefore, to reduce the financial liabilities of the intervenor than to safeguard the position of recaptives at a general level, even if recaptives in the *Sinceridade* were to all intents and purposes free. The legal vulnerabilities of recaptives are further evident when the *Sinceridade* is compared with the slightly later case of the *Hiroina/Heroina*.

In January 1827, British Commissioners condemned the Brazilian ship the *Hiroina*. The *Hiroina* had been captured north of the equator with no slaves on board (HM Commissioners to Canning 2 February 1827). The ship's passport authorised the *Hiroina* to slave trade but only to enter ports where the slave trade was permitted. Since the Portuguese were forbidden to slave trade north of the equator, the *Hiroina* had violated its passport. However, the seizure of the *Hiroina* was problematic because there were no slaves on board when the ship was captured. Even so, British Commissioners decided that the requirement that slaves had to be on board when a ship was captured only protected lawful slave traders (ibid. 53). Despite Brazil's objections, the *Hiroina* was the source of a series of controversial subsequent decisions and authority for the principle that 'a Vessel guilty of a breach of Passport, whether with or without Slaves, is equally liable to Capture with one found with an irregular License to the North of the Line' (HM Commissioners to Aberdeen 16 February 1829: 43). As the King's Advocate commented on the *Hiroina*, an anomaly resulted. The *Hiroina* permitted the confiscation of slave ships north of the equator when no slaves were on board, whereas the *Sinceridade* affirmed that illegally trading slave ships unlawfully captured south of the equator should be restored with recaptives (King's Advocate, on the case of the 'Heroina': 323–324). Notwithstanding the formal legal position, the in-person restoration of recaptives was avoided in the *Sinceridade*. However, the precariousness of the resolution in the *Sinceridade* was evident in a series of subsequent cases explored in Chapter 5. These are the cases of the Brazilian ships the *Activo* and the *Perpetuo Defensor* and the notorious case of the Portuguese ship the *Maria da Gloria*.

Conclusion

The development of prize into a tool for abolition was inventive. Nevertheless, it came at a cost because international slave trade repression law was directed at questions of intervention rather than the rights of recaptives per se (Haslam 2016: 424–425). Commissioners and captors had to balance their adherence to the Conventions against their concerns to limit the slave trade. They had to weigh unlawful slave trading against unlawful capture (ibid: 442). As Fitzgerald observed in the case of the *Sinceridade*:

> The Commissioners are, it is to be hoped, never insensible to the feelings of humanity, never wanting in sympathy for the sufferings of the oppressed, nor

> in aversion for the oppressors. But under the Treaties which form the law of these Commissions, enslaved Africans can be liberated, and nefarious Slave-traders can be punished, only so far as the Treaties will admit.
>
> (Gregory and Fitzgerald to Canning 22 April 1823: 120)

It might be thought that Mixed Commissioners, Vice Admiralty Judges and Royal Naval Officers did their best to advance abolition with inherently imperfect legal tools (Haslam 2016: 443). Moreover, it should be acknowledged whatever the formal legal position, the in-person restoration of recaptives was avoided in the *Sinceridade*. However, this is the kind of progress narrative that risks relegating the ambiguities and injustices of abolition to an unfortunate by-product of overall progressive legal change. In contrast, this book argues that although factually exceptional, the *Maria da Gloria* was integral to the logic of the law. This logic stemmed from the law of prize, the very instrument that served as the mechanism for legal change. Within this context, it was easier for Commissioners to expand captors' rights to intervene than to expand the circumstances in which recaptives could be formally emancipated, as the following chapter shows.

Notes

1 For example, on the question of the legality of seizing ships colourably flying the American flag, see, for example, (Foreign Office to the Secretary to the Admiralty 29 August 1839).

2 Subsequently the Registrar, Hamilton, admitted to having been involved in drafting the petition.

3 For example, in Sierra Leone the convictions of Joseph Peters and his partner William Tufft rested on African testimony, including that of individuals they had enslaved (*The Trials of the Slave Traders* 1813; Haslam 2014).

4 Including in the trial against Reverend John Smith for his role in the Demerara rebellion.

5 The *Arogante Mayaguesana* was the first Spanish slave ship captured south of the equator and condemned after the Spanish abolition of the slave trade following Government advice to this effect in 1832 (HM Commissioners to Palmerston 13 October 1834: 13).

6 Bethell suggests that the Anglo-Brazilian Mixed Commission at Rio de Janeiro would have condemned the *Maria da Gloria* had they found it to be a Brazilian ship (Bethell 1970:137).

7 In 1838 Macaulay and Doherty declared themselves incompetent to adjudicate the *Mary Anne Cassard*, a slave ship which was flying an American flag but was in all other respects Spanish (HM Commissioners to Palmerston 30 November 1838), although there some differences in the approach on this general point between Mixed Commissioners and the government's legal advisers. See, for example, (Foreign Office to the Secretary to the Admiralty 29 August 1839). However, in some cases the ostensible American master, notwithstanding the crews' objections broke up the ship anyway, thereby taking it out of action, achieving close to the same end as if the ship had been condemned.

8 Debate over the right to visit gave rise to significant diplomatic controversy (Wheaton 1936). Eventually in 1842 the USA agreed to an antislavery contingent off the coast of Africa (Webster-Ashburton Treaty). In 1862 the USA agreed to a mutual right of search and the establishment of Mixed Commissions

in New York and Cape Town (Shaikh 2012: 57–58). These were terminated by agreement in 1870 having heard no cases (Van Niekerk 2004: 434).

9 This account of the *Sinceridade* case draws on Haslam (2016: 431–433).

10 Article 9 stated that a claimant 'shall in no case be entitled to claim for more than the number of Slaves which his vessel was, by the Portuguese laws, authorised to carry, which number shall always be declared in his Passport' (Portuguese Instructions).

References

Alston, P. (2013) 'Does the Past Matter? On the Origins of Human Rights Law', *Harvard Law Review* 126(7): 2043–2081.

Anonymous. *The Trials of the Slave Traders, Samuel Samo, Joseph Peters and William Tufft before the Hon Robert Thorpe, LLD with Two Letters on the Slave Trade from a Gentleman Resident at Sierra Leone to an Advocate for the Abolition in London* (1813), London: Sherwood.

Benton, L. and Ford, L. (2016) *Rage for Order: The British Empire and the Origins of International law 1800–1850*, Cambridge and London: Harvard University Press.

Bethell, L. (1966) 'The Mixed Commissions for the Suppression of the Transatlantic Slave Trade in the Nineteenth Century', *Journal of African History* 7(1): 79–93.

Bethell, L. (1970) *The Abolition of the Brazilian Slave Trade: Britain, Brazil and the Slave Trade Question 1807–1869*, Cambridge: Cambridge University Press.

Haslam, E. (2014) 'Silences in International Criminal Legal Histories and the Construction of the Victim Subject of International Criminal Law: The Nineteenth-Century Slave Trading Trial of Joseph Peters', in C. Schwöbel (ed.), *Critical Approaches to International Criminal Law: An Introduction*, London: Routledge.

Haslam, E. (2016) 'International Criminal Law and Legal Memories of Abolition: Intervention, Mixed Commission Courts and "Emancipation"', *Journal of the History of International Law* 18: 420–447.

Lovejoy, P. E. and Schwarz, S. (2015) 'Sierra Leone in the Eighteenth and Nineteenth Centuries', in P. E. Lovejoy and S. Schwarz (eds.), *Slavery, Abolition and the Transition to Colonialism in Sierra Leone*, Trenton: Africa World Press.

Martinez, J. (2012) *The Slave Trade and the Origins of International Human Rights Law*, Oxford: Oxford University Press.

Moyn, S. (2014) *Human Rights and the Uses of History*, London: Verso.

Scott, D. (2004) *Conscripts of Modernity: The Tragedy of Colonial Enlightenment*, Durham and London: Duke University Press.

Shaikh, F. (2012) 'Judicial Diplomacy', in K. Hamilton and P. Salmon (eds.), *Slavery, Diplomacy and Empire Britain and the Suppression of the Slave Trade, 1807–1975*, Eastbourne: Sussex Academic Press.

Van Niekerk, J.-P. (2004) 'British, Portuguese, and American Judge in Adderley Street: The International Legal Background to and Some Judicial Aspects of the Cape Town Mixed Commissions for the Suppression of the Transatlantic Slave Trade in the Nineteenth Century (Part 3)', *Comparative and International Law Journal of South Africa* 37: 404–435.

Wheaton, H. (1936) *Elements of International Law*, R. H. Dana (ed.), Boston: Little Brown and Oxford: Clarendon.

Zacek, N. (2003) 'Voices and Silences: The Problem of Slave Testimony in the English West Indian Law Court', *Slavery and Abolition* 24(3): 24–39.

International instruments

Additional Convention to the Treaty of the 22 January 1815, between His Britannic Majesty and his Most Faithful Majesty, for the Purpose of Preventing Their Subjects from Engaging in Any Illicit Traffic in Slaves, 1817 (Additional Convention (Portugal)), The National Archives: FO 84/2, pp. 3–5.

Instructions for the British and Spanish Ships of War Employed to Prevent the Illicit Traffic in Slaves 1817 (Spanish Instructions), The National Archives: FO 84/2, pp. 14–15.

Instructions Intended for the British and Portuguese Ships of War Employed to Prevent the Illicit Traffic in Slaves 1817 (Portuguese Instructions), The National Archives: FO 84/2, pp. 6–8.

Regulations for the Mixed Commissions Which Are to Reside on the Coast of Africa, in the Brazils and London 1817 (Portuguese Regulations), The National Archives: FO 84/2, pp. 8–10.

Webster-Ashburton Treaty, 10 August 1842 8 Stat. 572 T.S. No. 119.

Mixed commission cases

Findlay and Smith to Palmerston, 10 November 1831 in the Case of the *Rapido*, No 10 with Enclosure *Class A Correspondence with the British Commissioners at Sierra Leone, the Havana, Rio de Janeiro and Surinam Relating to the Slave Trade, 1832* PP 1833 (007) XLIII.1.

Gregory and Fitzgerald to Canning, 1 January 1823 in the Case of the *San Antonio de Lisboa*, No 31 with Enclosure *Class B Correspondence with the British Commissioners at Sierra Leone, the Havana, Rio de Janeiro and Surinam Relating to the Slave Trade 1822* PP 1823 (008) XIX.311.

Gregory and Fitzgerald to Canning, 31 January 1823 in the Case of the *Magdalena*, No 34 with enclosures *Class B Correspondence with the British Commissioners at Sierra Leone, the Havana, Rio de Janeiro and Surinam Relating to the Slave Trade 1822* PP 1823 (008) XIX.311.

Gregory and Fitzgerald to Canning, 22 April 1823 with Enclosures in the Case of the *Sinceridade*, The National Archives: FO 84/22, 89.

Gregory and Fitzgerald to Canning, 25 March 1826 in the Case of the *Sam Joao Segunda Rosalia*, No 39 with Enclosure *Class A Correspondence with the British Commissioners at Sierra Leone, the Havannah, Rio de Janeiro, and Surinam, Relating to the Slave Trade 1826–1827* PP 1826–27 (010) XXVI.127.

Gregory and Fitzgerald to the Marquess of Londonderry, 17 March 1822 in the Case of the *Rosalia*, No. 10 with Enclosures *Class B Correspondence with the British Commissioners at Sierra Leone, the Havana, Rio de Janeiro and Surinam Relating to the Slave Trade 1822* PP 1823 (008) XIX.311.

Gregory and Fitzgerald to the Marquess of Londonderry, 15 September 1822, in the Case of the *Nymfa Del Mar*, No 29 with Enclosures *Class B Correspondence with the British Commissioners at Sierra Leone, the Havana, Rio de Janeiro and Surinam Relating to the Slave Trade 1822* PP 1823 (008) XIX.311.

Gregory to Canning, 7 June 1823 in the Case of the *Nova Sorte*, Nos 46–48 with Enclosures *Class B Correspondence with the British Commissioners at Sierra Leone, the Havana, Rio de Janeiro, and Surinam, Relating to the Slave Trade 1823* PP 1824 (002) XXIV.215.

Gregory to Castlereagh, 21 February 1820 in the Case of the *Marie*, No 31 with Enclosure *Class A Correspondence with Her Majesty's Commissioners at Sierra Leone Relative to the Slave Trade* PP 1821 (003) XXXII.165.

Gregory to Castlereagh, 27 June 1820 in the Case of the *San Salvador*, No 35 with Enclosure *Class A Correspondence with Her Majesty's Commissioners at Sierra Leone Relative to the Slave Trade* PP 1821 (003) XXXII.165.

Hamilton to Canning, 12 October 1826, in the Case of the *Perpetuo Defensor*, No 46. with Enclosures in *Class A Correspondence with the British Commissioners at Sierra Leone, the Havannah, Rio de Janeiro, and Surinam, Relating to the Slave Trade 1826–1827* PP 1826–27 (010) XXVI.127.

HM Commissioners to Canning, 9 November 1824 in the Case of the *Fabiana*, No 42 *Class A Correspondence with the British Commissioners at Sierra Leone, the Havana, Rio de Janeiro, and Surinam, Relating to the Slave Rrade 1824–1825* PP 1825 (011) XXVII.281.

HM Commissioners to Canning, 10 June 1826, in the Case of the *Activo*, No. 42 with Enclosures in *Class A Correspondence with the British Commissioners at Sierra Leone, the Havannah, Rio de Janeiro, and Surinam, Relating to the Slave Trade 1826–1827* PP 1826–27 (010) XXVI.127.

HM Commissioners to Canning, 2 February 1827 in the Case of the *Hiroina*, No 51 with Enclosure *Class A Correspondence with the British Commissioners at Sierra Leone, the Havana, Rio de Janeiro, and Surinam, Relating to the Slave Trade 1827*, 1828 PP (542) XXVI.281.

HM Commissioners to Castlereagh, 27 June 1820 in the Case of the *St Salvador* No 36 *Class A Correspondence with Her Majesty's Commissioners at Sierra Leone Relative to the Slave Trade* PP 1821 (003) XXXII.165.

HM Commissioners to Palmerston, 18 July 1833 in the Case of the *Segunda Socorro* No 18 with Enclosure *Class A Correspondence with the British Commissioners at Sierra Leone, the Havana, Rio de Janeiro, and Surinam, 1833* PP 1834 (471) XLIV.577.

HM Commissioners to Palmerston, 31 March 1834, in the Case of the *Maria da Gloria* No. 34 with Enclosures in *Class A Correspondence with the British Commissioners at Sierra Leone, the Havana, Rio de Janeiro, and Surinam, Relating to the Slave Trade 1834* PP 1835 (006) LI.1.

HM Commissioners to Palmerston, 5 September 1834 in the Case of the *Despique*, No. 43 with Enclosure *Class A Correspondence with the British Commissioners at Sierra Leone, the Havana, Rio de Janeiro, and Surinam, Relating to the Slave Trade 1834* PP 1835 (006) LI.1.

HM Commissioners to Palmerston, 13 October 1834 in the Case of the *Arogante Mayaguesana*, No 10 with Enclosure *Class A Correspondence with the British Commissioners at Sierra Leone, the Havana, Rio de Janeiro, and Surinam, Relating to the Slave Trade 1835*, PP 1836 (005) L.1.

HM Commissioners to Palmerston, 14 November 1837 in the Case of the *Vibora de Cabo Verde*, No 11 with Enclosure *Class A (Father Series) Correspondence with the British Commissioners at Sierra Leone, the Havana, Rio de Janeiro, and Surinam, Relating to the Slave Trade* 1837 PP 1837–38 (132) L.181.

HM Commissioners to Palmerston, 20 October 1838 in the Case of the *Diligente*, No 10 with Enclosures *Class A (Further Series) Correspondence with the British Commissioners at Sierra Leone, the Havana, and Rio de Janeiro Relating to the Slave Trade from February 2 to May 31, 1839*, 1839 PP (188) XLIX.99.

HM Commissioners to Palmerston, 30 November 1838 in the Case of the *Mary Anne Cassard*, No 17 with Enclosures *Class A Correspondence with the British Commissioners at Sierra Leone, the Havana, Rio de Janeiro, and Surinam, Relating to the Slave Trade from June 30 to December 31 1839* PP 1840 (265) XLVI.9.

HM Commissioners to Palmerston, 2 September 1839, in the Case of the *Emprehendedor*, No 77 with Enclosures *Class A Correspondence with the British Commissioners at Sierra Leone, the Havana, Rio de Janeiro, and Surinam, Relating to the Slave Trade from June 30 to December 31 1839* PP 1840 (265) XLVI.9.

Documents and correspondence

Aberdeen to HM Commissioners, 29 June 1842, The National Archives: FO 315/6, pp. 517–526.

Castlereagh to HM Commissioners at Sierra Leone, 19 February 1819, *Class A Correspondence with Her Majesty's Commissioners at Sierra Leone Relative to the Slave Trade* PP1821 (003) XXXII.165.

Castlereagh to HM Commissioners at Sierra Leone with Memoranda for the Guidance of the Commissions Appointed for Carrying into Effect the Treaties for the Abolition of the Slave Trade, 20 February 1819, *Class A Correspondence with Her Majesty's Commissioners at Sierra Leone Relative to the Slave Trade* PP1821 (003) XXXII.165.

Commission for a British Commissary Judge, a Commissioner of Arbitration, and a Secretary or Registrar, to Reside at Sierra Leone, *Class A Correspondence with Her Majesty's Commissioners at Sierra Leone Relative to the Slave Trade* PP 1821 (003) XXXII.165.

Count de Palmella to Castlereagh, 29 October 1819, *Class A Correspondence with Her Majesty's Commissioners at Sierra Leone Relative to the Slave Trade* PP 1821 (003) XXXII.165.

Dodson to Aberdeen, 27 September 1843, The National Archives: FO 83/2350, pp. 328–321.

Foreign Office to King's Advocate, 11 November 1826, The National Archives: FO 83/2344, pp. 96–99.

Foreign Office to the Secretary to the Admiralty, 29 August 1839, The National Archives: FO 315/5, pp. 205–207.

HM Commissioners to Aberdeen, 16 February 1829, The National Archives: FO 84/90, pp. 41–49.

Jenner to Aberdeen, 16 November 1830, The National Archives: FO 83/2345, pp. 203–206.

King's Advocate, on the Case of the 'Heroina', The National Archives FO 83/2344, pp. 318–325.

King's Advocate Report on the *Fabiana*, 11 May 1824, The National Archives: FO 83/2343, pp. 208–209.

Palmerston to HM Commissioners, 8 October 1934, in *Correspondence with British Commissioners Relating to the Slave Trade 1834* PP 1835 (006) LI.1.

Robinson to Canning, 18 November 1826, The National Archives: FO 83/2344, pp. 107–110.

5 After seizure

The hazards of recaptivity

Introduction

Slave trade repression treaties bestowed emancipation on victims of the slave trade who were found on slave ships which had been lawfully captured and detained. To be emancipated it was not therefore enough that recaptives had been the victims of unlawful slave trading. As Chapter 4 showed, interventions that took place in violation of the international treaties left recaptives legally vulnerable because Commissioners were in theory obliged to order recaptives' restoration in many cases when slave ships had been captured unlawfully (Haslam 2016: 424). Commissioners were constrained by their governing legal instruments. However, in many cases of unlawful capture Commissioners were able to avoid ordering in-person restoration. Yet, this chapter argues that when recaptives were subject to ownership claims in such cases it seems that Mixed Commissions were able as a matter of law to do more to minimise the liabilities of captors to pay damages (and in turn the government as guarantor) than to expand the circumstances in which recaptives could be formally emancipated as a matter of general legal principle (Haslam 2016: 435). Moreover, sometimes, it was recaptives' resistance that led to liberation, despite, not as a result of, slave trade repression law. However, for the most part such resistance has been lost to international legal history, specifically international criminal legal history. This chapter inscribes two such cases which demonstrate the legal significance of recaptives' resistance: the *Activo* and the *Perpetuo Defensor*. Recaptives' resistance was central to the legal arguments and the legal resolution in the *Activo* and the *Perpetuo Defensor* even if it was not formally acknowledged as such. However, tragically, the legal resolution in these cases also set the conditions for the disastrous case of the *Maria da Gloria* with which this book opened.

It might be objected that this argument draws too broad and bleak a conclusion about international slave trade repression law from a small handful of cases when set against the number of recaptives emancipated at Sierra Leone and the efforts of Commissioners to mitigate some of the more difficult and troubling aspects of slave trade repression treaties. Jenny Martinez, for example, concludes her discussion of the *Maria da Gloria* with the observation that:

> The purpose of the regime was to benefit the victims of the slave trade – to preserve the freedom of the millions of Africans who might otherwise be

> torn from their homes and carried to slavery on the other side of the globe. Ultimately, this goal was achieved. But along the way, many individual Africans were harmed.
>
> (Martinez 2012: 113)

In that sense she claims Mixed Commissions delivered 'imperfect justice at best' (ibid: 113). How far should the *Maria da Gloria* be considered to exemplify international slave trade repression law? Should slave trade repression be judged by the exceptional case, such as the *Maria da Gloria*, or more typical cases at Sierra Leone, in which recaptives were emancipated? This inquiry raises questions about the purpose and politics of history more generally as well as the specific purpose of my project.[1] As regards the latter, from the perspective of an account focused on the legal construction of the recaptive, the *Maria da Gloria* is central. Whilst the legal construction of recaptives is not the only factor by which international slave trade repression law should be assessed, it is an important one and could, as the case shows, have material consequences. The approach to recaptives adopted in this case was a direct consequence of the logic and frameworks of international slave trade repression law. In that sense, it and the *Activo* and *Perpetuo Defensor* cases reveal the preoccupations of the law and understanding the law's preoccupations is central to assessing the many legacies of international slave trade repression law today.

This chapter begins by setting the legal discussion of recaptivity in its broader factual context, arguing that recaptivity was precarious in fact and law. It then turns to the law's preoccupation with intervention, rather than enslavement, showing how this focus excluded certain categories of enslaved Africans from the law's largesse. Mixed Commissioners were able to sidestep the obligation to restore recaptives in person in many cases when slave ships were captured in violation of the international treaties. However, their creative ad hoc responses to unlawfully captured slave ships with recaptives on board, which the following section explores, involved an element of chance. Commissioners were generally unable to expand directly the circumstances in which formal emancipation was granted as a matter of law. This stands in stark contrast to their expansion of captors' rights to intervene, explored in Chapter 4. The chapter then turns to the cases of the *Activo* and *Perpetuo Defensor*, cases in which recaptives effectively liberated themselves, achieving de facto, albeit not formal emancipation. Whilst recaptives' freedom is clearly to be welcomed, I argue that in the end the jurisprudence of Mixed Commissions here did more to minimise the liability of intervenors to pay damages than to enhance the protection of recaptives as a matter of general principle. If this argument seems to overstate the difference between de facto and legal emancipation, the case of the *Maria da Gloria* demonstrates the serendipity of de facto emancipation. The misfortune of recaptives' resistance is that the legal resolution in the *Activo* and *Perpetuo Defensor* failed to prevent the catastrophic outcome of the *Maria da Gloria*. The chapter ends with some brief reflections on how recaptives' resistance might be written into international (criminal) legal histories as a result.

The precariousness of recaptivity

Far from representing a smooth legal transition from capture to liberation, the seizure of slave ships impelled recaptives into an uncertain factual and legal terrain. For one thing, recaptivity was physically and psychologically hazardous. For another, it did not necessarily augur emancipation.

The appearance of a Royal Naval Ship did not – and could not – put an end to the misery of those stowed on board slave ships. When crews of slave ships resisted detention, they endangered their own lives, the lives of slaves on board and the crew of the intervening vessel. The Spanish slave ship, *El Almirante*, was captured in February 1829 after a bloody skirmish in which 11 slaves were slain or went missing and the master and all the officers except the third mate of the *El Almirante* were killed (HM Commissioners to Aberdeen 23 March 1829: 22–23).[2] Chapter 3 showed how prize crews sometimes exercised disciplinary violence against recaptives. Prize crews sometimes used restraints against recaptives to keep them alive. When four recaptives threw themselves into the sea and drowned, the prize crew put on board the Spanish slave ship, the *Norma*, restrained the male recaptives in irons in order to prevent further suicide. The Mixed Commissioners considered this had been a wise course of conduct (Macaulay and Lewis to Palmerston 8 January 1836: 86).

Prize crews faced very real difficulties for which they had limited resources and training to respond. Conditions on the journey to Sierra Leone were often appalling. Although from the early 1830s medical personnel accompanied prize crews wherever possible, diseases such as ophthalmia, craw craw, dysentery and smallpox had often already taken hold before slave ships were captured. Even before they were loaded onto slave ships, many recaptives had been forced to march to the coast and had been detained in barracoons (Burroughs 2010: 101). Added to which, most slave ships were captured in the Bights of Benin and Biafra from where they had to travel around a thousand miles to reach the nearest Mixed Commission (Bethell 1966: 81). Alternative plans to move the Sierra Leone Mixed Commissions to Fernando Po came to nothing because of disputes over the sovereignty of the island (ibid).

When a prize crew brought a slave ship to Sierra Leone, adjudication was to take place within 20 days where practicable (Article 1 Portuguese Regulations; Article 1 Spanish Regulations). However, delays in adjudication often compounded the misery of recaptives on board, with the period between the capture and adjudication of a slave ship considerably lengthened when a ship was first taken to a Mixed Commission without jurisdiction, as in the case of the *Maria da Gloria* (HM Commissioners to Palmerston 31 March 1834). Pending adjudication, recaptives were landed only in the case of 'sickness or other sufficient cause'. When recaptives were landed, they were technically still considered slaves until adjudication otherwise (Doctors Commons to Bathurst 26 January 1827; Haslam 2016: 427) – at least, that is, possibly until the abolition of slavery.[3] If recaptives were emancipated, the principle was that the proceeds of the sale of the cargo and ship on which they were found were used to pay for their subsistence pending adjudication. If these proceeds were insufficient, the government that eventually had '*the advantage of the labour of the slaves*' paid for subsistence (Dudley to HM Commissioners 13 December 1827: 23 emphasis added). Whilst this ensured recaptives' subsistence, the rationale highlights the economic importance of liberated African labour (albeit referred to here as slaves).

In practice, captors typically requested Mixed Commissions to permit the landing of recaptives prior to adjudication. Whether the colonial authorities had the right to order the landing of recaptives on their own initiative was a source of disagreement. Following controversy in the *Anna Maria* and the *Donna Eugenia* cases, it was affirmed that the colonial authorities should not ordinarily interfere with the Mixed Commissions' disposition of recaptives (Hamilton to Goulburn 29 October 1821; McCarthy to Bathurst 10 March 1822). Notably, however, the colonial authorities' refusal to return the recaptives in the *Activo* and *Perpetuo Defensor*, discussed later in this chapter, played an important role in preventing the recaptives from being returned to slavery. In general, Mixed Commissions seem to have ordered the landing of recaptives on medical advice, but even so granting such requests was not always possible. Fever raged through the colony when the captured slave ship the *Panchita* was brought to Sierra Leone on 18 May 1829 with 282 recaptives. Thirty recaptives were suffering from serious medical complaints. Although the sick were landed, the remaining recaptives were not initially brought ashore because of overcrowding at the Department of Liberated Africans.[4] The midshipman, the prize master and the majority of the prize crew subsequently died, which the British Commissioners, who condemned the *Panchita* for illegally slave trading, felt compelled to deny was a result of the delayed landing (HM Commissioners to Aberdeen 15 September 1829: 26).

Beyond questions of practicability, requests to land recaptives were not always granted. The captor's proctor petitioned the Mixed Commission to land recaptives in the case of the *Maria da Gloria*. However, Mixed Commissioners were concerned that unrest might break out in the colony if they went on to decide (as indeed they did) to order in-person restoration, and instead they arranged with the Governor to have the sick recaptives placed on board a government ship (HM Commissioners to Palmerston 31 March 1834: 37). Captors might also object to the landing of recaptives if they were concerned that recaptives might be claimed or that the Mixed Commission might order the restoration of the ship and its cargo not least because captors could in theory be liable to pay damages in these circumstances if recaptives could not be returned (Haslam 2016: 427). Commissioners considered that the possibility that the recaptives might become 'objects of adjudication' may have been amongst the reasons why Lieutenant Rothery of the *Snapper* did not request the landing of recaptives in the case of the *Nova Sorte*. With the captor opposed to landing the recaptives (and after discussion between Rothery and the Clerk of the Mixed Commission about the health of the recaptives), the Commission did not pursue it further, even though the master of the *Nova Sorte* did not claim them (Gregory to Canning 7 June 1823: 107–108). Captors may have felt they had little choice but to look after their interests in this way. That they needed to do so reveals much about the preoccupations of the law.

Unsurprisingly given all the above, mortality rates between the capture of a slave ship and its adjudication by a Mixed Commission could be very high. For example, 214 recaptives on board the Brazilian ship *Umbelina* died between capture and adjudication. One hundred and sixty-three individuals were still surviving when Commissioners ordered emancipation (Findlay and Smith to Aberdeen 15 May 1830: 64). One hundred and twelve of the 361 recaptives on board the Brazilian ship the *Uniao* perished between capture and arriving at Sierra Leone, many dying from smallpox and dysentery (Rendall to Canning 21 November 1825: 39). One hundred and seventy-nine of the 448 recaptives found on board the Brazilian ship the *Arcenia* died between capture and adjudication (Jackson to Aberdeen 20 December 1828: 37). The Brazilian slaver the *Sam Joao Segunda Rosalia* was captured with 258 slaves on board. It took 65 days for the ship to reach Sierra Leone, but there was only enough food for 30 days. Seventy-two recaptives died mostly because of the lack of food as a result (Williams to Canning 25 March 1826: 43).[5]

Naturally, intervention also improved the lot of some, indeed many, recaptives. Captain Bullen of the *Maidstone* captured the Brazilian ship the *Creola* in 1827 (Lumley and Smith to Canning 18 June 1827). Although the ship was only authorised to carry 214, 308 were on board at the time of its capture. In these circumstances, expectations of mortality were inevitably low. Commissioners noted the 'praiseworthy care and attention' given to the recaptives, because of which 19 individuals – and not more – died on their way to Sierra Leone (ibid: 15–16). Similarly, the fact that 13 recaptives – and not more – died between capture and adjudication in the *Conde de Los Andes* case was understood to be a credit to the prize master (Macaulay and Lewis to Palmerston 3 December 1835: 80–81).

If they were emancipated, recaptives were handed over to the Sierra Leone government 'to be employed as servants or free labourers' (Article 7 Portuguese Regulations; Article 7 Spanish Regulations). In practice, the eventual disposition of recaptives depended much on the governor in charge (Asiegbu 1969: 32). From the early days of abolition, recaptives freed by the Vice Admiralty Court were bound to largely unregulated apprenticeships (African Institution 1815: 51–52).[6] There was evidence that some of these apprentices were cruelly treated and indentures were bought and sold (Schwarz 2012: 193–199). Early on, when liberated Africans resisted and left the colony, adverts were placed for their return, seemingly similar in tone to adverts for runaway slaves (Schwarz 2012: 203). In this respect, the injunction that forfeiture operated to deprive others of property in the slaves (s 7 Abolition Act 1807) appears not to have been observed. The first governor of the colony, Thomas Perronett Thompson, trenchantly criticised the apprenticeship system, including the treatment of some of the 167 recaptives recaptured by HMS *Derwent* in March 1808 who were made available to purchase as 'apprentices' and restrained in irons for seeking to run away (Turner 1997: 335–336; Schwarz 2012: 195–199). Thompson's criticisms brought him into dispute with prominent abolitionists and ultimately led to his recall by the government in 1809 (Turner 1997). Robert Thorpe, Chief Justice of Sierra Leone, raised similar charges in a bitter pamphlet dispute with the African Institution (Macaulay 1815; Thorpe 1815a, 1815b, 1815c).[7] Even with the shift to Mixed Commissions, concerns persisted that the status of free labourers was often in effect the continuation of a form of slavery (Shaikh 2012: 48).[8] Some liberated Africans referred to the 'apprenticeship' of liberated African children as slavery (Olusoga 2016: 315). By the late 1830s, Sierra Leonean liberated Africans made up, arguably not always fully consensually, all of the African Corps and much of the West Indian Regiments (Asiegbu 1969: 31–33). Recaptives were also recruited as indentured labourers to British West Indian colonies especially after the abolition of the slave trade (Mamigonian 2009: 42; Asiegbu 1969).[9] Sierra Leone, therefore, it has been argued moved from being a place of settlement to a 'source of indentured labourers for the British West Indies' (Mamigonian 2009: 44). Johnson Asiegbu notes that liberated African emigration seemed to 'perpetuate the slave trade in a new guise' and that, while it continued, other European states had less of an incentive to suppress the trade carried out by their nationals (Asiegbu 1969: 34).

Overall, whilst some liberated Africans did achieve worldly success (Fyfe 1961), the situation for many was precarious. Liberated Africans escaped the trauma of further shipment and enslavement in the Americas. However, they would likely, as Northrup observes, have been in a similar physical and mental state on their arrival at Sierra Leone as those arriving in the Americas (Northrup 2006: 5). Having experienced capture (and recapture), recaptives arriving at Sierra Leone would have been separated from their communities after a long and agonising sea passage (ibid.: 3). They had not chosen to come to Sierra Leone, a colonial territory in which they were exposed to forced labour to a greater or lesser degree (Lovejoy and Schwarz 2015: 21). They were also vulnerable to further enslavement.[10] Reports exist of the kidnap of liberated Africans and some liberated Africans turned to the slave trade themselves. It was observed that some slavers considered liberated Africans in Sierra Leone to be amongst the easiest Africans to enslave (Lieutenant Governor Findlay to Hay 20 December 1830). In December 1830, four liberated Africans were seized on board the French ship the *Caroline*. These were 'individuals who on a former occasion had been made free at the expense of the British Government' (Governor Findlay to Commandant of Goree 22 December 1830). As such they were re-recaptives. One of them, John Davis, claimed that he had been put in chains for six days before he was sold to the master of the *Caroline*. His protestations that he was a 'Sierra Leone boy', a 'King's boy' were to no avail (Deposition of Liberated African Boy Named John Davis December 1830). George, another liberated African, claimed he had been kept in irons for three months, compelled to 'lick his food off the ground' because his hands were tied up and then sold to the Captain of the *Caroline* (Deposition of Liberated African Boy named George Found on Board).

The capture of the *Caroline* with re-enslaved liberated Africans was not an isolated example. Lieutenant Smithers of HM brig the *Conflict* captured the Portuguese ship the *Ninfa* after a bloody engagement. Stowed on board were 167 recaptives, four of whom were liberated Africans who had been kidnapped from Sierra Leone. Before he had been re-enslaved two years previously, one of these liberated Africans had apparently been 'an apprentice *belonging* to Mr Macaulay' (emphasis added). It was said that Macaulay's agent had not reported his loss, a fact described as 'most extraordinary' by Lieutenant Governor Findlay. It was claimed that a settler had sold Macaulay's apprentice and that liberated African residents of Freetown had sold the other three (Lieutenant Governor Findlay to Hay 3 December 1830).[11]

The status of liberated Africans was also unclear. Attempts to prosecute liberated Africans who traded slaves outside the territory of Sierra Leone gave rise to debates about jurisdiction because, as Misevich explains, the precise scope of the Sierra Leone Company Transfer Act 1807, which had declared slave trading within Freetown illegal, was unclear (Misevich 2015: 191). One point of contestation was whether liberated Africans could be considered British subjects and, therefore, amenable to British law when they were outside the colony of Sierra Leone. It was not until 1853 that legislation finally made them British (Misevich 2015: 205–206).

Recaptivity was not just factually perilous. While it held open the promise of liberation, it threatened potentially devastating sentences of restoration in which recaptives were returned to slave owners and not to their original state of freedom. In this sense, recaptivity was a liminal status between two more fixed legal identities. Pointing to the liminal nature of recaptivity emphasises the distinct legal challenges and contradictions inherent in 'rescue'. Recaptivity was a perilous liminal legal status because international slave trade repression law linked emancipation to the question of the legality of intervention, rather than to the fact of illegal slave trading or slavery. However much Mixed Commissioners tried to avoid in-person restoration in cases in which slave ships had been detained unlawfully, their ability to do so was largely serendipitous (Haslam 2016: 433).

Emancipation and its beneficiaries

International slave trade repression law's preoccupation with intervention, rather than enslavement, excluded certain categories of enslaved Africans from the law's largesse. Mixed Commissioners were able to sidestep the obligation to restore recaptives in person in a number of cases in which slave ships were captured in violation of the international treaties. However, their ability to do so was largely down to chance factors.

Central to Mixed Commission's ability to order emancipation was the question whether recaptives had been the object of lawful intervention. Capture was generally lawful if the recaptives on board had been regularly trafficked in areas of Africa where the trade was forbidden and if the slave ship was captured within particular geographical limits and in a prescribed manner. Since it was only lawful to detain a ship where recaptives had been brought on board for the object of trafficking, the presence of domestic slaves (or sailors) did not justify captors detaining a slave ship. Mixed Commissions were not an assault on slavery per se. This can be seen in cases in which it was debated whether recaptives had been brought on board for the purposes of trafficking. These cases are revealing for the ways in which Mixed Commissioners represented slavery.

Whether an individual was a domestic slave depended upon a number of circumstances, including how, and where, he or she had been put on board, and by and with whom. The status of 38 recaptives was contested in the case of the Portuguese ship the *Aurelia*, captured by HMS *Primrose* in January 1829 and condemned for unlawful slave trading (HM Commissioners to Aberdeen 4 March 1829). The master of the *Aurelia* claimed that the recaptives were domestic slaves belonging to passengers. Most of the recaptives were ordered to appear before the British-Portuguese Mixed Commission. Having examined them, the Commission held that 13 men, 6 women, 4 boys and 6 girls were eligible for emancipation. However, 9 recaptives, 2 women and 7 girls, were considered 'long domesticated in the respective families'. As regards these, the court would 'not interfere, *any more than with the bona fide private baggage and effects of those on board*' (ibid: 71, emphasis added).

Similar controversy arose as to whether Franco, Antonio and Manoel were loaded on board the Portuguese ship *Nymfa del Mar* for the purposes of trafficking or whether they were domestic slaves of the captain (Gregory and Fitzgerald to Marquess of Londonderry 15 September 1822). Franco, Antonio and Manoel explained how they had been detained naked and in irons and only released and clothed on the appearance of the capturing ship the *Iphigenia* (ibid: 67). As the British and Portuguese Commissary Judges disagreed, the case went to arbitration. The British judges thought that Franco and Antonio were more reliable witnesses than the ship's master and emancipated them (ibid: 69). However, Manoel was found to be the slave of the supercargo for six years (ibid: 70). British arbitrator, Fitzgerald, thought that the fact that Manoel had been imprisoned before embarkation and had been detained in irons on the ship did not alone entitle him to emancipation (ibid: 75). But whilst Manoel was on British soil, Gregory and Fitzgerald made clear, the slave owner could not interfere with him. Therefore, domestic slaves in his position were advised not to put themselves a 'within the grasp of their Masters' (ibid: 70). Manoel's position was undoubtedly precarious but significantly less so than that of slaves illegally trafficked and brought to Sierra Leone in unlawfully detained ships, as in the case of the *Maria da Gloria*.[12]

Admittedly, in-person restoration (as opposed to damages) was unusual,[13] and there seems to have been some judicial disquiet about it.[14] The sorts of decisions which expanded captors' rights to intervene, which the previous chapter explored (Chapter 4), increased the circumstances in which Mixed Commissioners could order recaptives' emancipation. In other cases, Mixed Commissioners tried to sidestep in-person restoration. However, their ability to do so was largely down to chance factors. In general, where slave ships were captured in violation of the international treaties, Mixed Commissioners were more successful in expanding the protection accorded to captors as a matter of law than they were in directly expanding the circumstances for the grant of legal emancipation.

In the case of the Spanish ship, the *Dichosa Estrella*, Commissioners took the bold step of emancipating recaptives whom the captor had put on board the ship in his attempt to create the conditions for intervention (Gregory and Fitzgerald to the Marquess of Londonderry 24 July 1822). For simplicity's sake, initially forfeiture was limited to cases in which slaves were on board at the time of detention in order to minimise abuse of power and disagreement amongst governments (King's Advocate Report on Condemnation of the *Rosalia* 23 July 1822: 93),[15] but it rendered slaves vulnerable to being re-landed when antislavery patrols came into view. Cases arose where captors placed slaves on board slave ships themselves in an attempt to justify intervention. In the *Dichosa Estrella*, Commissioners considered that a special decision of emancipation was appropriate where captors had embarked slaves themselves. In such cases they considered that claimants could not claim restitution given that they had purchased the slaves unlawfully. At the same time, the circumstances of capture meant that emancipation could not be ordered. They did, however, request further instructions on this point (Gregory and Fitzgerald to the Marquess of Londonderry 24 July 1822: 26). In response, the King's Advocate emphasised the case's special circumstances but disagreed with the broader principle Commissioners had suggested (King's Advocate, Case of the *Dichosa Estrella* 10 October 1822). Commissioners had taken the view that captors could procure slaves who were being detained on shore so that they could be emancipated under the slave trade repression treaties (Gregory and Fitzgerald to the Marquess of Londonderry 24 July 1822: 26). The King's Advocate disagreed, affirming that 'demanding. . . slaves from native chiefs on the plea that they were held under contract for embarkation in vessels on the coast was. . . not within the provisions of the treaty' (King's Advocate 28 October 1823: 158).

Despite this, Commissioners were able to sidestep these limitations by in effect de facto acts of emancipation. For example, in the *Pepita*, the British-Spanish Mixed Commission refused to emancipate recaptives whom the captors had put on board. However, having refused to recognise the recaptives judicially, the Commission delivered them to the colonial government to enjoy in effect the same freedom granted to emancipated slaves (HM Commissioners to Palmerston 21 November 1834: 23). The King's Advocate approved of this course of conduct, observing that indemnification should have been awarded, but since the claimant denied title to the slaves, he 'can have no right to demand compensation for the loss of them' (Dodson to Wellington 15 April 1835: 248).

Such orders – effectively emancipation by the back door – depended on masters refraining from claiming recaptives, as Commissioners openly acknowledged. The Portuguese ship, the *Camoes*, was seized with 138 slaves on board. The agent of the *Camoes* had brought them on board in cooperation with the captor because although the *Camoes* had landed its cargo, it had not yet loaded slaves (HM Commissioners to Palmerston 24 January 1835: 15). As a result, the capture of the ship was unlawful. The state of the recaptives was such that, by the time the case was adjudicated, around only half of those originally shipped were alive (ibid: 17). The surgeon put the poor state of the recaptives down to inadequate food during the passage – when the ship had been captured the crew had not yet loaded provisions for the onward journey, having only just landed its cargo. The Court ordered the restoration of the ship with costs, damages and expenses.[16] Since the recaptives were not claimed, they were handed over to the colonial government 'to be employed as servants, or free labourers, but without a decree of emancipation' (ibid: 18). Commissioners noted that the sentence of restoration would have no impact on the recaptives' freedom because the recaptives were not subject to ownership claims (ibid: 15, 18). Recaptives were, therefore, handed over to the Liberated African Department to enjoy the same freedom as those actually emancipated (ibid:15). Had the master claimed them, the outcome would have been very different, but had the master claimed the recaptives, it would have undermined his argument that he had done nothing to violate the Additional Convention (Portugal) 1817. The Court was relieved from the 'disagreeable necessity' of restoring the recaptives (ibid: 18).[17]

In practice, since emancipation did not inevitably always protect liberated Africans from re-enslavement as the previous section showed, the absence of a formal grant of emancipation might not be thought a significant loss (Haslam 2016: 433). Liberated Africans were able to claim the protection of the British flag, but it is unlikely that this advantage extended only to those with emancipation certificates, although emancipation certificates may have made proof of entitlement to this protection easier. However, such legal niceties may also have been irrelevant in practice. According to Misevich, liberated Africans were often identified by the fact of their being able to speak English. This effectively ensured that 'any English-speaking slaves' could claim 'British protection' and gave officials wide discretion (Misevich 2015: 199).[18] But even if the distinction between freedom with or without emancipation might have been insignificant in many instances, it is revealing for it shows how emancipation was linked to the question of lawful intervention, and not to unlawful slave trading or to slavery (Haslam 2016: 433). The granting of freedom without legal emancipation can be seen as a creative response to the legal tools at Commissioners' disposal. However, Commissioners' ability to sidestep in-person restoration was not guaranteed (ibid). De facto orders of emancipation depended on ships' masters forgoing their rights to claim recaptives. However much they would have had it otherwise, there were situations in which Commissioners felt legally unable to do anything other than to order the restoration of recaptives, as the case of the *Maria da Gloria* shows. To that extent, recaptivity was a precarious legal state. This impoverished legal state contrasted with the more favourable legal situation of fugitive slaves who reached the territory of Sierra Leone: in practice, with some exceptions, the territory's governors granted freedom to them (Misevich 2015: 191).[19] The legal vulnerability of recaptives on board unlawfully captured slave ships is graphically illustrated by the cases of the *Activo* and the *Perpetuo Defensor*, where actual restoration of slaves was avoided, and in the notorious case of the *Maria da Gloria* where it was not.

The *Activo, Perpetuo Defensor* and *Maria da Gloria* cases[20]

When recaptives on board unlawfully detained ships were claimed by the ship's master, they were vulnerable to orders of in-person restoration. In these cases, Commissioners were able to do more to minimise the liabilities of captors to pay damages than to expand rights of recaptives as a matter of law. The desire to reduce damages was predicated on the assumption that this would discourage the unlawful slave trade. However, read alongside the failure to protect against in-person restoration as a matter of law, the reduction of captors' liabilities to pay damages is problematic. However, while the resolution in the *Activo* and *Perpetuo Defensor* cases laid the ground for the disastrous case of the *Maria da Gloria* with which this book opened, they also show the importance of recaptives' resistance.

During a few days in April 1826, over 160 recaptives who had been awaiting adjudication, resisted their detention on board the captured Brazilian slave ship, the *Activo* and made it to the shore of Sierra Leone in groups (HM Commissioners to Canning 10 June 1826; Hamilton to Canning 25 July 1826). Two mariners, George Springle and Bob Leigh testified that recaptives had threatened violence against those overseeing them, leaving the mariners in fear for their lives (Hamilton to Canning 25 July 1826: 56–57). Some had armed themselves with knives, wood and iron hoops and threatened anyone who resisted them, according to Leigh. In the end six recaptives, who Springle claimed had previously helped to calm earlier disturbances, took control of the ship's jollyboat and longboat under the protection of armed recaptives, enabling them all to escape (ibid.). This was, Commissioners observed, the first case in which slaves rebelled in the Sierra Leone harbour (ibid: 50).

The recaptives had been detained on board pending the Mixed Commission's adjudication of Captain Murray's capture of the *Activo* on 1 February 1826. They certainly had good reason to fear, as had been intimated to them, that the Mixed Commission might not emancipate them. Although the testimony of six recaptives 'clearly established' that the *Activo* had traded in slaves north of the equator and therefore illegally, according to the Additional Convention of 1817 between Britain and Portugal (HM Commissioners to Canning 10 June 1826: 49), Captain Murray of HMS *Atholl* had captured the *Activo* south of the equator. There was, therefore, a significant risk that the ship and the recaptives would be restored.

Faced with potential personal liability for the loss of the recaptives, the captor unsuccessfully requested the colonial authorities to return the recaptives to the ship. The Acting Governor's view was that the recaptives were free by virtue of their presence in a British colony. However, the British-Portuguese Mixed Commission ordered the ship and its recaptives to be restored, with damages, to the owner. Had it not been for recaptives' resistance ensuring they reached the shore, and the refusal of the Acting Governor of Sierra Leone, Macaulay, to return them once they had landed, the recaptives would most likely have been transported to the Americas as slaves.

In the *Activo*, Commissioners were faced with essentially the same legal problem which had confronted Commissioners in the case of the *Sinceridade* discussed in chapter 4 (Gregory and Fitzgerald to Canning 22 April 1823). The Brazilian ship the *Activo* had been trading unlawfully north of the equator, but its capture south of the equator was unlawful. In the *Activo*, unlike in the *Sinceridade*, the parties did not enter into an agreement to avoid in-person restoration. However, since the recaptives could not in fact be returned, the question became whether the claimants were entitled to damages for their loss. Alternatively, as the captor tried to argue, should the fact that the recaptives mutinied mitigate his liability? Just as in the case of the *Sinceridade*, Commissioners made an award of unconditional and conditional damages, the latter including a sum for the loss of the slaves, subject to the British and Brazilian governments' agreement (Hamilton to Canning 25 July 1826: 50).

Mixed Commissioners reached a similar accommodation in the case of the *Perpetuo Defensor*. This Brazilian slave ship and its 424 recaptives had also been captured unlawfully south of the equator in April 1826, having illegally laden slaves north of the equator (Hamilton to Canning 12 October 1826). Many of the surviving recaptives were in a 'wretched' condition when they reached Sierra Leone (ibid: 62). The sick recaptives were quarantined on the *Perpetuo Defensor* and the healthy were quartered on a colonial government ship, the *Susan*. When Captain Bullen, the British captor, learnt that he had no grounds to detain the ship – he had sought to defend the capture because the *Perpetuo Defensor* had enslaved a British subject Cacow/Cackau – he tried to restore the ship and the recaptives to the master, Antonio Mauricio de Mendonça. De Mendonça sought damages and therefore insisted that the Mixed Commission hear the case. The Acting Governor was determined that the recaptives should not be restored. He ordered those on the *Susan* to be landed in early July, without the permission or knowledge of the Mixed Commission. Eighty-eight recaptives remained on the *Perpetuo Defensor*. Armed with sticks, wood and cannon shot, they demanded to be put ashore, purportedly having been encouraged by recaptives from the *Susan* and a black sailor of the *Maidstone* (ibid: 67). The acting master of the *Perpetuo Defensor* was unable to control the recaptives. Thinking that lives were at risk and having received no assistance to his distress call, he landed the recaptives on 6 July 1826 without the permission of the Mixed Commission.

The Mixed Commission adopted the same approach to this case as it had to the *Activo*. On 28 September 1826, in the absence of the Portuguese Commissioner it awarded, on top of an unconditional sum of damages, an amount for the total loss of 364 slaves, subject to the British and Brazilian governments' agreement. The captor had argued that the claimant should only be recompensed for the loss of 276 slaves because the claimant himself had landed the recaptives from the *Perpetuo Defensor*. The Mixed Commission rejected the captor's argument that the circumstances did not justify the landing of the recaptives. The report of the case acknowledges recaptives' 'revolt and violence' (Hamilton to Canning 12 October 1826: 70). Thus, recaptives' resistance played a role in debates about the quantification of damages. It was legally significant to that extent at least.

To all intents and purposes, in these cases the recaptives were treated as if they had been emancipated. However, the cases did little to safeguard the rights of recaptives at a more general level. The Sierra Leone government thought that *Somerset*'s case applied to the recaptives in the *Activo* (*Somerset v Stewart* 1772) and had considered that the recaptives in the *Perpetuo Defensor* were free by virtue of being on a British government ship, propositions with which the Mixed Commission and the government's legal advisers disagreed.[21] The Government received legal advice that *Somerset*'s case could not be applied as an 'abstract or universal principle' to recaptives in these circumstances (Doctors Commons to Canning 26 January 1827: 133–134). Although it was considered doubtful that recaptives were entitled to liberation (Robinson to Canning 18 November 1826: 109), it was not thought that compensation awards for the loss of slaves in the situation of the *Activo* and *Perpetuo Defensor* cases were within the 'object and spirit of the treaties' (Doctors Commons to the Earl of Dudley 23 May 1828: 276). However, it was advised that the British government should agree with Brazil that compensation should be refused in these circumstances rather than issue general guidance to that effect (Doctors Commons to the Earl of Dudley 23 May 1828: 277). What results from Mixed Commissioners' approach here is an unhappy distinction, as the King's Advocate noted, between the approach taken to the slaves (whom it was determined could not be emancipated) and their economic worth (which it was determined was not compensable) (King's Advocate Memo 22 September 1828: 310, 317). The King's Advocate thought it would have been better if the Commissioners, instead of ordering the recaptives to be restored, had first asked whether claimants should be able to claim restitution when slaves had been illegally traded (King's Advocate Memo 22 September 1828: 311). This might have breached the link between lawful intervention and emancipation, lessening the legal precariousness of recaptivity. The reasons for the failure to ask this question can really only be inferred. Commissioners no doubt felt constrained – as did the government's legal advisers – by the legal tools at their disposal which focused on questions of intervention (and resulting financial liabilities) rather than recaptives' rights. The question however, cannot be avoided: had such a question been asked, would the outcome in the case of the *Maria da Gloria* have been different?

In the case of the *Maria da Gloria*, commissioners felt that it was accepted that claimants were not entitled to damages for the loss of illegally traded slaves when restoration was ordered, but still felt they had no choice but to order the restoration of the recaptives, who unlike the recaptives in the *Activo* and *Perpetuo Defensor* cases did not make it to the shore.[22] In fact, after some initial disagreement, Commissioners extended previous practice: they denied the claim for the loss of the slaves which in the *Activo* and *Perpetuo Defensor* cases had been provisionally granted and made an award for costs and other damages, which had been granted unconditionally before, provisional upon the agreement of the British and Portuguese governments (HM Commissioners to Palmerston 31 March 1834: 40–42). The legal accommodation in the *Activo* and *Perpetuo Defensor* cases, whilst paving the way for further reductions in damages, did not therefore stop the disastrous outcome in the case of the *Maria da Gloria*.

Recaptives' resistance

By resisting their detention pending adjudication, recaptives in the *Activo* and *Perpetuo Defensor* cases secured their own freedom and shone a light on the contradictions in the slave trade repression treaties and their application in Sierra Leone, which had been set up as a territory for freed slaves. International abolition law did not formally recognise recaptives as legal subjects, let alone their agency or resistance. However, as these cases show, resistance influenced the legal argument and outcomes. Yet, as noted earlier, the legal solution in these cases and the resistance which provoked such legal dilemmas did not prevent the disaster of the *Maria da Gloria*.

The provisions of the slave trade repression treaties that provided for restoration rested upon a contradiction in the context of Sierra Leone, a colony which the British had established for freed slaves. This contradiction opened a space for recaptives to challenge the logic of slave trade repression treaties. The extent to which recaptives in the *Activo* and *Perpetuo Defensor* cases intentionally deployed the paradoxes inherent in international slave trade repression law and the contradictions between British obligations under the slave trade repression treaties on the one hand and the promise of *Somerset*'s case on the other is of course unknown. Expressed in those terms it is probably unlikely. However, in the *Perpetuo Defensor* it was claimed that interaction between liberated Africans and recaptives was among the factors that made the recaptives rebellious (Hamilton to Canning 12 October 1826: 65). At least some recaptives then may have understood the potential legal significance of making it to the shore.

The colonial authorities' actions supported recaptives' resistance. The Acting Governor was determined to avoid recaptives' in-person restoration and arranged for the landing of the recaptives on board the *Susan* and may have tried to prevent obstacles to recaptives leaving the *Perpetuo Defensor* (Hamilton to Canning 12 October 1826: 70). The Acting King's Advocate and the Deputy Inspector of Hospitals were also active in seeking recaptives' freedom, twice unsuccessfully making an application for habeas corpus of the recaptives on the *Perpetuo Defensor*. Their actions contributed to recaptives' liberation. However, without recaptives' resistance, recaptives would not have reached the shore or been landed and would not, therefore, have attained their freedom. To that extent, Mixed Commissioners acknowledged the significance of recaptives' resistance. Thus, the Mixed Commission's view was that recaptives had been incited to revolt and had they not been so incited they would not have been landed (ibid). Had they not been landed, recaptives would most likely have faced the fate of recaptives in the *Maria da Gloria*. Secretary of State Canning also appears to have acknowledged resistance – even if only implicitly – in his advice to Mixed Commissioners. Noting that that restoration in the *Activo* and *Perpetuo Defensor* cases was appropriate, he also directed that when restoration was impossible by 'unforeseen circumstances' the court should use its discretion and hand recaptives over to the local government (Canning to HM Commissioners 30 December 1826: 9–10). Here then the unforeseen circumstance was recaptives' resistance, which Canning can be read here as having effectively licenced. However, although recaptives' resistance led to recaptives' own freedom from enslavement, thereby indirectly contributing to changes in compensation practices, it did not lessen the legal precariousness of recaptivity more generally, as the catastrophic case of the *Maria da Gloria* demonstrates. In fact, tragically it was the fear of the outbreak of resistance in the colony that influenced the Mixed Commission in its decision not to land the recaptives in the *Maria da Gloria* pending adjudication.

Recaptives' resistance was significant both legally and factually. However, for the most part it has been written out of international (criminal) legal histories. This writing-out can be contrasted with the voluminous literature on *Somerset*'s case upon which some of the arguments in the protracted legal disputes in the *Activo* and *Perpetuo Defensor* cases drew. A variety of reasons can explain why the *Activo* and *Perpetuo Defensor* cases have not gone down in international legal histories as leading cases, including the limited accessibility of Mixed Commission reports and the status and geographical location of Mixed Commissions. More than this, recaptives were not given their freedom in the *Activo* and *Perpetuo Defensor* cases. Instead, they seized it for themselves, thereby liberating themselves and challenging the conditions that slave trade repression treaties set for their freedom. Consequently, the *Activo* and *Perpetuo Defensor* cases do not lend themselves to the sort of myth-making that has grown up around abolition. These cases confronted those myths by shining a vital light on the limits of freedom under international abolition law and by illuminating the productive role of recaptives' violent resistance. As Chapter 3 suggested, this offers a counter-narrative to the narratives surrounding the use of force by the British Royal Navy.

However, if recaptives' resistance is written into international criminal legal history, the question remains as to the ends to which it is inscribed. The history of the recaptive provides a critical starting point for thinking about the ways in which agency and resistance can be mobilised in international (criminal) legal history and its present. As David Scott masterfully reminds us, accounts of agency and resistance must be alert to the politics and purposes behind their inscription (Scott 2004). Inscribing recaptives' agency and resistance can serve as a critique of the limitations and structures of international abolition law and/or a memorialisation of the struggles of recaptives. Inscribing recaptives' agency and resistance can also be deployed within a progress narrative to affirm the responsiveness of international abolition law to recaptives' resistance. In other words, resistance can be written in as a narrative of inclusion or exclusion, the limitations of the law or its potential. Ultimately, this is a political choice. However, for this author at least it is impossible to read the *Activo* and *Perpetuo Defensor* cases without taking account of the later case of the *Maria da Gloria*.

Conclusion

Far from being universally granted to unlawfully trafficked slaves, slave trade repression treaties effectively privileged particular victims of the slave trade by granting legal emancipation to recaptives who were the objects of lawful intervention (Haslam 2016: 443). Whether a slave ship had been captured lawfully raised often complex legal and evidential questions. Recaptivity was, therefore, inherently risky. All recaptives entered this intrinsically perilous and liminal legal state, some for longer than others. While they remained on prize ships, recaptives were particularly vulnerable.

Unlawful interventions left recaptives legally exposed. Under these circumstances, Commissioners might be considered to have done what they could to ensure recaptives' de facto emancipation within the limited framing of the law. At the same time, recaptives' resistance also played a vital role in recaptives' self-liberation in the cases of the *Activo* and *Perpetuo Defensor* (Haslam 2016: 441). This chapter has argued that as a matter of law Mixed Commissions were able, in situations of unlawful captures when recaptives were claimed, to do more to protect captors from damages claims than they were to safeguard the formal legal position of recaptives, for example by expanding emancipation. In the majority of cases this did not significantly affect what happened to recaptives who were granted de facto freedom. However, the *Maria da Gloria* shows how the focus on the circumstances surrounding intervention could lead to disastrous consequences. Whilst recaptives' resistance should be remembered in accounts of the *Activo* and *Perpetuo Defensor* cases, the outcome of these cases did not alleviate the legally precarious position of recaptives found in unlawfully captured ships in all cases.

Finally, awards of damages – even to avoid the in-person restoration – exemplify the focus of prize on property rights. The next chapter (Chapter 6) shifts gear to explore this aspect of international slave trade repression further. It moves from considering how the focus on intervention explored in this and the previous chapters framed the legal construction of recaptives to examining the property relations underpinning slave trade repression and their effects on the construction of recaptives.

Notes

1 As regards the former, in general terms then this might be seen as a question of whether injustice is determined by 'average rather than with particularity' (Kapczynski 2004–2005: 1086 (commenting on Walter Benjamin)).

2 *El Almirante* was captured by the *Black Joke*, a former slave ship and one of the most celebrated ships in the squadron. When the ship was finally decommissioned and burnt liberated Africans are said to have wept. See Olusoga (2016: 297).

3 After the abolition of slavery the Queen's Advocate advised that recaptives who were disembarked in the West Indies prior to adjudication should not be detained as slaves, even if a sentence of restoration were subsequently ordered (Dodson to Palmerston 30 August 1838, 29 September 1838).
4 Fett observes that between 1838 and 1850 the average annual mortality rate of recaptives at the Sierra Leone recaptive hospital was 50% (Fett 2017: 85).
5 Sherwood notes that it has been estimated that 25% of recaptives died before they left slave ships (Sherwood 2007: 119–120).
6 For discussion of the disposition of liberated Africans under the Abolition Act see also Chapter 2.
7 The African Institution was established in 1807. Its members were well-known British abolitionists, including William Wilberforce, James Stephen, Granville Sharp, Thomas Fowell Buxton and Zachary Macaulay. Their aim was to contribute to the 'civilisation' of Africa through Christianity and legitimate trade. The African Institution recognised the potential for abuse of apprenticeships, but claimed that 'much more has been effected' for the benefit of recaptives than required by law (African Institution 1815: 51), and that overall liberated Africans were treated in a 'kind and liberal manner' (ibid: 62). For an account of the different approaches towards liberated Africans in Sierra Leone over time see Christopher (2018).
8 Here Shaikh is referring to Madden's 1836 Parliamentary Select Committee testimony. On concerns about the '*de facto* servitude' of recaptives in Brazil, the so-called emancipados, see Conrad (1973: 51), who describes them as 'living in a kind of legal purgatory between slavery and freedom' (ibid: 69).
9 On the transportation of emancipados from Cuba to the Caribbean, see Martinez-Fernandez (1995).
10 See further, for example, the trial of Jousiffe, described by Mixed Commissioners as a 'notorious offender' (Doherty and Lewis to Palmerston 23 September 1837: 8) found guilty of slave trading under the Slave Trade Amendment and Consolidation Act 1824 and sentenced to 14 years' transportation (ibid: 5–8).
11 It is not clear whether the reference to Macaulay here is a reference to a member of the Macaulay family prominent in Sierra Leone.
12 Later, in the case of the *Arogante Mayaguesana*, Commissioners explained their practice when faced with domestic slaves: to explain that individuals had the choice of remaining with their master or joining the rest of the liberated slaves. In that case, one young boy, a domestic slave, chose to stay with his master (HM Commissioners to Palmerston 13 October 1834: 16).
13 On the question of restitution, in the *Amedie* Sir William Grant doubted the rectitude of a claim for in-person restitution observing that: 'We are of opinion, upon the whole, that persons engaged in such a trade cannot, upon principles of universal law, have a right to be heard upon a claim of this nature in any court' (The *Amedie* 1810: 96–97).
14 For example, British Commissioner Fitzgerald suggested in the *Rosalia*, that recaptives should not be restored even where restoration was ordered (Gregory and Fitzgerald to the Marquess of Londonderry 17 March 1822: 25). This suggestion was later criticised, however, and contradicted by subsequent cases, including the *Maria da Gloria*.
15 This requirement was loosened over the life of Mixed Commissions, for example, over time to encompass situations where slaves had been on board. Spain agreed an equipment clause in 1835 and Portugal in 1842.
16 The King's Advocate also approved of the decision of the Mixed Commission not to emancipate the slaves that captors had placed on board the *Ninfa Habunera* and advised against awarding bounties (Jenner to Palmerston 20 June 1833).

17 Sometimes masters agreed to manumit recaptives. The master of the Spanish ship *Pajarito* that had been irregularly captured by a tender which did not have authority to make captures voluntarily manumitted 233 surviving recaptives (293 had originally been trafficked) (HM Commissioners to Aberdeen 30 October 1830: 45).

18 The manager of the Liberated Africans Department, having been sent to rescue liberated Africans sold to a Frenchman outside the territory of Sierra Leone, felt obliged not to intervene in the case of a woman in irons, who did not claim liberated African status. All he could do was to request the King that she was not put in irons again (Pratt to Cole 19 November 1830).

19 This practice was not uncontested. Responding to a complaint from Samo, a slave owner on the Isles de Los, the governor observed the appropriate way to prevent such losses was to indent individuals, who could then be returned as fugitive apprentices (MacCarthy to Goulburn 30 September 1820), thereby demonstrating some of the shifting legal sands between slavery and 'free' labour.

20 This and the following section draw on the discussion of the *Activo, Perpetuo Defensor* and *Maria da Gloria* cases in Haslam (2016: 433–445).

21 *Somerset*'s case has come to occupy a key legal place in Anglo-American histories of abolition. At the time, many interpreted the case to have abolished slavery in England. It is widely accepted that this construal was not justified by a strict reading of the decision. Lord Mansfield, the presiding judge, sought to distance himself from more expansive readings of the case (*Somerset v Stewart* 1772; Nadelhart 1966; Shyllon 1974; Wiecek 1974–1975; Finkelman 1981; Fryer 1984; Harris, 2006–2007). In fact, what Lord Mansfield decided was that a slave could not be removed from England without his consent. See further Wiecek (1974–1975: 86, 141–146). He later sought to emphasise the limitations of his decision in *Somerset*'s case to counsel in *R* v *the Inhabitants of Thames Ditton* (1785).

22 Although 64 recaptives who had been landed previously due to sickness remained in Sierra Leone.

References

African Institution (1815) *Ninth Report of the Directors of the African Institution*, Fleet Street: Ellerton & Henderson.

Asiegbu, J. U. J. (1969) *Slavery and the Politics of Liberation 1787–1861: A Study of Liberated African Emigration and British Anti-Slavery Policy*, London and Harlow: Longmans.

Bethell, L. (1966) 'The Mixed Commissions for the Suppression of the Transatlantic Slave Trade in the Nineteenth Century', *Journal of African History* 7(1): 79–93.

Burroughs, R. (2010) 'Eyes on the Prize: Journeys in Slave Ships Taken as Prizes by the Royal Navy', *Slavery and Abolition* 31(1): 99–115.

Christopher, E. (2018) 'Tis Enough That We Give Them Liberty'? Liberated Africans at Sierra Leone in the Early Era of Slave-Trade Suppression', in R. Burroughs and R. Huzzey (eds.), *The Suppression of the Atlantic Slave Trade*, Manchester: Manchester University Press.

Conrad, R. (1973) 'Neither Slave Nor Free: The Emancipados of Brazil, 1818–1868', *Hispanic American Historical Review* 53(1): 50–70.

Fett, S. M. (2017) *Recaptured Africans: Surviving Slave Ships, Detention, and Dislocation in the Final Years of the Slave Trade*, Chapel Hill: University of North Carolina Press.

Finkelman, P. (1981) *An Imperfect Union: Slavery, Federalism and Comity*, Chapel Hill: University of North Carolina Press.
Fryer, P. (1984) *Staying Power: The History of Black People in Britain*, London and Sydney: Pluto Press.
Fyfe, C. (1961) 'Four Sierra Leone Recaptives', *Journal of African History* 2(1): 77–85.
Harris, C. (2006–2007) '"Too Pure an Air": Somerset's Legacy from Anti-Slavery to Colorblindness', *Texas Wesleyan Law Review* 13: 439–458.
Haslam, E. (2016) 'International Criminal Law and Legal Memories of Abolition: Intervention, Mixed Commission Courts and "Emancipation"', *Journal of the History of International Law* 18: 420–447.
Kapczynski, A. (2004–2005) 'Historicism, Progress, and the Redemptive Constitution', *Cardozo Law Review* 26: 1041–1117.
Lovejoy, P. E. and Schwarz, S. (2015) 'Sierra Leone in the Eighteenth and Nineteenth Centuries', in P. E. Lovejoy and S. Schwarz (eds.), *Slavery, Abolition and the Transition to Colonialism in Sierra Leone*, Trenton: Africa World Press.
Macaulay, Z. (1815) *A Letter to HRH the Duke of Gloucester, President of the African Institution, from Zachary Macaulay Esq, Occasioned by a Pamphlet Lately Published by Dr Thorpe, Late Judge of the Colony of Sierra Leone, Entitled: 'A Letter to William Wilberforce Esq'*, London: Ellerton & Henderson.
Mamigonian, B. G. (2009) 'In the Name of Freedom: Slave Trade Abolition, the Law and the Brazilian Branch of the African Emigration Scheme (Brazil – British West Indies, 1930s – 1950s)', *Slavery and Abolition* 30(1): 41–66.
Martinez, J. (2012) *The Slave Trade and the Origins of International Human Rights Law*, Oxford: Oxford University Press.
Martinez-Fernandez, L. (1995) 'The Havana Anglo-Spanish Mixed Commission for the Suppression of the Slave Trade and Cuba's Emancipados', *Slavery and Abolition* 16(2): 205–225.
Misevich, P. (2015) 'Freetown and "Freedom?" Colonialism and Slavery in Sierra Leone 1790s to 1861', in P. E. Lovejoy and S. Schwarz (eds.), *Slavery, Abolition and the Transition to Colonialism in Sierra Leone*, Trenton: Africa World Press.
Nadelhart, J. (1966) 'The Somersett Case and Slavery: Myth, Reality and Repercussions', *Journal of Negro History* 51: 193–208.
Northrup, D. (2006) 'Becoming African: Identify Formation among Liberated Slaves in Nineteenth-Century Sierra Leone', *Slavery and Abolition* 27(1): 1–21.
Olusoga, D. (2016) *Black and British: A Forgotten History*, London: Macmillan.
Schwarz, S. (2012) 'Reconstructing the Life Histories of Liberated Africans: Sierra Leone in the Early Nineteenth Century', *History in Africa* 39: 175–207.
Scott, D. (2004) *Conscripts of Modernity: The Tragedy of Colonial Enlightenment*, Durham and London: Duke University Press.
Shaikh, F. (2012) 'Judicial Diplomacy British Officials and the Mixed Commission Courts', in K. Hamilton and P. Salmon (eds.), *Slavery, Diplomacy and Empire Britain and the Suppression of the Slave Trade, 1807–1975*, Eastbourne: Sussex Academic Press.
Sherwood, M. (2007) *After Abolition: Britain and the Slave Trade since 1807*, London: I.B. Tauris & Co. Ltd.
Shyllon, F. O. (1974) *Black Slaves in Britain*, London, New York, Ibadan: Oxford University Press.

Thorpe, R. (1815a) *A Letter to William Wilberforce, ESQ: MP Vice President of the African Institution Containing Remarks on the Reports of the Sierra Leone Company, and African Institution with Hints Respecting the Means by Which an Universal Abolition of the Slave Trade Might Be Carried into Effect*, London: Law & Gilbert.

Thorpe, R. (1815b) *A Reply, Point by Point to the Special Report of the Directors of the African Institution*, London: R & R Gilbert.

Thorpe, R. (1815c) *Postscript to the Reply 'Point by Point' Containing an Expose of the Misrepresentation of the Treatment of the Captured Negroes at Sierra Leone; and Other Matters Arising from the Ninth Report of the African Institution*, London: R & R Gilbert.

Turner, M. J. (1997) 'The Limits of Abolition: Government, Saints and the "African Question", c. 1780–1820', *English Historical Review* 112: 319–357.

Wiecek, W. M. (1974–1975) '*Somerset:* Lord Mansfield and the Legitimacy of Slavery in the Anglo-American World', *University of Chicago Law Review* 42: 86–146.

International instruments

Additional Convention to the Treaty of the 22 January 1815, between His Britannic Majesty and his Most Faithful Majesty, for the Purpose of Preventing Their Subjects from Engaging in Any Illicit Traffic in Slaves (Additional Convention (Portugal)), 18 July 1817, The National Archives: FO 84/2, pp. 3–5.

Regulations for the Mixed Commissions, Which Are to Reside on the Coast of Africa, and in a Colonial Possession of His Catholic Majesty (Spanish Regulations), The National Archives: FO 84/2, pp. 15–18.

Regulations for the Mixed Commissions Which Are to Reside on the Coast of Africa, in the Brazils and London (Portuguese Regulations) 1817, The National Archives: FO 84/2, pp. 8–10.

Legislation

An Act for the Abolition of the Slave Trade (Abolition Act 1807) 47 Geo 3 c 36.

An Act to Amend and Consolidate the Laws Relating to the Abolition of the Slave Trade (Slave Trade Amendment and Consolidation Act 1824) 5 Geo 4 c 113.

English cases

The Amedie (1810) 12 Eng Rep 92.

R v the Inhabitants of Thames Ditton (1785) 99 ER 891.

Somerset v Stewart (1772) 98 Eng Rep 499.

Mixed commission cases

Findlay and Smith to Aberdeen, 15 May 1830 with Enclosures in the Case of the *Umbelina*, No. 52 *Class A Correspondence with the British Commissioners at Sierra Leone, the Havana, Rio de Janeiro and Surinam Relating to the Slave Trade, 1830* PP 1831 (004) XIX.321.

Gregory and Fitzgerald to Canning, 22 April 1823 with Enclosures in the Case of the *Sinceridade*, The National Archives: FO 84/22, 89.
Gregory and Fitzgerald to the Marquess of Londonderry, 17 March 1822 in the *Case of the Rosalia*, No. 10 with Enclosures *Class B Correspondence with the British Commissioners at Sierra Leone, the Havana, Rio de Janeiro and Surinam Relating to the Slave Trade 1822* PP 1823 (008) XIX.311.
Gregory and Fitzgerald to the Marquess of Londonderry, 24 July 1822 in the Case of the *Dichosa Estrella*, No. 11 with Enclosures *Class B Correspondence with the British Commissioners at Sierra Leone, the Havana, Rio de Janeiro and Surinam Relating to the Slave Trade* 1822. PP 1823 (008) XIX.311.
Gregory and Fitzgerald to the Marquess of Londonderry, 15 September 1822, in the Case of the *Nymfa Del Mar*, No 29 with Enclosures *Class B Correspondence with the British Commissioners at Sierra Leone, the Havana, Rio de Janeiro and Surinam Relating to the Slave Trade 1822* PP 1823 (008) XIX.311.
Gregory to Canning, 7 June 1823 in the Case of the *Nova Sorte*, Nos. 46–48 with Enclosures *Class B Correspondence with the British Commissioners at Sierra Leone, the Havana, Rio de Janeiro, and Surinam, Relating to the Slave Trade 1823* PP 1824 (002) XXIV.215.
Hamilton to Canning, 25 July 1826, in the Case of the *Activo*, No 43 with Enclosures in *Class A Correspondence with the British Commissioners at Sierra Leone, the Havannah, Rio de Janeiro, and Surinam, Relating to the Slave Trade 1826–1827* PP 1826–27 (010) XXVI.127.
Hamilton to Canning, 12 October 1826, in the Case of the *Perpetuo Defensor*, No 46 with Enclosures in *Class A Correspondence with the British Commissioners at Sierra Leone, the Havannah, Rio de Janeiro, and Surinam, Relating to the Slave Trade 1826–1827* PP 1826–27 (010) XXVI.127.
HM Commissioners to Aberdeen, 4 March 1829 in the Case of the *Aurelia*, No 65 with Enclosure *Class A Correspondence with the British Commissioners at Sierra Leone, the Havana, Rio de Janeiro, and Surinam, Relating to the Slave Trade 1829* PP 1830 (014) XXX111.23.
HM Commissioners to Aberdeen, 23 March 1829 in the Case of the *El Almirante*, No 29 with Enclosure *Class A Correspondence with the British Commissioners at Sierra Leone, the Havana, Rio de Janeiro, and Surinam, Relating to the Slave Trade 1829* PP 1830 (014) XXXIII.23.
HM Commissioners to Aberdeen, 15 September 1829 in the Case of the *Panchita*, No 32 with Enclosures *Class A Correspondence with the British Commissioners at Sierra Leone, the Havana, Rio de Janeiro, and Surinam, Relating to the Slave Trade 1829* PP 1830 (014) XXX111.23.
HM Commissioners to Aberdeen, 30 October 1830 in the Case of the *Pajarito*, No 35 with Enclosure *Class A Correspondence with the British Commissioners at Sierra Leone, the Havana, Rio de Janeiro and Surinam Relating to the Slave Trade, 1830* PP 1831 (004) XIX.321.
HM Commissioners to Canning, 10 June 1826, in the Case of the *Activo*, No 42 with Enclosures in *Class A Correspondence with the British Commissioners at Sierra Leone, the Havannah, Rio de Janeiro, and Surinam, Relating to the Slave Trade 1826–1827* PP 1826–27 (010) XXVI.127.
HM Commissioners to Palmerston, 31 March 1834, in the Case of the *Maria da Gloria* Nos 34 and 35 with Enclosures in *Class A Correspondence with the British*

Commissioners at Sierra Leone, the Havana, Rio de Janeiro, and Surinam, Relating to the Slave Trade 1834 PP 1835 (006) LI.1.

HM Commissioners to Palmerston, 13 October 1834 in the Case of the *Arogante Mayaguesana*, No 10 with Enclosure *Class A Correspondence with the British Commissioners at Sierra Leone, the Havana, Rio de Janeiro, and Surinam, Relating to the Slave Trade 1835* PP 1836 (005) L.1.

HM Commissioners to Palmerston, 21 November 1834 in the Case of the *Pepita*, No 11 with Enclosure *Class A Correspondence with the British Commissioners at Sierra Leone, the Havana, Rio de Janeiro, and Surinam, Relating to the Slave Trade 1835* PP 1836 (005) L.1.

HM Commissioners to Palmerston, 24 January 1838 in the Case of the *Camoes*, No 24 with Enclosures *Class A Correspondence with the British Commissioners at Sierra Leone, the Havana, Rio de Janeiro, and Surinam, Relating to the Slave Trade from May 1 1838 to February 2 1839* PP 1839 (180) XLVIII.1.

Jackson to Aberdeen, 20 December 1828 in the Case of the *Arcenia*, No 41 with Enclosure *Class A Correspondence with the British Commissioners at Sierra Leone, the Havana, Rio de Janeiro, and Surinam, Relating to the Slave Trade 1929* PP 1830 (014) XXX111.23.

Lumley and Smith to Canning, 18 June 1827 and Report of the Brazilian Brigantine *Creola*, The National Archives: FO 84/66, 14.

Macaulay and Lewis to Palmerston, 3 December 1835 in the Case of the *Conde de Los Andes*, No. 39 with Enclosure *Class A Correspondence with the British Commissioners at Sierra Leone, the Havana, Rio de Janeiro, and Surinam, Relating to the Slave Trade 1835* PP 1836 (005) L.1.

Macaulay and Lewis to Palmerston, 8 January 1836 in the Case of the *Norma*, No 43 with Enclosure *Class A Correspondence with the British Commissioners at Sierra Leone, the Havana, Rio de Janeiro, and Surinam, Relating to the Slave Trade 1835* PP1836 (005) L.1.

Rendall to Canning, 21 November 1825 in the Case of the *Uniao*, No 34 with Enclosure *Class A Correspondence with British Commissioners at Sierra Leone, Havana, Rio de Janeiro and Surinam Relating to the Slave Trade, 1826–27*, PP 1826–27 (010) XXVI.127.

Williams to Canning, 25 March 1826 in the Case of the *Sam Joao Segunda Rosalia*, No. 39 with Enclosure *Class A Correspondence with British Commissioners at Sierra Leone, Havana, Rio de Janeiro and Surinam Relating to the Slave Trade, 1826–27*, PP 1826–27 (010) XXVI.127.

Documents and correspondence

Canning to HM Commissioners, 30 December 1826, The National Archives: FO 84/49, pp. 7–10.

Deposition of Liberated African Boy Named George Found on Board the *Caroline*, The National Archives: CO 267/105.

Deposition of Liberated African Boy Named John Davis, December 1830, The National Archives: CO 267/105.

Doctors Commons to Bathurst, 26 January 1827, The National Archives: CO 267/85.

Doctors Commons to Canning, 26 January 1827, The National Archives: FO 83/2344, pp. 132–134.

Doctors Commons to the Earl of Dudley, 23 May 1828, The National Archives: FO 83/2344, pp. 275–277.
Dodson to Palmerston, 30 August 1838, The National Archives: FO 83/2347, pp. 383–385.
Dodson to Palmerston, 29 September 1838, The National Archives: FO 83/2347, pp. 408–410.
Dodson to Wellington, 15 April 1835, The National Archives: FO 83/2346, pp. 247–248.
Doherty and Lewis to Palmerston, 23 September 1837, No 9 *Class A Correspondence with the British Commissioners at Sierra Leone, the Havana, Rio de Janeiro, and Surinam, Relating to the Slave Trade 1837* PP 1837–1838 (124) L.I.
Dudley to HM Commissioners, 13 December 1827, The National Archives: FO 84/64, pp. 22–24.
Governor Findlay to Commandant of Goree, 22 December 1830, The National Archives: CO 267/105.
Hamilton to Goulburn, 29 October 1821, The National Archives: CO 267/55.
Jenner to Palmerston, 20 June 1833, The National Archives: FO 83/2346, pp. 124–125.
King's Advocate, 28 October 1823, The National Archives: FO 83/2343, pp. 157–159.
King's Advocate, Case of the *Dichosa Estrella* 10 October 1822, The National Archives: FO 83/2343, pp. 100–101.
King's Advocate Memo on the Cases of the *Activo* and the *Perpetuo Defensor*, 22 September 1828, The National Archives: FO 83/2344, pp. 303–317.
King's Advocate Report on Condemnation of the *Rosalia*, 23 July 1822, The National Archives: FO 83/2343, pp. 92–93.
Lieutenant Governor Findlay to Hay, 3 December 1830, The National Archives: CO 267/105.
Lieutenant Governor Findlay to Hay, 20 December 1830, The National Archives: CO 267/105.
MacCarthy to Goulburn, 30 September 1820, The National Archives: CO 267/51.
McCarthy to Bathurst, 10 March 1822, The National Archives: CO 267/56.
Pratt to Cole, 19 November 1830, The National Archives: CO 267/105.
Robinson to Canning, 18 November 1826, The National Archives: FO 83/2344, pp. 107–109.

6 Prize, property and the economies of slave trade repression

Introduction

This chapter shows how questions of property continued to play a role in determining recaptives' formal legal status during slave trade repression, alongside questions about intervention that the previous chapters have explored. The deployment of prize for abolition was a creative and pragmatic response to the limited legal tools available to further abolition, but, as the previous chapters have made clear, it came at a price. In some respects, of course, slave trade repression law subverted prize for more humane ends. However, prize focused on the 'adjudication of property rights rather than on the protection of rescued slaves' (Benton and Ford 2016: 125), and as a result the law continued to treat recaptives and liberated Africans in many respects as subjects who had an economic value – albeit not to themselves. This framing was not only of theoretical interest. It could impact upon the grant of legal emancipation. This commodification of recaptives also contributed to the uneven distribution of the 'material' benefits of slave trade repression to borrow from Guyora Binder's criticism of the US Thirteenth Amendment (Binder 1993: 473). As the following chapter argues (Chapter 7), the uneven distribution of the benefits of slave trade repression contributes to international law's indebtedness to recaptives.

This chapter mainly analyses the way that international slave trade repression law framed its subjects but, like the chapters before it, it also provides an opportunity to acknowledge recaptives' resistance. The general thrust of this narrative aligns with established critiques. Scholars have emphasised the ways that abolition commodified the African body (Wood 2010: 14) and the limitations of prize in challenging the construction of slaves as property (Benton and Ford 2016: 122). This chapter contributes an analysis of how the commodification of recaptives and the property relations running through international slave trade repression law impacted on the legal construction of recaptives. In so doing, like the previous chapter, it provides some broader historical context to contemporary debates about the construction and representation of victims in international criminal law today.

The chapter begins by showing how slave trade repression law commodified slaves and recaptives directly by placing an economic value on them through awards of compensation and indirectly by enabling conditions by which recaptives generated wealth for others. This construction of recaptives left little space for the law to acknowledge recaptives as legal subjects. This contrasted sharply with its approach to captors whose responsibility for capturing slave ships positioned them in a potentially invidious position between state and individual responsibility. Tellingly, however, as the next section shows, the commodification of recaptives could also operate as a limit to the liabilities of captors. The following section explores how bounties commodified recaptives. However, paradoxically, it is in the context of a claim for bounties that one of the fullest narratives of resistance and survival read in the research for this book emerges. Finally, on occasion the prospect of an award of bounties could play a role in determining whether emancipation should be granted or withheld. The last section argues that formal legal emancipation, therefore, was a particular kind of freedom infused with the economy of slave trade repression. This was a political economy which distributed the profits of slave trade repression unequally and as a result has contributed to the indebtedness of international law to the recaptive (Chapter 7).

From human cargo to prize

Included amongst the instructions to the Spanish master of the ship, the *Gertrudis La Preciosa*, to purchase 400 men and 100 women was the injunction that:

> [t]he men ought to be from 12 to 18 years, and the women from 12 to 15; the colour of both sexes ought to be the blackest possible, of a regular stature, considering those that are very tall and very small faulty; they must also be robust and vigorous; none are to be received that have any corporeal defect, and much less those that may discover any contagious infirmity.
>
> (*Gertrudis La Preciosa* 1816: 409)

These instructions epitomise some of the ways that the slave trade commodified its victims. Litigation contains other such examples.[1]

However, although slave trade repression limited the traffic in slaves, it still allowed for the commodification of slaves and recaptives to a greater or lesser extent – albeit of course in different ways to the slave trade. Prize, the basis for international slave trade repression law, as Benton and Ford have shown, was concerned with questions about property rights (Benton and Ford 2016: 125). Within this legal worldview, recaptives were potentially compensable property. In addition to which, slave trade repression created the conditions by which others (not recaptives and liberated Africans) gained resources. These are amongst the reasons why international law remains indebted to recaptives.

Vice Admiralty Courts were obliged to order compensation to slave and ship owners when captors detained ships unlawfully, but liberated Africans received no compensation for their enslavement. Mixed Commissions were embedded in this compensation culture from the outset. As Chapter 2 showed, the London Slave Trade Commission was established solely to compensate Portuguese ship and slave owners for losses arising from unlawful captures. Its records brim with calculations about the price of slaves, the cost of insurance premiums for slave-trading journeys, the price of slaves at destination ports and the cost of import duties on slaves, a particular point of controversy during its operation being whether indemnification could include any anticipated profits on slave trading voyages (Marsden to Castlereagh 31 May 1820).

The Regulations for Mixed Commissions provided extensive guidance about quantifying damages resulting from the loss of slaves. In cases in which restoration was ordered, claimants were entitled to recover 'all losses and damages' arising out of capture and detention. Where this included the loss of slaves on board detained ships, an award was made according to the value of the slaves at the final destination. Commissioners were instructed to take account of 'the usual fair average mortality for the unexpired period of the regular voyage' and any charges due on sale. Where slaves were not lost to owners, owners could still claim compensation. This could include a sum for the extra subsistence detention required, an amount representing the 'deterioration' of slaves, and compensation for any decrease in the slaves' worth as a result of increased mortality or sickness resulting from the ship's detention (Article 8 Spanish Regulations; Article 8 Portuguese Regulations; Haslam 2016: 428). The grant of such compensation treated individuals as property. Previous chapters showed that Commissioners tried to mitigate the worst effects of slave trade repression treaties by avoiding in-person restoration. On occasion they were also able to reduce the damages payable (the *Sinceridade*, the *Activo* and the *Perpetuo Defensor*). However, in the *Maria da Gloria*, compensation was avoided, but in-person restoration was not.

The sums paid to slave and ship owners can be seen as the 'price' paid for liberating slaves where slave ships were detained unlawfully. However, recaptives and liberated Africans received none of it.[2] As Wood notes, the £20 million pounds compensation Britain paid to slave owners after the abolition of slavery 'cut the slave out of the equation', at the same time as it was supposed to leave him indebted (Wood 2010: 10).[3] Much the same could be said about slave trade repression. Compensation perpetuated the commodification of recaptives and liberated Africans. Bounties (see the following) brought funds to individuals, including captors and their agents, and the colony of Sierra Leone also benefited financially from abolition activity (Fyfe 1962: 116; Sherwood 2007: 119).[4] Slave trade repression therefore led to the emancipation of many recaptives, but it remained infused with some of the legal structures that had also supported the slave trade which treated individuals as property. This framing left little space for the law to recognise recaptives as subjects in stark contrast to the law's recognition of the agency of captors.

Commodification and responsibility

In effect prize positioned recaptives as commodified objects of intervention to a greater or lesser extent, contributing to their erasure as legal subjects. In contrast, it emphasised the agency of individual naval officers. Captors were accountable for losses arising out of unlawful seizures, although these were underwritten by the Government in many cases. Captors operated against the backdrop of a complex web of international treaties that were subject to changing international legal interpretations. This cannot have been an enviable legal starting point from which to embark on potentially dangerous interventions against slave ships,[5] but the measures captors were compelled to take to reduce their own liabilities could operate at the expense of recaptives, as Chapter 5 showed.

In the case of the partly successful appeal of the *Gertrudis La Preciosa* from the Vice Admiralty Court in Sierra Leone, it was argued that compensation for the loss of the (now liberated) slaves should be reduced. The Registrar had recommended compensation based at a rate of £60 per man, £45 per woman and £20 per child. It was argued that the award should have taken account of 50 slaves who had died before emancipation. The calculation of the purchase price of the slaves at the intended destination was also challenged on the basis that at least a third of them would have died on the journey to Havana. As regards the remainder, it was argued that their value would have been reduced to the extent of them becoming largely 'unsaleable, until, by great Expense to the Proprietors, such Slaves, in Progress of Time, became fit to endure the Labour for which they were designed by the Purchasers' (*Gertrudis La Preciosa* 1816: 390). Prize was a double-edged sword. It facilitated slave trade repression but still allowed for slaves (and recaptives) to be treated and/or represented as property. In the attempt to reduce damages, the slaves were represented as a set of depreciating assets.

Despite the awkwardness of their legal position, captors did not always bear sole responsibility for loss. States underwrote the damages awarded by Mixed Commissions against the captors of their own state and were obliged to indemnify claimants within a year of the date of sentence (Article 6 Portuguese Regulations; Article 6 Spanish Regulations).[6] Sometimes captors were indemnified. Roffery, the slave trade advisory to the Treasury who had been Registrar to the London Slave Trade Commission, advised in the case of the *Gavao*, that captors should be indemnified only if they were 'fully justified' in seizing a ship in the first place. To indemnify all such cases would be 'dangerous'. Whether captors should be indemnified should depend upon the circumstances (Roffery to Lords Commissioners of the Treasury 12 August 1822: 25). For example, Roffery advised in the case of the *Calypso*, condemned by the Sierra Leone Vice Admiralty Court (and not under the Mixed Commission regime), that the captor might be indemnified. Although the Prize Appeal Court had overturned the Vice Admiralty Court's decision, the captor had acted according to the Vice Admiralty Court's erroneous views of the 1810 Treaty of Friendship and Alliance with Portugal (Roffery to Lords Commissioners of the Treasury 31 May 1826: 44).

The commodification of the labour of liberated Africans could also place a brake on captors responsibilities. This is demonstrated by the case of the *San Juan Nepomuceno*, again decided outside the Mixed Commission regime. Hagan captured this Spanish slave ship in December 1817 (*San Juan Nepomuceno* 1824). The prize crew sailed the ship with 268 recaptives, including 81 children, to Sierra Leone. In February 1818, the Sierra Leone Vice Admiralty Court condemned the ship. The appeal against the decision was delayed. Therefore, it was not until 1824 that the Court of Appeal, applying the case of the *Le Louis*, 'reluctantly' (ibid: 95) overturned the decision of the Vice Admiralty Court in Sierra Leone. The Court reserved the question of the captor's liability for costs and damages. Hagen had already raised this question with the Treasury prior to the appeal, but Roffery, who thought Hagan's seizure of the *San Juan Nepomuceno* was unjustified, had advised the government against intervening to indemnify Hagan at that stage (Roffery to Lords Commissioners of the HM Treasury 22 April 1823: 64). The King's Advocate's view was that it would be unjust for Hagan to be compelled to pay costs and damages. The case of *Le Louis* had been decided after Hagan's capture of the *San Juan Nepomuceno* and the slaves who had been condemned as prize had been 'delivered over to the Crown for emancipation'. This presented Lord Stowell with a dilemma. On the one hand, the claimant was entitled to compensation. On the other hand, Hagan could no longer restore the property (in this case the liberated Africans) since the government had the benefit of it/them. The Court's view was that, as the government had the benefit of the slaves' labour, and because Hagan was not in a position to restore the property, restitution should come from the government (Nicholl to Lords Commissioners of the Treasury 7 July 1824: 230–231). Lord Stowell sought an assurance from the government that it would indemnity Hagan.

Here, the commodification of the labour of liberated Africans set legal limits to the responsibility of the intervenor. This outcome was not unreasonable. It would have been unjust to have required the captor to pay damages. However, the rationale for the Court's decision shows the open recognition of the value of the labour of liberated Africans to the government and the significance of that recognition for the purposes of allocating legal responsibility. Liberated Africans remained legally commodified at least to that extent. That recaptives and liberated Africans had economic value (to someone else) can also be seen in the bounties awarded to captors.

Bounties

Bounties provided an important economic incentive to captors and potentially encouraged (lawful) interventions. Their payment provided additional non-judicial oversight of intervenors' activities, as well as indirectly that of the Vice Admiralty and Mixed Commission Courts. The bounty system encouraged lawful interventions by placing an economic value on recaptives, in contrast to awards of compensation, which discouraged unlawful interventions. Whilst bounties can be read as commodifying recaptives by enabling the generation of funds for captors, compensation claims effectively treated recaptives as property. Either way, recaptives received none of the money. Despite the fact that bounties commodified recaptives, one of the most detailed accounts of survival found in the research for this book was contained not in a case about emancipation but in a petition for bounties.

The system of bounties was complex and developed over time. Working out the correct bounty payment could be a problem when the judgments of the Vice Admiralty Court in Sierra Leone did not sufficiently clearly identify the grounds for condemnation (Nicholl to Lords Commissioners of the Treasury 8 May 1818) because different sums were awarded by either the navy or treasury depending on whether slaves were liberated as prize, under the Abolition Act 1807 or international treaties.[7] Bounties were distributed amongst the crew according to varying formulae over time (Lloyd 1968: 83), but in practice it seems that those actually involved in the seizure often received little or none of the awards due (Van Niekerk 2004: 37). Even so, this incentive was significant, as is evident when joint captors litigated over bounties (*The Aviso* 1826; *The Zepherina* 1830; *The Sociedade Feliz* 1843). William Roffery exerted considerable power in his capacity as advisor to the Treasury. After his appointment in September 1821, bounties were payable after he had considered and commented on them first (Roffery to Harrison 29 March 1823).

Thus, bounties commodified recaptives, but, notwithstanding, it is in a claim for bounties that one of the most detailed accounts of resistance – and arguably a claim evidencing legal agency – was read in the research for this book.

After a hazardous 18-hour chase, Captain Kelly and his crew of HMS *Pheasant* captured the Portuguese slave ship, the *Vulcano* with 270 recaptives, on 6 October 1819 (Memorial of Captain Kelly: 124). Kelly put a prize crew on board the *Vulcano* to sail the ship to Sierra Leone for adjudication. Amongst the prize crew were a number of black Africans, including Sam. The *Vulcano* never reached Sierra Leone because six weeks into the journey Xavier, the master of the *Vulcano,* retook the *Vulcano,* killing the prize master and the prize crew with the exception of Sam and an unnamed black sailor who hid below the hatches (ibid: 125). In his deposition (ibid: 127–130), Sam recounts how when the hatches were opened about ten hours later, Xavier told him and the other black sailor that he would sell them as slaves in Brazil, but he would kill them if they met an English ship first. In Brazil Sam refused food, was flogged and sold a number of times and worked twisting tobacco for about sixteen months. Eventually he managed to run away when he found out he was going to be sold again. He made contact with an English merchant vessel in Bahia. The crew, however, sent him back ashore. Sam stayed in the bush for about two weeks until he heard that an English war ship the *Morgiana* had arrived in Bahia escorting a slave ship. By pretending to sell fowl to the *Morgiana*, Sam managed to access the ship. The *Morgiana* took Sam to Sierra Leone where he swore his deposition which was attached to Kelly's memorial and on which this account is based.[8]

Section 72 of the Slave Trade Amendment and Consolidation Act allowed bounty payments in cases in which recaptives were not actually condemned because of circumstances such as sickness or death. Separating the fate of the recaptives from decisions to make bounty payments was not usual. Commenting on the case of the *Sinceridade* considered in previous chapters, Roffery cautioned against the 'dangerous' precedent of permitting bounties just because slaves had been liberated (Roffery to Lords Commissioners of the Treasury 30 March 1827: 2). The availability of bounties notwithstanding the re-enslavement of recaptives shows how the benefits of abolition were not always evenly spread and raises the question how the economy of slave trade repression might have appeared from the perspective of those at the receiving end of slave trade repression. Whilst the payment of bounties was not always linked to the freedom of recaptives, the spectre of an award of bounties could impact upon the circumstances in which emancipation was ordered or withheld, as the next section shows.

Kelly argued that he was entitled to bounties because the *Vulcano* had been unlawfully slave trading and because the prize crew had taken all precautionary measures to ensure that the ship arrived safely in Sierra Leone (Memorial of Captain Kelly: 126). The slave trade advisor to the Treasury, William Roffery, who thought that Kelly had taken proper care, advised that this situation fell within the Act and within the exercise of the Treasury's discretion (Roffery to Lords Commissioners of the Treasury 20 August 1825: 134). Kelly's claim was unusual for the extent to which slave resistance was recorded in the archival sources consulted for this book. As an original member of the prize crew, Sam should presumably also have received his share of any bounty for the capture of the *Vulcano*. Kelly was claiming on his own behalf and that of his crew. In so far as Sam's remarkable narrative has no other legal significance than to contribute to the generation of bounties for Kelly and the crew, one reading of this claim then is that even his resistance seems subsequently to have been commodified. However, another reading of the record that contains Sam's deposition positions him in effect as a joint petitioner alongside Captain Kelly, albeit not in name. From this perspective Sam was a critical legal agent whose testimony was essential for the crew's attempt to secure bounties. More than that, Sam was not only witnessing for others, he was also making a claim for himself. He was, therefore, someone who was calling in a debt which was owed to him. Sam's deposition can, therefore, be read both as evidence of his factual resistance to enslavement and also resistance to the commodification that ran through slave trade repression.

Emancipation and the economies of abolition

Within the political economy of slave trade abolition, formal legal emancipation did not simply denote the presence or absence of freedom. Decisions to grant or withhold emancipation were on occasion infused with economic considerations. First, the spectre of bounties could place a restraint on the grant of legal emancipation in some cases even where recaptives enjoyed freedom. Second, in certain cases in which the status of recaptives would be unaffected by emancipation, its grant could protect captors and the government from compensation claims. Economic considerations were not the only factors for the grant or refusal of emancipation in such situations and these situations themselves represented only a minority of cases. It is important to note that in these cases the grant or refusal of emancipation did not affect the freedom of recaptives. Therefore, it might be thought that withholding or granting emancipation was a wise move to avoid potentially adverse financial consequences for the government. Beyond the question of policy, however, these cases are important for what they demonstrate about legal subjectivity. The commodification of recaptives meant that economic, rather than for example rights-based imperatives, infused the grant of the full legal freedom of the law. Legal emancipation then operated within a broader economy of abolition which affected the legal construction of the subject.

The link between emancipation and its economic consequences can be seen in the way in which the spectre of bounties could limit emancipation awards in cases in which slave ships were unlawfully detained, but recaptives were not claimed, as the case of the *Rosalia* shows. Lieutenant Hagen captured the Spanish slave ship the *Rosalia* in January 1822 (Gregory and Fitzgerald to the Marquess of Londonderry 17 March 1822). Although the master of the ship had purchased slaves, he had not loaded them when Hagan first boarded the ship on 7 January. A few days later, the slaves were loaded at Hagan's instigation. Thereupon, Hagan seized the ship. As previously explained (Chapter 5), Hagan's actions were not out of the ordinary, but his conduct was not permitted by the British-Spanish Treaty. Had the master claimed the ship and the recaptives, they would have been restored to him. However, he did not do so. The Mixed Commission, therefore, emancipated the recaptives, as Fitzgerald explained, as 'a matter of propriety on general grounds' (ibid: 25). The King's Advocate criticised this outcome (Robinson to Marquis of Londonderry 23 July 1822). Secretary of State Canning was concerned that Mixed Commissioners had gone beyond the scope of the Additional Convention (Spain), but he was also cautious about the possibility that emancipation orders could enable captors to claim bounties 'as if they had made a meritorious seizure' (Canning to British Commissioners at Sierra Leone 25 September 1822: 36). It seems then that the economic consequences of formal legal emancipation may have also played a role in Canning's reluctance to envisage it in these circumstances.

In the *Nova Sorte*, Commissioners were also faced with the question of what to do with recaptives whom the captor had put on board. The master sought the return of his ship and damages, but he did not claim the recaptives. The question arose as to whether the recaptives should be emancipated (Gregory to Canning 7 June 1823). British arbitrator Fitzgerald was inclined to emancipate them, according to 'the spirit of the Convention' (ibid: 126). British Commissioner Gregory thought that 'the spirit of the Convention' indicated freedom for the recaptives, but this did not entitle them to emancipation certificates. Secretary of State Canning's criticism of the *Rosalia* decision influenced Gregory, who was concerned that an emancipation decree could provide the basis for a claim for bounties (ibid). It was not denied that the captor sought emancipation certificates in order to claim bounties (the recaptives were of course unable to seek emancipation themselves because they were not parties to proceedings). Taking all this into account, Gregory refused to grant emancipation. The Commissioners in the *Nova Sorte* ordered the recaptives to be handed over to the colonial government to 'share in the happiness of their brethren in [the] Colony' but without certificates of emancipation and sought further guidance from the government on the question of whether they should receive emancipation certificates (ibid).

In each of these cases recaptives became free even if not formally legally emancipated. The failure to emancipate them formally may not therefore have been a particularly grave legal loss. As already seen, emancipation did not prevent the re-enslavement of Africans in fact (Haslam 2016: 433). Moreover, it was observed at the time that at least some liberated Africans did not appreciate the value of emancipation certificates. Given the limited ability of emancipation certificates to protect liberated Africans from re-enslavement, as Chapter 5 showed, it was hardly surprising if liberated Africans did not value emancipation certificates. Nevertheless, in a climate in which an economic value was placed on liberated Africans, it was the economic consequences that contributed to setting the parameters of emancipation. Emancipation did not stem from an inherent or nascent right on the part of recaptives to freedom. It follows that bounties were not simply a consequence of emancipation. Their potential award contributed to determining the grant or otherwise of legal emancipation in circumstances which, whilst they were outside the formal treaty, might reasonably be considered to fall within its spirit. Legal emancipation was not simply about the grant of freedom. There were different degrees of freedom: freedom with or without full emancipation and its grant was linked to the broader economies of abolition.

The way in which orders of emancipation were influenced by the abolition economy can also be gleaned from situations in which orders of emancipation were, strictly speaking, not necessary to ensure recaptives' freedom but were considered wise to protect captors, and ultimately the government, from claims for damages. Sometimes recaptives too sickly to travel were landed in the nearest British port. After the abolition of slavery, the Governor of the Bahamas raised a hypothetical concern about the status of recaptives landed in the West Indies from Portuguese slave ships prior to adjudication by Mixed Commissions. The Queen's Advocate advised that recaptives entering a British port in the West Indies would be free. A Mixed Commission's decree would not affect their status because British law would have freed them. However, he advised, Portuguese slave ships and their crews should still be sent to Sierra Leone. If a Mixed Commission were to order recaptives' restoration, the captor and potentially the British government might be liable for damages. Thus whilst a decree of emancipation was unnecessary as far as the status of the recaptives was concerned as long as they remained on British territory, a decree of condemnation from the Mixed Commission could avoid a claim for damages (Dodson to Palmerston 30 August 1838: 384–385, 29 September 1838: 409). Here then emancipation can be read as having another function than simply determining the freedom or otherwise of recaptives. It contributed to determining liabilities for damages.

These decisions represent a handful of situations dealing with circumstances at the edges of the slave trade repression treaties that have been discussed in this book. However, they are revealing. In these situations, recaptives were or would be free from slavery. The preceding interpretations ensured both their freedom and the minimising of adverse financial consequences for the government. Taking account of the economic consequences of emancipation in cases that fell outside the strict letter of the treaties arguably falls within the judicial function. Yet, these cases are problematic in so far as they link the grant or otherwise of emancipation to its economic consequences. However it has come to be understood, emancipation was not simply a designator of freedom. In the situations outlined in this chapter, the broader economies of abolition contributed to conditioning the possibilities for the bestowal of the full legal freedom of the law and not any putative right to freedom on the part of recaptives.

The economy of abolition commodified recaptives directly and indirectly. Here the grant of emancipation was legally linked to the spectre of bounties or the obligation to pay compensation. The link between the political economy of abolition and emancipation puts a check on solely humanitarian narratives about abolition. It also highlights the historical importance of property in international law's construction of some of its subjects.

Conclusion

Slave trade repression litigation offered the promise of liberation. However, to a greater or lesser extent recaptives were still commodified. Slave trade repression operated within a political economy which contributed to the unequal status of recaptives and liberated Africans. Emancipation as a legal concept did not simply denote the presence or absence of freedom. The broader economy of abolition infused its application. These are among the limitations and compromises of the system of abolition that was bound in different ways to questions about property.

Tracing the property relations underpinning the construction of recaptives is important for what it shows about the constraints of the legal framing. However, it takes on additional significance in the context of discussions about victims today. Whilst the previous chapters have sought to provide a counter-history of international slave trade repression by illuminating the preoccupations of international abolition law with intervention and by providing a platform for remembering some of the victims of the slave trade, the final chapter pursues the question of what this history has to offer international criminal law today, more particularly for thinking about the construction and representation of victims. Chapter 7 also offers a provocation to contemporary debates by seeking to read the property relations underpinning slave trade repression that the current chapter has traced back on themselves.

Notes

1 See further the appeal in the case of the *St Joan* which included a list of various shippers' instructions: for examples 10 rolls of Gold Coast tobacco were to be exchanged for 'a little Black Girl, or young Black Slave that had had the Small Pox', smallpox being a major killer at the time. Forty pieces of cloth were to be traded 'for what might prove more beneficial to the Shipper's Interest', including possibly, slaves (*St Joan*, 258). The ambivalence of these instructions speaks to the exchangeability and interchangeability of individuals for any commodity.

2 That is not to say that, as Fyfe has shown, some liberated Africans did not go on to achieve success in worldly terms (Fyfe 1961).

3 See further on the compensation culture of the Slavery Abolition Act 1833: An Act for the Abolition of Slavery throughout British Colonies, and for Promoting the Industry of Manumitted Slaves, and for the Compensation of Persons hitherto entitled to the Services of Such Slaves, the ground-breaking work of Hall, Draper, McClelland, Donnington and Lang (2014).

4 See further, for example, Sherwood (2007: 117).

5 The complex interplay of state and individual liability can be seen in the well-known test case of *Buron v Denman*. In 1840, Captain Denman set out with three British ships for the Gallinas islands on the orders of the governor of Sierra Leone to rescue two British subjects, including one child, who were being held as slaves. Denman's threats against the king of the Gallinas induced the king to agree a slave trade abolition treaty. Following this Denman destroyed slave barracoons, including Buron's. He also took over 840 individuals out of the barracoons to Sierra Leone. Initially the government approved of his actions, and other officers followed Denman's actions in similar expeditions against slavers' factories. However, concerns were raised about the international legality of such actions. Palmerston was replaced as Foreign Secretary by Aberdeen, who ordered such conduct to cease. Even so, in Buron's action against Denman it was held that the government's subsequent ratification of Denman's intervention rendered it an act of state (*Buron v Denman* 1848; Lloyd 1968: 94–99).

6 See further, for example art 5 Additional Convention (Portugal) which obliged states 'to make good any losses which their respective Subjects may incur unjustly, by the arbitrary and illegal detention of their vessels'.

7 The Slave Trade Amendment and Consolidation Act (1824) reduced the bounties payable in 1824 to £10 per slave, with the proceeds of the sale of the ship divided between the Crown and the captors. In 1830, bounties were reduced further to £5 for each living slave (Lloyd 1968: 80). With the introduction of equipment clauses, it made less sense to calculate bounties according to the number of slaves delivered and in 1838, the incentive scheme was recalculated. However, this still offered greater rewards for ships with slaves than without and concerns were raised that captors might wait until ships were full before they intervened (Lloyd 1968: 81–82). In the end, a system of discretionary payments was introduced (ibid: 83).

8 This is not the only case in which resistance enters the legal record as the backdrop to a claim for someone else's compensation (albeit not in this case bounties). On 1 January 1811, the slave ship, the *Amelia*, left Angola bound for Havana. Two hundred and seventy-one slaves were pitilessly crammed beneath the deck of the ship. During the passage, the captain of the *Amelia* brutally flogged one of his own slaves, Jack White. In response, White opened the slave hatches and incited the slaves packed below to rebel against their captors. White and about 30 slaves were killed in the bloody uprising that followed. On 20 January 1811, the surviving slaves seized control of the *Amelia*. With the captain and most of the crew fleeing on a rowing boat, one of the victorious slaves, Ned Brown, persuaded the others to spare the lives of four of the crew to enable them to navigate the *Amelia*. By mid-May many of those on board, including many children, had died of starvation. The surviving slaves had no supplies on board and could barely move for hunger. John Roach, the master and owner of a merchant ship, the *Kitty*, boarded the *Amelia* after some resistance from the slaves. Roach procured provisions, landed those who were too sick to journey on, and navigated the ship to Sierra Leone. Eighty-five of the 271 slaves who were originally loaded onto the *Amelia* survived this final journey (*The Amelia* 1816; African Institution 1812: 39). Roach spent the next few years in a series of complicated legal wrangles unsuccessfully seeking compensation for his expenditure before he was allegedly murdered by the crew of another captured slave ship.

References

African Institution (1812) *Sixth Report of the Directors of the African Institution*, London: Ellerton & Henderson.

Benton, L. and Ford, L. (2016) *Rage for Order: The British Empire and the Origins of International Law 1800–1850*, Cambridge and London: Harvard University Press.

Binder, G. (1993) 'Did the Slaves Author the Thirteenth Amendment? An Essay in Redemptive History', *Yale Journal of Law and the Humanities* 5(2): 471–505.

Fyfe, C. (1961) 'Four Sierra Leone Recaptives', *Journal of African History* 2(1): 77–85.

Fyfe, C. (1962) *A History of Sierra Leone*, Oxford: Oxford University Press.

Hall, C., Draper, N., McClelland, K., Donnington, D. and Lang, R. (2014) *Legacies of British Slave Ownership: Colonial Slavery and the Formation of Victorian Britain*, Cambridge: Cambridge University Press.

Haslam, E. (2016) 'International Criminal Law and Legal Memories of Abolition: Intervention, Mixed Commission Courts and "Emancipation"', *Journal of the History of International Law* 18: 420–447.

Lloyd, C. (1968) *The Navy and the Slave Trade: The Suppression of the African Slave Trade in the Nineteenth Century*, London: Franck Cass & Co Ltd.

Sherwood, M. (2007) *After Abolition: Britain and the Slave Trade since 1807*, London: I.B. Tauris & Co. Ltd.

Van Niekerk, J.-P. (2004) 'British, Portuguese, and American Judges in Adderley Street: The International Legal Background to and Some Judicial Aspects of the Cape Town Mixed Commissions for the Suppression of the Transatlantic Slave Trade in the Nineteenth Century (Part 1)', *Comparative and International Law Journal of South Africa* 37: 1–39.

Wood, M. (2010) *The Horrible Gift of Freedom Atlantic Slavery and the Representation of Emancipation*, London and Georgia: University of Georgia Press.

International instruments

Additional Convention to the Treaty Concluded at Madrid on the 5th of July 1814, between His Britannic Majesty and His Catholic Majesty, for Preventing Their Subjects from Engaging in Any Illicit Traffic in Slaves, 23 September 1817 (Additional Convention (Spain)), The National Archives: FO 84/2, pp. 11–13.

Regulations for the Mixed Commissions, Which Are to Reside on the Coast of Africa, and in a Colonial Possession of His Catholic Majesty (Spanish Regulations), The National Archives: FO 84/2, pp. 15–18.

Regulations for the Mixed Commissions Which Are to Reside on the Coast of Africa, in the Brazils and London (Portuguese Regulations), The National Archives: FO 84/2, pp. 8–10.

Treaty of Friendship and Alliance between Great Britain and Portugal 1810, (Treaty of Amity) *British and Foreign State Papers*, 1812–1814, Volume 1: 547.

Legislation

An Act for the Abolition of the Slave Trade 1807 (Abolition Act), 47 Geo 3 c 36.

An Act for the Abolition of Slavery throughout British Colonies, and for Promoting the Industry of Manumitted Slaves, and for the Compensation of Persons Hitherto

entitled to the Services of Such Slaves 1833 (Slavery Abolition Act), 3 & 4 Will 4 c 73, as Amended 1838 1 & 2 Vict c 19.
Slave Trade Amendment and Consolidation Act 1824, 5 Geo 4 c 113.

English cases

The Amelia (1816) The National Archives: HCA 45/70, 310.
The Aviso (1826) 166 Eng Rep 155.
Buron v Denman (1848) 154 Eng Rep 450.
Gertrudis La Preciosa (1816) The National Archives: HCA 45/70, 389; HCA 45/69, 396.
San Juan Nepomuceno (1824) 166 Eng Rep 94.
The Sociedade Feliz (1843) 166 Eng Rep 713.
St Joan The National Archives HCA 45/66, 238; HCA 45/67, 205.
The Zepherina (1830) 166 Eng Rep 259.

Mixed commission cases

Gregory and Fitzgerald to the Marquess of Londonderry, 17 March 1822 in the Case of the *Rosalia*, No 10 with Enclosures *Class B Correspondence with the British Commissioners at Sierra Leone, the Havana, Rio de Janeiro and Surinam Relating to the Slave Trade 1822* PP 1823 (008) XIX.311.
Gregory to Canning, 7 June 1823 in the Case of the *Nova Sorte*, Nos 46–48 with Enclosures *Class B Correspondence with the British Commissioners at Sierra Leone, the Havana, Rio de Janeiro, and Surinam, Relating to the Slave Trade 1823* PP 1824 (002) XXIV.215.

Documents and correspondence

Canning to British Commissioners at Sierra Leone, 25 September 1822, No. 14 *Class B Correspondence with the British Commissioners at Sierra Leone, the Havana, Rio de Janeiro and Surinam Relating to the Slave Trade 1822* PP 1823 (008) XIX.311.
Dodson to Palmerston, 30 August 1838, The National Archives: FO 83/2347, pp. 383–385.
Dodson to Palmerston, 29 September 1838, The National Archives: FO 83/2347, pp. 408–410.
Marsden to Castlereagh, 31 May 1820, The National Archives: FO 84/5, pp. 106–109.
Memorial of Captain Kelly on Behalf of Himself, the Officers and Crew of HM Ship the *Pheasant*, The National Archives: HCA 35/7, pp. 123–134.
Nicholl to Lords Commissioners of the Treasury, 8 May 1818, The National Archives: HCA 35/2, pp. 2–3.
Nicholl to Lords Commissioners of the Treasury, 7 July 1824, The National Archives: HCA 35/6, pp. 227–232.
Robinson to Marquis of Londonderry, 23 July 1822, The National Archives: FO 83/2343, 92.
Roffery to Harrison, 29 March 1823, The National Archives: HCA 35/3, pp. 1–5.
Roffery to Lords Commissioners of the Treasury, 12 August 1822, The National Archives: HCA 35/2, pp. 24–26.

Roffery to Lords Commissioners of the Treasury, 22 April 1823, The National Archives: HCA 35/3, pp. 58–65.
Roffery to Lords Commissioners of the Treasury, 20 August 1825, The National Archives: HCA 35/7, pp. 130–134.
Roffery to Lords Commissioners of the Treasury, 31 May 1826, The National Archives: HCA 35/9, pp. 40–44.
Roffery to Lords Commissioners of the Treasury, 30 March 1827, The National Archives: HCA 35/11, pp. 2–3.

7 Back to the present

Recaptives, victims and creditors

Introduction

This book has offered a counter-legal history of international law and abolition by focusing on the figure of the recaptive. This historical narrative is important for its own sake, but one of the book's central claims is that the figure of the recaptive is relevant to discussions about the construction and representation of victims in international criminal law today.[1] On the basis of this claim I have proposed in this book that the recaptive should form part of the history of international criminal law, where international criminal legal history, as a reflection of current concerns, extends beyond the scope of international criminal law in a strict sense. The purpose of this chapter is to explore this claim further, that is to 'read' the construction of the recaptive alongside the victim in international criminal law today. In so doing, it returns to some of the broader questions about the politics and purposes of international criminal legal history that I discussed in Chapter 1.

As discussed in Chapter 1, despite the claim to centre victims in international criminal law, international criminal law has faced challenges in its quest to deliver justice for victims (Sagan 2010; Clarke 2015: 292; Fletcher 2015: 303; Schwöbel-Patel 2016: 252). A longer-term history of victims, which goes beyond the more orthodox progress narrative from Nuremberg to the Hague, can provide a useful source for reflection and provocation. The central aim of this chapter then is to deploy this history of the recaptive to reflect upon the framing of victims in international criminal law and legal discourse. In so doing, it seeks to temper progress narratives about victims in international criminal law and to suggest alternative ways of thinking about victims.

However, reading back to the figure of the recaptive to reflect on the construction of victims today is open to a number of criticisms. First, recaptives were not participants in criminal proceedings and, second, this exercise runs the risk of instrumentalising recaptives. Mixed Commissions were not criminal institutions. However, they were early international courts in which international law was confronted with tens of thousands of victims of the slave trade. As such, their construction of the recaptive provides a springboard for thinking about the law's approaches to subjecthood. Moreover, as I discussed in Chapter 1, the representation of victims in international criminal law has drawn on patterns of representation that exist beyond international criminal law (Schwöbel-Patel 2016: 248). So even though Mixed Commissions were not criminal courts, the recaptive can usefully be included in histories about victims in international criminal law, especially when international criminal law is understood as a historically contingent response to injustice. That said, the construction of victims in international criminal law is distinctive to the extent that the victim is constructed in opposition to a perpetrator figure (Schwöbel-Patel 2016: 256). Slaves and recaptives were to some extent also constructed in opposition to slave traders, although slave traders were not formally (at least in international law) criminal figures. Yet, as argued in Chapter 1, on another level the absence of the figure of the (internationally) criminal slave trader could offer critical potential.[2] Clarke has argued that the focus on individual criminal responsibility has directed attention to individual rather than structural cause of harm (Clarke 2015: 283). To the extent that the recaptive was not constituted in opposition to an internationally criminal figure (at least in law), an opportunity arises to also emphasise structural, and not just individual, roots of injustice. Inscribing the recaptive can, for example, challenge us to inscribe questions about the role of capital in histories of international criminal law.

Second, the arguments in this chapter are open to the criticism that they instrumentalise the past – and more particularly the recaptive – with the aim of redeeming current international criminal law.[3] The idea of *the recaptive* erases insofar as it effaces gender, class, culture and individuality. Deploying the figure of the recaptive to offer insights on the construction and representation of victims today can be charged with erasing the recaptive further, and with being animated by the same legitimating impulse as the legal progress narratives that this book has challenged. These concerns are very real. However, the recaptive can offer insights on the contemporary representation and construction of victims in international criminal law. As I have argued elsewhere in relation to histories of slavery more generally (Haslam 2019: 138), for the sake of the present therefore, inscribing the recaptive – even at some risk of instrumentalising the past – is overdue. The challenge is to do justice to the past and to the present. Doing justice in this sense then means being aware of the pitfalls of erasure, whilst recognising that these exist in relation to the present as well as to the past.

In sum, this chapter embodies a reflection upon some of the broader questions about history that were introduced in Chapter 1 by offering a series of different narratives about some of the ways in which the recaptive might be "read" alongside the figure of the victim in international criminal law today.[4] These narratives present a reflection on the diverse approaches to subjecthood that might underpin the construction – and potential construction – of victims that the history of the recaptive brings to the fore. Each narrative and each approach to subjecthood offers different possibilities and constraints.

These different narratives employ different approaches to the past and the present. They use the past as: a source of legitimacy; a critique of the present; and, more radically, a basis for transformation in the sense of providing provocation for alternative thinking. These different narratives represent discursive possibilities, but they rest on the assumption that accounts of the past and present are co-constitutive. Thus which, if any, might be favoured depends upon where the contemporary challenges of international criminal law's engagements with victims is thought to lie: for example, in institutional development, in the construction of the subject, in the broader political economy of justice? This is ultimately then a political question.[5] However, inscribing the recaptive is instructive whichever approach is adopted because it opens up a series of questions and reflections. Moreover, inscribing the recaptive lends historical urgency to the resolution of these questions.

The chapter turns first to consider progress narratives about victims in international criminal law. It also highlights some of the criticisms of these narratives that have emerged in recent years. Within this narrative frame, inscribing the recaptive is likely, albeit not inevitably, to be deployed to lend legitimacy to current developments. The next two sections read the recaptive alongside the construction and representation of victims in international criminal law more critically by rooting the contemporary representation and construction of victims within a longer legal history of intervention and property. This history suggests commonalities in aspects of the representation and construction of victims and the legal construction of recaptives, although they play out in historically contingent ways. The chapter then experiments with an alternative approach by positioning international law as indebted to recaptives – and by analogy to victims. In so doing, it draws inspiration from Guyora Binder's challenge to the gift narrative in the context of the Thirteenth Amendment to the US Constitution and Robert Meister's critique of transitional justice as it relates to historic injustice. This thinking is directed at the 'imagined' subject to borrow from Fletcher (Fletcher 2015: 303). Although thinking about the recaptive as creditor raises the question of reparations,[6] the primary concern is with the potential impacts of the debt framing on thinking about the constitution of the recaptive as subject. By analogy, thinking of the 'imagined' victim as creditor can offer a provocation to aspects of current representations of victims. Thinking of the 'imagined' victim as creditor can provide a way to centre critique in the constitution of the victim as subject. This does not necessarily lead to specific policy prescriptions, but it can temper taken-for-granted assumptions about victims which can infuse policy and practice and can go some way to meeting some of the criticisms that have been levelled against contemporary representations of victims that were outlined in Chapter 1. It also centres questions about distribution in the constitution of the victim as subject. The chapter turns first, however, to current narratives about victims in international criminal law.

From recaptives to victims: progress narratives

Narratives about the development of victims' rights in international criminal law generally take Nuremberg and Tokyo as their starting point and follow a progressive trajectory (Haslam 2014: 188–189). As such, they reflect a more orthodox approach to international criminal legal history. From this perspective, the limited opportunities provided to victim-witnesses at Nuremberg and Tokyo to testify and the inability of the International Criminal Tribunals for Rwanda and Yugoslavia to provide compensation and victim (as opposed to victim-witness) participation contrast with subsequent provisions of the Rome Statute which provide for victim participation and reparations (Article 15(3), Article 19(3), Article 68(3), Article 75 Rome Statute 1998). Victim participation permits victims, with the leave of the Court, to participate in proceedings independently from their role as defence or prosecution witnesses. The aim of victim participation was to turn victims from 'passive object' to 'potential subject matter' of international criminal proceedings (Jorda and de Hemptinne 2002: 1389, 1399). Accordingly, the Revised Strategy on Victims from the International Criminal Court (ICC) claims that a victim is 'a vital actor in the justice process rather than a passive recipient of services and magnanimity' (Assembly of States Parties, Court's Revised Strategy in Relation to Victims 2012: para 6). It emphasises a 'rights-based perspective' that entails duties on the part of the Court (ibid.)

Legal scholars have recognised that the Court faces substantial difficulties in making victim participation effective and in meeting victims' expectations around, and need for, justice. The sheer numbers of victims, their remoteness from the Court, resource constraints and more specifically the potential challenge of victim participation to defence rights and an expeditious trial, all present significant challenges. Drawing on Ian Edwards, Moffett has suggested that victims' roles have been 'more informational or expressive' rather than 'consultative' (Moffett 2015: 295). It has also been observed that the Revised Strategy in Relation to Victims is aspirational and faces considerable implementation challenges (Carayon and O'Donohue 2017: 570–571).[7] However, despite this, commentators and policy makers have generally welcomed victim participation for the avowed benefits it brings to survivors and proceedings more generally. Many commentators have therefore focused on highlighting limitations in the law and operation of victim participation and making suggestions for improvements.[8] As a result, notwithstanding criticisms, the progress narrative has remained strong overall.

Within the context of legal institutional progress narratives and in the context of the ICC's focus on situations in Africa, a history of the recaptive is likely to be used to lend further legitimacy to current developments.[9] By focusing on the inclusiveness of Mixed Commissions to African testimony and the attempts of Mixed Commissioners to subvert the limitations of slave trade repression treaties, a narrative can be constructed around international law's longer-term attempts to bring justice to (African) victims. Such a narrative is also likely to emphasise that in contemporary international criminal law the position of victims in the courtroom is significantly improved compared to that of recaptives. Even the fact of recaptives' testimony against white slave owners and ship masters, which might have challenged the apparent normalisation of the figure of the African defendant today, could be read less as a challenge to the present than for the absence today of the sorts of problematic assumptions that ran through Mixed Commissions' treatment of recaptives' testimony. Legal institutional narratives do not have to fit in this vein, of course. From another perspective, a history of Mixed Commissions which focuses on their non-criminal aspects might challenge assumptions about the centrality of international *criminal* law in delivering justice to victims. A history might also, as this book has sought to do, challenge assumptions about agency in international criminal legal history (and therefore the present) by emphasising how recaptives influenced proceedings independently of the law's grant of subjectivity.

Although progress narratives remain powerful, there has been criticism of them and commentators have emphasised the importance of going beyond what Schwöbel has described as 'the effectiveness critique' in international criminal law more generally (Schwöbel 2014: 3). As Chapter 1 outlined, scholarship has challenged the representation of victims (Kendall and Nouwen 2014; Schwöbel-Patel 2016) on the assumption that the representation of victims (both inside and outside the courtroom) affects the nature of international (criminal) justice. The next sections build on this critical approach, suggesting that aspects of the representation and construction of victims have some similarities to the construction of the recaptive. These commonalities play out in historically contingent ways. However, they might lead us to consider the extent to which some of the legal origins of current thinking about victims can be seen to lie in international slave trade repression law. Here I am not claiming direct legal and/or institutional links.[10] Rather my interest is in the way these legal forms might reflect and buttress particular configurations of power, which without challenge, remain rooted in current approaches. Moreover, my concern is the extent to which a broader approach to international criminal legal history might raise questions about these configurations. Thus, in thinking about origins I am interested in how the absence of the recaptive in international (criminal) legal history has erased a history of international law's engagement with recaptives, and thus one source for thinking about contemporary representations of victims; in other words, I am interested in the role that absences can play in origins.

Recaptives, victims and liminal subjects of intervention

This book has emphasised how international slave trade repression law read recaptives' paths to emancipation or restoration through the prism of intervention. Because the end legal status of recaptives was determined largely by questions about intervention, I have argued that the recaptive (as well as being the object of factual intervention) was effectively constructed in law as an object of intervention with the 'ideal' slave trade victim an object of lawful intervention, rather than simply a victim of unlawful slave trading.[11] A progress narrative might emphasise how international law has freed itself from these origins with victims not considered objects of intervention as a matter of law. However, as Kendall and Nouwen have shown, victims are still often represented as 'objects of the agency of heroic interveners' (Kendall and Nouwen 2014: 257). However well-intentioned – and notwithstanding their different context – such representations might be seen to harbour similarities to the construction of the recaptive, in so far as they reflect certain assumptions about agency in transition.

As objects of intervention recaptives were transitional figures:[12] from slave to recaptive to restored or liberated African with subjects' status dependent upon the circumstances of intervention, with the result that even recaptives who attained 'freedom' might attain it with or without full emancipation. Today transitions remain central to international criminal law. First, even though they no longer involve an explicit permanent change in victims' legal status, the victim remains a transitional figure par excellence. International criminal hearings are claimed to be transformative for victims and societies, aiding societies' transition to sustainable peace and the rule of law, a process in which the victim is assumed to play a special role,[13] although it should be noted that the claims made about the individual and collective transformations generated by international criminal law are not unproblematic.[14] Secondly and more concretely, victim participation, much like recaptivity, creates subjects who can be in a legally liminal state insofar as victims may transition in and out of victim participant status depending on the stage that the proceedings have reached.[15] Consequently, survivors may satisfy the conditions for victim participant status at some stages of the proceedings but may lose and (potentially) regain that status at another point.

To the extent that the representation and construction of a liminal subject is a consequence of law's transformative promise, it might be thought to be both inevitable and to be welcomed. Clearly, there are differences between the construction of recaptives and victims as liminal objects/subjects; the legal violence of restoration is not the same as the termination of victim participant status at the ICC, although some survivors may experience such termination as a kind of harm. Yet, reading contemporary representations of victims alongside the construction of recaptives highlights an inherent tension even in avowedly emancipatory projects: when recaptives/victims are framed as liminal subjects at the receiving end of, albeit different forms of, international intervention, the space for the recognition of their agency can be limited. Thus, as Chapter 1 outlined, the construction of international criminal interventions as transformative for victims can come at the expense of the idea of the political, critical or resisting victim. Whilst the law's failure to recognise recaptives as subjects with agency was one result of the law of prize, today as Chapter 1 discussed, limitations on the recognition of victims' agency are partly a paradoxical result of the centrality of the *idea* of the victim in international criminal legal discourse. In that respect, a progress narrative might emphasise the differences between the construction of recaptives and thinking about victims today. However, these similarities might also raise questions about the conditions of possibility for the recognition of agency within the context of current thinking about victims. They might also provoke an attempt to consider other framings of the subject which might contribute to setting different conditions of possibility. The history of the recaptive can provide one source for such rethinking.

Previous chapters have shown that a more complete history of slave trade repression can challenge the representation of the (African) victim-subject as object of intervention. Thus, one important lesson of recaptives' engagements with slave trade repression law is that recaptives could influence proceedings (and in some cases illuminate the law's limitations) even though the law did not formally recognise them as legal subjects. Reading the recaptive alongside the victim also provides a springboard for a more fundamental rethinking of those relations. Before exploring such a rethinking, the chapter turns to another important aspect of the construction of the recaptive: that is the role of property.

Recaptives, victims and property

Alongside the question of intervention, property played a vital role in setting the conditions of possibility for the constitution of recaptives and liberated Africans as legal subjects. This book has argued that legal emancipation was a particular kind of freedom. It was framed by a political economy of abolition, which was deployed to encourage particular forms of intervention. The award of compensation to slave owners and bounties to captors demonstrates the importance of property to slave trade repression. These awards commodified recaptives to a greater or lesser extent. Recaptives received no compensation but they could generate wealth for others, potentially enough for captors to consider it worth litigating over.

At first sight contemporary approaches to victims have fully transcended the property relations embedded in abolition. Today the construction of the victim is not linked legally to the question of property rights. However, the broader political economy may still continue to influence the representation and construction of victims today.[16] Thus, it has been convincingly argued that already existing representations of victims, on which international criminal legal discourse has drawn, have been driven by the image of a 'fundraising victim' (Schwöbel-Patel 2016: 256),[17] which deploys victims' suffering in racialized and gendered ways as a 'spectacle' (ibid: 250–251).[18] Moreover, property may still continue to exert an influence in determining legal subjectivity, albeit differently. Thus, Kamari Clarke has argued that that the 'protection of the victim has been driven by particular economic interests tied to the protection of private property' (Clarke 2015: 299). As already noted in the introduction to this chapter, Clarke argues that one result of the individualisation of responsibility and victimhood is that international criminal law focuses on physical, not structural, violence (Clarke 2015: 277). Robert Meister has raised similar concerns in the context of human rights. He argues that contemporary human rights discourse has contributed 'to the counterrevolutionary project of reassuring structural beneficiaries by focusing on violent crimes committed against the *bodies* of victims' (Meister 2012: 14). Clarke and Meister challenge us then to consider who/what benefits in this broader sense from the contemporary constitution of international criminal justice (and human rights). Moreover, for Clarke the construction of the victim as someone who has suffered individual bodily – and not structural – harm causes a 'substantive disjuncture' because institutions for victims, such as the Trust Fund, cannot make available to victims 'the basic necessities for addressing their suffering' (Clarke 2015: 277).[19] In these ways, questions of property and capital then continue to haunt international criminal law's ability to deliver justice.

The history of the recaptive shows that justice will be incomplete if the legal and economic structures that contributed to the conditions that enabled international crime in the first place continue to influence the responses to it. An alternative framing of victims in international criminal law might therefore usefully include a provocation to these structural conditions of possibility. The final sections experiment with one such alternative framing, drawing on a history of the recaptive as inspiration. In so doing, they read the property relations underpinning slave trade repression back upon themselves and suggest a more radical approach to recognising recaptives' agency than the one which results from the legal construction of recaptives as liminal objects of intervention. With that, they challenge contemporary representations of victims.

Recaptives as creditors

This section experiments with a framing of the relationship between recaptives and international slave trade repression law. In so doing it seeks to capture different aspects of recaptives' engagements with the legal process. It provides a framework to account alongside the more progressive aspects of slave trade repression law both for the law's limitations and for recaptives' contributions to the law. It also provokes a broader accounting of the legacies of international slave trade repression law, beyond for example (albeit highly important) questions about the numbers of Africans liberated and the resulting changes to international law. Critically, this framework subverts the property relations underpinning abolition to position the recaptive as a creditor.[20] This approach is inspired by Binder's subversion of the gift narrative in the context of the Thirteenth Amendment to the US Constitution. It also draws on Meister's powerful critique of transitional justice (Binder 1993; Meister 2012). In the next section, I continue this experiment by suggesting that thinking about recaptives as creditors offers a challenge to contemporary thinking about victims by analogy. Thus, the framing of 'imagined' victims (Fletcher 2015) could look very different if victims were thought of as the law's creditors, that is individuals to whom international law is indebted in various ways, rather than the law's beneficiaries. In that respect the term 'creditor' is directed not so much at a monetary claim (although that might be appropriate) than as a device to shift the lens: that is to inject critique into the constitution of the recaptive and victim as legal subjects, not least by asking what the present demands to minimise current and future debts, even if it cannot fully redeem past ones.

Framing the recaptive as creditor draws on some of the insights of Guyora Binder. Amongst the many rich arguments in his far-reaching provocation, 'Did the Slaves Author the Thirteenth Amendment? An Essay in Redemptive History', Binder criticises the portrayal of the abolition of slavery in the US as a gift to 'Southern blacks' from 'Northern whites', who in return benefited from increased standing 'as constitutional authors' (Binder 1993: 427–473).[21] Binder is not alone in critiquing the trope of the gift in accounts of abolition,[22] but his account is particularly valuable here for the way it engages with legal history.

The gift narrative, he claims, 'symbolically dispossesses the slaves' and their 'historical agency' (ibid: 473). The Thirteenth Amendment gave disproportionate 'moral capital' to white Americans compared to the small 'material capital' African Americans received (ibid: 473). In contrast, he argues the Thirteenth Amendment was 'the slaves' gift to the nation' (ibid: 474). Slaves 'authored their own emancipation' and redeemed the nation (ibid: 474). This framing of both the agents and objects of redemption offers a highly productive provocation to understand the trope of redemption here redemptively.[23] Inspired by Binder's acknowledgement of the slaves as beneficiaries of a debt,[24] I suggest one way of thinking about recaptives' relationship to international law is to position them as creditors, specifically here of international law. Thinking of international law as indebted to recaptives does not of course exclude the possibility that others might be indebted to them too. However, my focus is on thinking about the framing of international law–recaptive relations. This reframing represents a shift in mindset, but it is also critically based on the interpretation of international slave trade repression law that this book has put forward based on legal and archival sources.

In general, international law can be considered to be indebted to slaves, recaptives and liberated Africans in a number of ways. Fundamentally, of course, international law's support of the slave trade is a debt that can never be redeemed. Moreover, far from just benefiting slaves, international abolition law also benefited international law.[25] More specifically, in terms of being indebted to recaptives, slave trade repression (alongside its more progressive aspects) also gave rise to injustices, such as in the case of the *Maria da Gloria* (HM Commissioners to Palmerston 31 March 1834). As this book has shown, recaptives (amongst other victims of the slave trade) made a largely unrecognised contribution to international slave trade repression law (see Chapters 4 and 5) and the 'moral' and 'material capital' of slave trade repression to draw on Binder's analysis of the Thirteenth Amendment (Binder 1993: 473) was not evenly distributed.

Admittedly, positioning the *law* as indebted risks denying the agency of those who created and applied it. However, there are benefits to recognising the indebtedness of the law in the case of historic injustices. The legacies of historic injustice can be difficult to deal with because of the difficulty of allocating particular responsibility, although that is not to say that should not take place as well. In this vein for example, in arguing that 'historical injustice should be viewed, primarily, as a form of property – the creation of an asset – rather than as personal liability for a harm' (Meister 2012: 237), Meister has emphasised that positioning 'present beneficiaries of past injustice' as 'constructive trustees' renders the question of personal guilt irrelevant (Meister 2012: 17). Pointing to the indebtedness of international law may also enable a conversation about (and challenge to) the structures of international law which the focus on individual – even individual state – responsibility may not encompass. Thus, although focusing on agency and/or structure does different work, they can be complementary.

However, there is a fundamental paradox in the position advocated here. Positing the recaptive as creditor subverts the property relations running through abolition. Yet, it does not escape them. Alberto Toscano considers Meister's commodification of 'past injustice' to be a 'tactical proposal, a lesser evil, or even a symbolic intervention' rather than a 'real challenge to the transitological paradigm' Meister addresses (Toscano 2014: 133).[26] Toscano contrasts Meister's approach with other justice movements which reject the enunciation of political subjectivity 'as the claim of property owners' (ibid). Framing the recaptive as creditor is also open to Toscano's important criticism. The depiction of recaptives as creditors fails to conceive of legal personhood free from property relations, even if it subverts them in its constitution of the subject.[27] However, in this context subverting (even if not transforming) the property relations that underpinned abolition can offer a challenge to them. In that sense, framing the recaptive as creditor challenges assumptions underpinning the construction of the recaptive (amongst other victims of the slave trade) as subjects in international (criminal) legal history. In so doing, the fundamentally irredeemable nature of the debt owed to the recaptive lends urgency to critical thinking about the present, including by challenging us to ask what the recaptive might make of contemporary justice efforts. Thinking of the recaptive as creditor then offers a provocation to the contemporary framing of victims.

Victims as creditors

This thinking is directed at, in Fletcher's words, an 'imagined' victim (Fletcher 2015: 303). As such, it is open to the criticism that it is both removed from – again to return to Fletcher – the 'real' victim (ibid) and moreover, that it is not directed at substantive legal argument before an international criminal court. However, in so far as this chapter represents an attempt to explore different approaches to subjecthood, it rests on the premise that alternative thinking about victims can usefully challenge some of the assumptions about the 'ideal' victim which infuse representations of victims and which can in turn feed into substantive (legal) argument.[28] Thinking of the recaptive as creditor, that is a figure to whom a debt is owed, offers a provocation to think through an alternative 'imagined' victim today, and with that the attendant responsibilities this framing might bring. Thinking of the victim as creditor can centre questions about distribution in the very constitution of the victim as subject.

There are parallels in the argument about the indebtedness of international law to the recaptive and the indebtedness of international (criminal) law to the victim today. At its broadest, international law may have played a role in facilitating some of the conditions that contribute to international crime in the first place, not least through its legacies of colonialism. Moreover, the claim to act in the name of the victim has contributed to the expansion of international law. Survivor testimony makes a critical contribution to international criminal law. And survivors have contributed to the development of international criminal law – inside and outside the courtroom – even if some of their contributions, such as Rwandan survivor group protests, are less often acknowledged in histories of victims' rights (Haslam 2007, 2014: 189). International criminal law, like any law, gives rise to its own set of injustices. It overlooks certain harms and, however well-intentioned, can risk instrumentalising survivors to some degree – for the demands of a particular trial, or more broadly, as Chapter 1 has shown in the service of a broader international criminal justice project. Moreover, to return to Binder again the 'moral' and 'material' benefits of international criminal justice are unevenly spread.

The focus on the indebtedness of the *law* offers a critical counterpoint to the tendency of international criminal courts and their supporters to make an abstraction of international criminal justice in a way which can denude it of the power relations that underpin its political and economic contexts.[29] However, the danger is that it can work to gloss over other responsibilities. These very different responsibilities might include that of those who commit crime and those who may benefit from the law's limitations, including from the forms of violence it insulates.[30] As with the recaptive, these different responsibilities and the indebtedness of international law are not mutually exclusive. However, in the current context in which the dominant representation of victims as explained in Chapter 1 has become coupled with justifications for international criminal law itself, thinking about the indebtedness of international law can do useful work. The term 'creditor' is preferred here to the term 'beneficiary'. The term beneficiary may work to presume a particular configuration of international criminal justice as an inherent good or benefit, whereas thinking of victims as creditors more readily leaves open the possibility that victims' interests may not inevitably always align with those of international criminal institutions, or that as creditors victims might call on a different kind of justice to the one that might be called for in their name. Any justice outcome will of course inevitably involve compromise, but thinking of victims as creditors shifts the starting point for its determination. Thinking of victims as creditors rather than beneficiaries also implies agency on the part of victims in a way that the word beneficiary may not, including by recognising what victims have contributed to international law.[31] At the same time, the term also allows for the recognition of victims' suffering as a source of obligation. Finally, thinking of victims as creditors (and not beneficiaries) enables international law also to be thought of as a beneficiary of international criminal justice, just as the previous section positioned international law also as a beneficiary, rather than just a progressive agent, of abolition.

Critically thinking of victims as creditors also requires an alertness to the 'moral' and 'material' benefits (to return to Binder) of international criminal justice, where they lie and how they relate to each other, and it emphasises that obligations flow from this interconnectedness.[32] Thinking about the 'moral' and 'material' benefits of international criminal justice in turn centres questions about distribution in the constitution of the figure of the victim.[33] This does not necessarily lead directly to individual monetary claims, but it can operate as further provocation to the material conditions that work to limit justice. Inscribing the slave trade into international criminal legal history then provokes us to centre questions about distribution, including in the constitution of the subject. A rights-based approach which is linked to the international criminal justice process does not easily encompass such (structural) concerns.[34]

The inscription of the recaptive lends historical urgency to these questions because the warning of the irredeemable debt of the recaptive stands alongside the debts owed to victims today. All this is not to ignore the progressive possibilities in international criminal justice, but it does seek to hold them to account in the constitution of an 'imagined' victim as legal (and critical) subject. In so doing, it also goes some way to meeting some of the criticisms that have arisen with the representation of victims today.

Conclusion

This chapter has suggested a series of overlapping narratives about recaptives and victims. In so doing, it has embodied a reflection on the telling of international criminal legal histories. It has shown how a longer legal history of victims in international criminal law can provide a springboard for thinking about the construction and representation of victims in international criminal law today. The approaches put forward here offer an account of various approaches to subjecthood that underpin the construction and potential constructions of victims, each with attendant advantages and disadvantages. These different narratives are in themselves of course an abstraction but the chapter has suggested that reading the recaptive alongside the representation of victims today gives rise to a history of international law's engagement with victims in which firstly, the representation of victims as liminal subjects of intervention and transformation might be read as having some *legal* roots in international slave trade repression law and which secondly, points to the role of property in contributing to framing (and potentially challenging) legal subjectivity as well as the constraints of capital in the delivery of justice. These roots lend historical urgency to alternative thinking about victims today which can offer a provocation to the conditions of possibility which constrain each of these approaches in their different ways.

Finally, the chapter has asked how else might the 'imagined' victim (Fletcher 2015) be imagined and with what implications? At the least, inscribing the recaptive offers a springboard to challenge representations of victims as passive by emphasising, as I have sought to do throughout this book, recaptives' agency and resistance. The chapter has also turned to international law's encounter with recaptives to reflect upon how else the victim might be framed – and the attendant challenges that might bring. Following Binder's provocation, it has argued that international law is indebted to the recaptive (amongst other victims of the slave trade). Whilst the full ramifications of this approach stand to be developed further, applied to victims, this shifting of the lens can challenge some of the assumptions that underpin current representations of victims in international criminal law. It also centres critique and questions about distribution (and relative distribution) in the constitution of the victim as subject, without the resolution of which justice will only ever be incomplete.

Notes

1 For a discussion which seeks to draw parallels between the methodological challenges in writing about slaves and victims see further Haslam (2019).
2 For debates about the criminal nature of the slave trade see Chapter 3.
3 For an exploration of the dangers of instrumentalising victims of the slave trade in the context of drawing lessons for contemporary international criminal law from writings on the slave trade about representation, witnessing, voice and agency see Haslam (2019: 138). For further discussion of the dilemmas attendant on seeking to draw present lessons from the past lives of slaves see Hartman (2008: 14).
4 To recap, my focus is on international criminal legal history as opposed to, for example, human rights law, although a history of the recaptive is also relevant to other areas of international law. I focus on the figure of the victim in international criminal law because of the current centrality of the international criminal legal response to widespread violations of human rights; the centrality of the claim to centre victims in international criminal law, and current concerns about the representation and construction of victims in international criminal law (Chapter 1).
5 See further, Scott (2004), on history writing and the 'problem-space' (ibid: 97) that frames it.
6 See further on reparations, Barkan (2007), Miller and Kumar (2007), Tan (2007), Valls (2007), Gross (2008: 305), and Beckles (2012).
7 The revised strategy notes of its four central policy objectives (communication, protection and support, participation and representation, and reparations and assistance) that

> while it is not always possible to achieve these ambitious goals due to the reality in the field, resource limitations etc., the Court continually strives to do its utmost and remains committed to achieving the best possible outcomes within the limits imposed by existing resources and our operating environment.
>
> (Assembly of States Parties, 'Court's Revised Strategy in Relation to Victims' 2012: para 16)

8 See further on victim participation, for example, Moffett (2015), Smith-Van Lin (2012), Funk (2015), and Vasiliev (2015).
9 On the past as a source of authority and legitimacy for lawyers, see Gordon (1997: 1023) and Kapczynski (2004–2005: 1041).
10 Although some such links may be broadly traceable. For example, Martinez traces the early use of the concept of a crime against humanity to abolition (Martinez 2012: 114–116), a claim which has been contested (Alston 2013: 2050–2051).
11 On the ideal victim, see Christie (1986). For the application of the idea of the ideal victim to international criminal law, see Van Wijk (2013). For discussion of the ideal victim in the context of victim participation, see Haslam and Edmunds (2014). See further, Schwöbel-Patel (2018).
12 For a masterful account of the lived experiences and liminality of the American recaptive, see Fett (2017).
13 Thus, the ICC Revised Victims Strategy on Victims states that:

> victims' participation empowers them, recognises their suffering and enables them to contribute to the establishment of the historical record. . . . Victims play an important role as active participants in the quest for justice. . . . Moreover, their participation in the justice process contributes to closing the impunity gap and is one step in the process of healing for individuals and societies.
>
> (Assembly of States Parties, 'Court's Revised Strategy in Relation to Victims' 2012: para 10)

14 Not least because international criminal hearings are not inevitably therapeutic (Dembour and Haslam 2004).

15 Rule 85(a) of the Rules of Procedure and Evidence (2002) of the ICC defines a victim as a natural person who has suffered harm from a crime that falls within the jurisdiction of the Court where there is a casual link between the crime and the harm suffered. The application of these conditions may vary according to the stage of proceedings reached, including whether proceedings relate to a situation or a case (*Prosecutor v Thomas Lubanga Dyilo* 17 January 2006, 29 June 2006). On the way that the legal process narrows the range of victim participants it recognises see further, Kendall and Nouwen (2014: 241).

16 For further and important discussion of the impact of the political economy on the construction and representation of victims, see Schwöbel-Patel (2016, 2018).

17 For a discussion of the construction of victims 'in the "attention economy"' see Schwöbel-Patel (2018: 721–723). On commodification in international criminal law more generally, see Kendall (2015: 114).

18 Thereby failing to recognise their agency (Schwöbel-Patel 2016: 250).

19 In a related vein, William Schabas has observed: 'One suspects that if the victims understood that many millions had been invested – mainly in professional salaries and international travel – in order to ensure the respect of their rights, they might ask if they could simply be given the money instead' (in Carayon and O'Donohue 2017: 587). To be clear I am not criticising the motives or professionalism of those who work with victims. Rather this is an observation about the structural constraints within which such work takes place.

20 I use the term creditor here as shorthand for creditor or potential creditor. Although in this section I work from the assumption that international law is indebted to recaptives, the debt framework itself implies that in theory at least international law could redeem these debts, although given the circumstances in which these debts have arisen (and the constraints on justice) this is unlikely. In fact, as I argue later it is precisely the irredeemable nature of this historical debt which offers such provocation today. Even so, the framework does allow for recognition of international law's progressive potential.

21 For further discussion of the application of Binder's insights to international criminal law, see Haslam (2019: 141–142).

22 See further for example Wood (2010: 2) and Gross (2008: 320).

23 In general, the trope of redemption is double-edged in this context. Justifications for British colonialism drew partly upon the need for Britain to redeem its involvement in the slave trade. Elsewhere, I have argued that a redemptive framing of the first prosecution for slave trading at Sierra Leone supported a broader colonial project (Haslam 2012). Binder argues that interpreting the Thirteenth Amendment redemptively requires giving it a meaning 'in light of the visions of freedom and the critiques of slavery enunciated by the slaves' (Binder 1993: 478).

24 Thus, he puts forward an interpretation that sees 'the Thirteenth Amendment as the slaves' gift to the nation, a gift that, like all gifts, cements a relationship and incurs a debt' (Binder 1993: 474). This is only one part of Binder's rich argument which positions slaves as 'benevolent founders of the new nation' and 'authors' of 'its new Constitution' (ibid).

25 The origins of many contemporary human rights campaigning techniques are traceable to the abolition movement and the rhetoric of abolition proved foundational for subsequent human rights campaigns; these have in turn contributed to the expansion and development of international law (Haslam 2014: 182).

26 Significantly, Meister links his proposal to recognise historic injustices as 'options held in a constructive trust' to market economies (Meister 2012: 250), with 'economic equality (socialism)' possibly setting restrictions on such claims (Meister 2012: 235).

27 One question a history of the recaptive leaves us with, therefore, is to what extent are property relations inescapable in the legal constitution of the human subject, even in avowedly emancipatory legal projects?

28 For a discussion of the impact of the ideal victim on debates about collective representation see Haslam and Edmunds (2014).

29 On international criminal justice as an abstraction, see further Mégret (2015: 26).

30 In his ground-breaking work *After Evil*, Meister distinguishes between victims, perpetrators and beneficiaries of human rights abuse. His aim is to interrogate what he sees as a key difficulty in in political transitions which is 'how to view ongoing beneficiaries of an injustice now regarded as past' (Meister 2012: viii). Meister's concern is with 'the question of *who* benefits and *how* benefits accumulate' (ibid: 14). He argues for 'an explicit or implicit *accounting* that connects the gains of the defendant to the losses of the plaintiff in a way that supplements the separate accounts maintained by each' (ibid: 239 original emphasis). Meister's concern is that in the contemporary context a beneficiary can see himself 'as a would-have-been rescuer rather than a would-be perpetrator' (Meister 2012: viii). Such 'compassion for past suffering' can justify 'ones' continuing to benefit from past conditions that one now would have opposed' (Meister 2012: x).

31 Binder also argues that slaves should be recognised as authors of the social contract, not just beneficiaries (Binder 1993: 478).

32 Thinking of the victim as a creditor does not work to prioritise victims' rights over those of defendants in international criminal proceedings. An accounting of victim–defendant relations is in any case already built into the structure of the law.

33 Critically here this thinking can extend beyond the relative benefits and burdens of international criminal justice (both 'material' and 'moral' to return to Binder) to international law on the one hand and victims on the other. For example, following the logic of Kamari Clarke and Robert Meister discussed in the previous section, the beneficiaries of international criminal justice might be thought to include those who profit/and or benefit from the structural violence international criminal law currently insulates. This opens up a different angle on the fundamental question of who is the constituency of international criminal justice: or, as Tallgren and Mégret have asked in different ways, who are the 'we' in international criminal law and justice (Tallgren 2014; Mégret 2015: 23).

34 Positioning the victim as creditor goes further than the rights-based perspective adopted by the ICC in its revised strategy on victims, which has perhaps unsurprisingly linked victims' rights very closely to the legal process. Thus, although the strategy claims that the rights-based approach 'enables one to look at the fundamental structural causes that underlie the failure to realise one's rights if and when that occurs' (Assembly of States Parties, 'Court's Revised Strategy in Relation to Victims' 2012: para 6), it is not clear how the strategy addresses structural issues in the challenge to victims' rights beyond the admittedly important issue of legal aid. However, even here positioning the 'imagined' victim as a creditor could provide a basis from which to argue that states have stronger obligations to make up the significant shortfall in funding that Carayon and O'Donohue, for example, have observed (Carayon and O'Donohue 2017: 584). It might also offer a challenge to the solely voluntary nature of contributions to the Trust Fund for Victims.

References

Alston, P. (2013) 'Does the Past Matter? On the Origins of Human Rights Law', *Harvard Law Review* 126(7): 2043–2081.

Barkan, E. (2007) 'Introduction: Reparation: A Moral and Political Dilemma', in J. Miller and R. Kumar (eds.), *Reparations: Interdisciplinary Inquiries*, Oxford: Oxford University Press.

Beckles, H. (2012) *Britain's Black Debt: Reparations for Caribbean Slavery and Native Genocide*, Kingston: University of West Indies Press.

Binder, G. (1993) 'Did the Slaves Author the Thirteenth Amendment? An Essay in Redemptive History', *Yale Journal of Law and the Humanities* 5(2): 471–505.

Carayon, G. and O'Donohue, J. (2017) 'The International Criminal Court's Strategies in Relation to Victims', *Journal of International Criminal Justice* 15(3): 567–591.

Christie, N. (1986) 'The Ideal Victim', in E. A. Fattah (ed.), *From Crime Policy to Victim Policy*, Basingstoke: Macmillan.

Clarke, K. M. (2015) '"We as for Justice, You Give Us Law": The Rule of Law, Economic Markets and the Reconfiguration of Victimhood', in C. De Vos, S. Kendall and C. Stahn (eds.), *Contested Justice: The Politics and Practice of International Criminal Court Interventions*, Cambridge: Cambridge University Press.

Dembour, M.-B. and Haslam, E. (2004) 'Silencing Hearings? Victim-Witnesses at the ICTY', *European Journal of International Law* 15(1): 151–177.

Fett, S. M. (2017) *Recaptured Africans: Surviving Slave Ships, Detention, and Dislocation in the Final Years of the Slave Trade*, Chapel Hill: University of North Carolina Press.

Fletcher, L. (2015) 'Refracted Justice: The Imagined Victim and the International Criminal Court', in C. De Vos, S. Kendall and C. Stahn, (eds.), *Contested Justice: The Politics and Practice of International Criminal Court Interventions*, Cambridge: Cambridge University Press.

Funk, M. R. (2015) *Victims' Rights and Advocacy at the International Criminal Court*, Oxford and New York: Oxford University Press.

Gordon, R. W. (1997) 'Foreword: The Archive of Critical Historicisim', *Stanford Law Review* 49(5): 1023–1029.

Gross, A. (2008) 'When Is the Time of Slavery: The History of Slavery in Contemporary Legal and Political Argument', *California Law Review* 96(1): 283–321.

Hartman, S. (2008) 'Venus in Two Acts', *Small Axe* 1–14.

Haslam, E. (2007) 'Law Civil Society and Contested Justice at the International Criminal Tribunal for Rwanda', in M.-B. Dembour and T. Kelly (eds.), *Paths to International Justice*, Cambridge: Cambridge University Press.

Haslam, E. (2012) 'Redemption, Colonialism and International Criminal Law: The Nineteenth Century Slave Trading Trials of Samo and Peters', in D. Kirkby (ed.), *Past Law, Present Histories: From Settler Colonies to International Justice*, Canberra: Australian National University e-Press.

Haslam, E. (2014) 'Silences in International Criminal Legal Histories and the Construction of the Victim Subject of International Criminal Law: The Nineteenth-Century Slave Trading Trial of Joseph Peters', in C. Schwöbel (ed.), *Critical Approaches to International Criminal Law: An Introduction*, London: Routledge.

Haslam, E. (2019) 'Writing More Inclusive Histories of International Criminal Law: Lessons from the Transatlantic Slave Trade', in I. Tallgren and T. Skouteris (eds.), *The New Histories of International Criminal Law: Retrials*, Oxford: Oxford University Press.

Haslam, E. and Edmunds, R. (2014) 'Victim Participation, Politics and the Construction of Victims at the International Criminal Court: Reflections on Proceedings in Banda and Jerbo', *Melbourne Journal of International Law* 14: 727–747.

Jorda, C. and de Hemptinne, J. (2002) 'The Status and Role of the Victim', in A. Cassese, P. Gaeta and J. R. W. D. Jones (eds.), *The Rome Statute of the International Criminal Court: A Commentary*, Volume 2, Oxford: Oxford University Press.

Kapczynski, A. (2004–2005) 'Historicism, Progress, and the Redemptive Constitution', *Cardozo Law Review* 26: 1041–1117.

Kendall, S. (2015) 'Commodifying Global Justice: Economies of Accountability at the International Criminal Court', *Journal of International Criminal Justice* 13: 113–114.

Kendall, S. and Nouwen, S. (2014) 'Representational Practices at the International Criminal Court: The Gap between Juridified and Abstract Victimhood', *Law and Contemporary Problems* 76: 235–262.

Martinez, J. (2012) *The Slave Trade and the Origins of International Human Rights Law*, Oxford: Oxford University Press.

Mégret, F. (2015) 'In Whose Name? The ICC and the Search for Constituency', in C. De Vos, S. Kendall and C. Stahn (eds.), *Contested Justice: The Politics and Practice of International Criminal Court Interventions*, Cambridge: Cambridge University Press.

Meister, R. (2012) *After Evil: A Politics of Human Rights*, New York: Columbia University Press.

Miller, J. and Kumar, R. (2007) *Reparations: Interdisciplinary Inquiries*, Oxford: Oxford University Press.

Moffett, L. (2015) 'Elaborating Justice for Victims at the International Criminal Court beyond Rhetoric and the Hague', *Journal of International Criminal Justice* 13: 281–311.

Sagan, A. (2010) 'African Criminals/African Victims: The Institutionalised Production of Cultural Narratives in International Criminal Law', *Millennium Journal of International Studies* 39(1): 3–21.

Schwöbel, C. (2014) 'Introduction', in C. Schwöbel (ed.), *Critical Approaches to International Criminal Law: An Introduction*, Abingdon: Routledge.

Schwöbel-Patel, C. (2016) 'Spectacle in International Criminal Law: The Fundraising Image of Victimhood', *London Review of International Law* 4(2): 247–274.

Schwöbel-Patel, C. (2018) 'The "Ideal" Victim of International Criminal Law', *European Journal of International Law* 29(3): 703–724.

Scott, D. (2004) *Conscripts of Modernity: The Tragedy of Colonial Enlightenment*, Durham and London: Duke University Press.

Smith-Van Lin, L. (2012) 'Victims' Participation at the International Criminal Court: Benefit or Burden?', in W. Schabas, Y. McDermott and N. Hayes (eds.), *Ashgate Research Companion to International Criminal Law: Critical Perspectives*, London and New York: Ashgate.

Tallgren, I. (2014) 'Who Are "We" in International Criminal Law? On Critics and Membership', in C. Schwöbel (ed.), *Critical Approaches to International Criminal Law: An Introduction*, Abingdon: Routledge.

Tan, K.-C. (2007) 'Colonialism, Reparations, and Global Justice', in J. Miller and R. Kumar (eds.), *Reparations: Interdisciplinary Inquiries*, Oxford: Oxford University Press.

Toscano, A. (2014) 'The Tactics and Ethics of Humanitarianism', *Humanity: An International Journal of Human Rights, Humanitarianism, and Development* 5(1): 123–147.

Valls, A. (2007) 'Reconsidering the Case for Black Reparations', in J. Miller and R. Kumar (eds.), *Reparations: Interdisciplinary Inquiries*, Oxford: Oxford University Press.

Van Wijk, J. (2013) 'Who Is the "Little Old Lady" of International Crimes? Nils Christie's Concept of the Ideal Victim Reinterpreted', *International Review of Victimology* 19(2): 159–179.
Vasiliev, S. (2015) 'Victim Participation Revisited: What the ICC Is Learning about Itself', in C. Stahn (ed.), *The Law and Practice of the International Criminal Court*, Oxford: Oxford University Press.
Wood, M. (2010) *The Horrible Gift of Freedom: Atlantic Slavery and the Representation of Emancipation*, Athens: University of Georgia Press.

International instruments

Assembly of States Parties, International Criminal Court, 'Court's Revised Strategy in Relation to Victims', ICC-ASP/11/38 5 November 2012.
Rome Statute of the International Criminal Court 1998, 2187 UNTS 3.
Rules of Procedure and Evidence 2002, International Criminal Court, ICC Doc ICC-ASP/1/3.

International criminal court cases

Prosecutor v Thomas Lubanga Dylio 'Decision on the Applications for Participation in the Proceedings of VPRS 1, VPRS 2, VPRS 3, VPRS 4, VPRS 5 and VPRS 6', 17 January 2006, ICC-01/04-101.
Prosecutor v Thomas Lubanga Dylio 'Decision on the Applications for Participation in the Proceedings Submitted by VPRS1 to VPRS 6 in the Case the Prosecutor v. Thomas Lubanga Dylio', 29 June 2006, ICC-01/04-172.

Mixed commission cases

HM Commissioners to Palmerston, 31 March 1834, in the Case of the *Maria da Gloria*, No 34 with Enclosures in *Class A Correspondence with the British Commissioners at Sierra Leone, the Havana, Rio de Janeiro, and Surinam, Relating to the Slave Trade 1834* PP 1835 (006) LI.1.

8 Conclusion

This book has offered a reflection on international criminal legal history writing through its examination of the figure of the recaptive. In so doing, it has sought to contribute to scholarly literature that seeks to broaden existing approaches to international criminal legal histories.[1] To this end it has emphasised substantively the importance of inscribing slavery and abolition into international criminal legal histories, and methodologically it has highlighted some of the challenges inherent in critical international criminal legal history writing. International criminal law is fundamentally influenced by its histories – both those that are told and those that remain as yet untold. It follows that how the slave trade is written into or out of international criminal legal histories, can play a key role in defining the nature of international criminal law – and its potential (Haslam 2019: 132).

There are many reasons for inscribing the slave trade and abolition into international criminal legal histories. However, despite these, the slave trade and abolition are generally omitted. This is because international criminal legal histories have typically focused on the prosecution of international crimes, the development of individual criminal responsibility on the international level and the establishment and operation of international criminal institutions. Even though the slave trade might not at first sight 'fit' into an international criminal legal history directed at these concerns, this book has argued that the slave trade forms a vital part of international criminal legal history. It has contended that what is omitted from categories of international crimes, and the processes by which this exclusion takes place, reveals much about the parameters and politics of the discipline. Thus, the exclusion of the slave trade from the category of international crimes was not inevitable, but was a political and contingent decision, the consequences of which still reverberate in the politics of contemporary international criminal justice and in the constitution and shape of international criminal law. More generally, this book has also emphasised that the focus on Nuremberg and Tokyo as the origins of modern international criminal law reflects not just international criminal legal doctrine but is also a product of ultimately political choices. More concretely, one way in which the political nature of international criminal legal history writing manifests is in the contradictions inherent in the application of the piracy analogy to slave trading (Chapter 3). At a doctrinal level, the piracy analogy resulted in the exclusion of the transatlantic slave trade from the category of international crimes. At the same time, international law has benefitted rhetorically from the reiteration of the piracy analogy to the slave trader. I have argued that these contradictions have operated to relieve international criminal law from accounting for the slave trade. The assumption behind this book has been that the exclusion of modernity's foundational crime from international criminal law haunts contemporary international criminal law and its practice and will continue to do so without a more fundamental accounting of the slave trade in international criminal legal history. This accounting can offer transformative potential in thinking about the figure of the victim in international criminal law.

Since the choices involved in history writing inevitably reflect current concerns and preoccupations, I have argued that international criminal legal histories can – and should – extend beyond the operation of international criminal law in a strict sense. International criminal law is after all also a historically contingent approach to injustice. Thus, the slave trade and abolition should be included in international criminal legal histories not just because of the enormity of the transatlantic slave trade and its significance for understanding the contemporary constitution of international criminal law and its politics (although these would be reason enough). Inscribing the slave trade and abolition into international criminal legal history introduces a missing historical perspective to contemporary constructions, and critiques thereof, of victims in international (criminal) law, features that have become central to contemporary international criminal legal discourse. The concern to contribute a historical perspective to debates about victims in international criminal law impels an analysis of the legal construction of the victims of the slave trade, with an account of the figure of the recaptive one starting point.[2] It follows that a history directed at a different set of contemporary concerns might have led to a different historical starting point.

Reading the figure of the recaptive alongside the victim, therefore, roots the contemporary construction of victims within a longer *legal* history. This narrative also tempers humanitarian accounts of international law and abolition.[3] Thus, I have argued that international slave trade repression law focused on questions of intervention sometimes at the expense of recaptives (Chapters 4 and 5), constructing them in effect as still commodified objects of intervention (Chapters 5 and 6). As a result, when slave ships were captured in violation of the international treaties, Mixed Commissioners were able to do more to expand captors' rights to intervene and to reduce captors' financial liabilities than they were able to formally safeguard the legal position of recaptives (for example, by expanding the circumstances for a grant of legal emancipation) (Chapter 5). Whilst Commissioners avoided in-person restoration orders in most such cases, liberation in these circumstances was to some extent fortuitous and not guaranteed as the case of the *Maria da Gloria* demonstrates. Finally, despite the failure of international slave trade repression law to recognise recaptives as legal subjects, recaptives' testimony and resistance contributed to the enforcement and development of the law and illuminated its limitations. By emphasising recaptives' roles in litigation in this way, the book has also sought to contribute to broader efforts to capture the roles of the victims of the slave trade in abolition.

The choices involved in history writing affect not just the question whether the slave trade and abolition should be included in international criminal legal histories but also the terms on which they could and/or should be inscribed. How legal histories should account for recaptives' roles in slave trade repression is a question, therefore, not just of the possibilities of the archival sources. It is also an issue of identifying what each of a number of different narratives might offer for the present.[4] In other words, should an account focus on: inclusion or exclusion; the recaptive as resisting subject or commodified object of intervention; the limitations of international law and the constraints on Mixed Commissioners (as well as the limitations of some of the approaches Mixed Commissioners took) or the law's potential (along with Commissioners' attempts to disrupt those limitations); the deployment by slave trade repression of prize, a legal instrument that had supported the slave trade; or the strategic subversion of prize for more humane ends? Should we focus on the judicial creativity which operated to sidestep the limitations of international law and ensure recaptives' freedom in many cases or the limited – and potentially devastating – positioning of the recaptive in slave trade repression? How the relationship between international slave trade repression law and recaptives is framed contributes to determining how we might understand the potential of international (criminal) law today as well as its relationship with, and responsibilities to, the past.

In the context of a history which is focused on the construction and representation of victims, I have argued that inscribing the recaptive works to emphasise the legal origins of tropes of intervention and foregrounds questions about property. I have suggested that progress narratives about victims in international (criminal) law are likely to consider that subsequent legal development has transcended some of the more problematic aspects of the legal construction of recaptives. In contrast, I have raised questions about the legacy of some of these origins today (Chapter 7). For example, in so far as international criminal law can struggle to recognise the agency of critical or resisting victims, I have suggested causal links between the stories told – and not told – about the past and the present. These similarities lend historical urgency to the quest to think critically about the way the figure of the victim is framed today. The history of the recaptive provides a springboard for alternative thinking about victims in international criminal law. I have drawn on the history of slave trade repression and the work of Guyora Binder (1993) and Robert Meister (2012) to suggest that framing the figure of the recaptive – and by analogy the contemporary victim – as a creditor can perform useful work by shifting the lens. In general, I have argued that there needs to be an accounting of the slave trade in histories of international criminal law, but the specific claim that international law is indebted to recaptives has run through this book in a number of different ways. Whilst the full implications of such a framing as applied to contemporary thinking about victims remains to be developed, it offers to centre critique and questions about distribution and relative distribution in the constitution of the figure of the victim as legal subject. The recaptive then offers inspiration for critical thinking in the present. The figure represents a powerful symbol of international law's promise of (and limitations around) transformation and stands as a potent reminder of the multiple ways in which slavery and abolition remain present and absent in the different registers and current constitution of international criminal law.

Notes

1 See further for example Tallgren and Skouteris (2019).
2 Like any law, international criminal law's origins are not to be found in one particular site or moment (Haslam 2016: 422). Writing abolition into international criminal legal histories is not, therefore, aimed at replacing the centrality of one historical starting point – that is the Nuremberg and Tokyo Tribunals and the legal principles they generated – with another – that is the slave trade and abolition. While narratives about victims in international criminal law should encompass the slave trade and abolition, they should also extend beyond them.
3 It is doubtful that anyone would now take seriously as a simple historical truth Lecky's famously celebratory description of British abolition that it 'may probably be regarded as among the three or four perfectly virtuous pages comprised in the history of nations' (in Hurwitz 1973: 20). For example, Marike Sherwood powerfully criticises the ways that Britain benefited from the slave trade after abolition, see Sherwood (2007). Even so Wood warns, the 'emancipation archive constitutes a set of blue-prints' that states can draw upon when they wish to gloss over 'horrible things' that have been 'done in the brilliant brush strokes of the gift of freedom' (Wood 2010: xi).
4 This question is inspired by David Scott's discussion of tragic and romantic narrative framings, see further Scott (2004).

References

Binder, G. (1993) 'Did the Slaves Author the Thirteenth Amendment? An Essay in Redemptive History', *Yale Journal of Law and the Humanities* 5(2): 471–505.
Haslam, E. (2016) 'International Criminal Law and Legal Memories of Abolition: Intervention, Mixed Commission Courts and "Emancipation"', *Journal of the History of International Law* 18: 420–447.
Haslam, E. (2019) 'Writing More Inclusive Histories of International Criminal Law: Lessons from the Transatlantic Slave Trade', in I. Tallgren and T. Skouteris (eds.), *The New Histories of International Criminal Law: Retrials*, Oxford: Oxford University Press.
Hurwitz, E. F. (1973) *Politics and the Public Conscience: Slave Emancipation and the Abolitionist Movement in Britain*, London: George Allen & Unwin Ltd.
Meister, R. (2012) *After Evil: A Politics of Human Rights*, New York: Columbia University Press.
Scott, D. (2004) *Conscripts of Modernity: The Tragedy of Colonial Enlightenment*, Durham and London: Duke University Press.
Sherwood, M. (2007) *After Abolition: Britain and the Slave Trade since 1807*, London: I.B. Tauris & Co. Ltd.
Tallgren, I. and Skouteris, T. (eds.) (2019) *The New Histories of International Criminal Law: Retrials*, Oxford: Oxford University Press.
Wood, M. (2010) *The Horrible Gift of Freedom: Atlantic Slavery and the Representation of Emancipation*, Athens: University of Georgia Press.

Index

For Product Safety Concerns and Information please contact our EU
representative GPSR@taylorandfrancis.com
Taylor & Francis Verlag GmbH, Kaufingerstraße 24, 80331 München, Germany

www.ingramcontent.com/pod-product-compliance
Ingram Content Group UK Ltd.
Pitfield, Milton Keynes, MK11 3LW, UK
UKHW011019180926
475701UK00004B/827
* 9 7 8 1 0 3 2 0 8 8 7 4 7 *